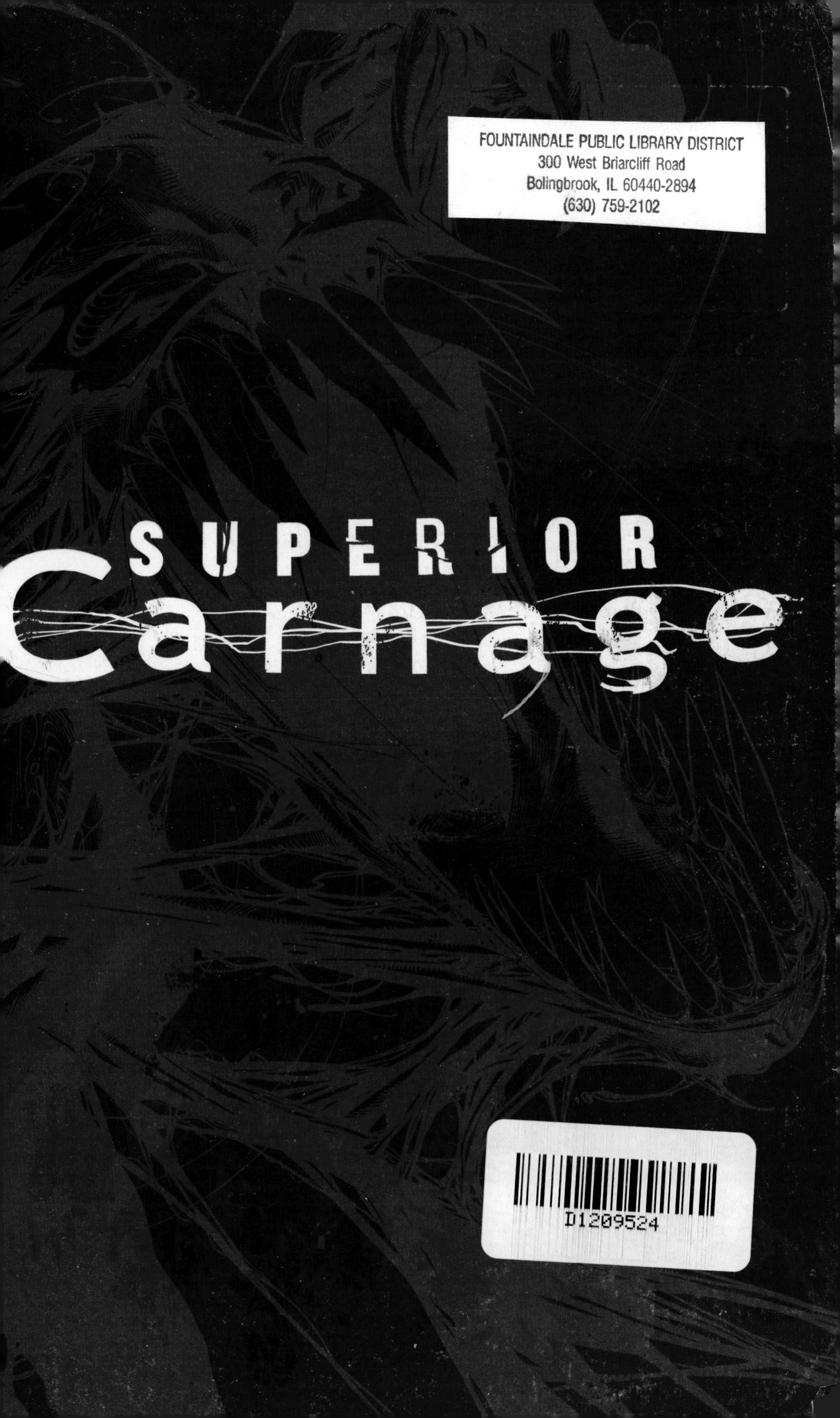
SUPERIOR
Carnage

SUPERIOR Carnage

WRITER
KEVIN SHINICK

PENCILERS
STEPHEN SEGOVIA (#1-5)
& DAN MEXIA (#4-5)

INKERS
STEPHEN SEGOVIA (#1-2),
DENNIS CHRISOSTOMO (#3-5),
DAN MEXIA (#4-5) & DON HO (#5)

COLORISTS
JAY DAVID RAMOS (#1-5)
WITH VERO GANDINI (#4),
RACHELLE ROSENBERG (#4) & REX LOKUS (#5)

LETTERER
VC'S JOE CARAMAGNA

COVER ARTIST
CLAYTON CRAIN

ASSISTANT EDITOR
DEVIN LEWIS

ASSOCIATE EDITOR
TOM BRENNAN

EDITOR
SANA AMANAT

SENIOR EDITOR
STEPHEN WACKER

COLLECTION EDITOR & DESIGN
CORY LEVINE
ASSISTANT EDITORS
ALEX STARBUCK & NELSON RIBEIRO
EDITORS, SPECIAL PROJECTS
JENNIFER GRÜNWALD & MARK D. BEAZLEY
SENIOR EDITOR, SPECIAL PROJECTS
JEFF YOUNGQUIST
SVP OF PRINT & DIGITAL PUBLISHING SALES
DAVID GABRIEL

EDITOR IN CHIEF
AXEL ALONSO
CHIEF CREATIVE OFFICER
JOE QUESADA
PUBLISHER
DAN BUCKLEY
EXECUTIVE PRODUCER
ALAN FINE

SUPERIOR CARNAGE. Contains material originally published in magazine form as SUPERIOR CARNAGE #1-5. First printing 2014. ISBN# 978-0-7851-6560-6. Published by MARVEL WORLDWIDE, INC., a subsidiary of MARVEL ENTERTAINMENT, LLC. OFFICE OF PUBLICATION: 135 West 50th Street, New York, NY 10020. Copyright © 2013 and 2014 Marvel Characters, Inc. All rights reserved. All characters featured in this issue and the distinctive names and likenesses thereof, and all related indicia are trademarks of Marvel Characters, Inc. No similarity between any of the names, characters, persons, and/or institutions in this magazine with those of any living or dead person or institution is intended, and any such similarity which may exist is purely coincidental. **Printed in the U.S.A.** ALAN FINE, EVP - Office of the President, Marvel Worldwide, Inc. and EVP & CMO Marvel Characters B.V.; DAN BUCKLEY, Publisher & President - Print, Animation & Digital Divisions; JOE QUESADA, Chief Creative Officer; TOM BREVOORT, SVP of Publishing; DAVID BOGART, SVP of Operations & Procurement, Publishing; C.B. CEBULSKI, SVP of Creator & Content Development; DAVID GABRIEL, SVP of Print & Digital Publishing Sales; JIM O'KEEFE, VP of Operations & Logistics; DAN CARR, Executive Director of Publishing Technology; SUSAN CRESPI, Editorial Operations Manager; ALEX MORALES, Publishing Operations Manager; STAN LEE, Chairman Emeritus. For information regarding advertising in Marvel Comics or on Marvel.com, please contact Niza Disla, Director of Marvel Partnerships, at ndisla@marvel.com. For Marvel subscription inquiries, please call 800-217-9158. Manufactured between 12/6/2013 and 1/13/2014 by QUAD/GRAPHICS, VERSAILLES, KY, USA.

10 9 8 7 6 5 4 3 2 1

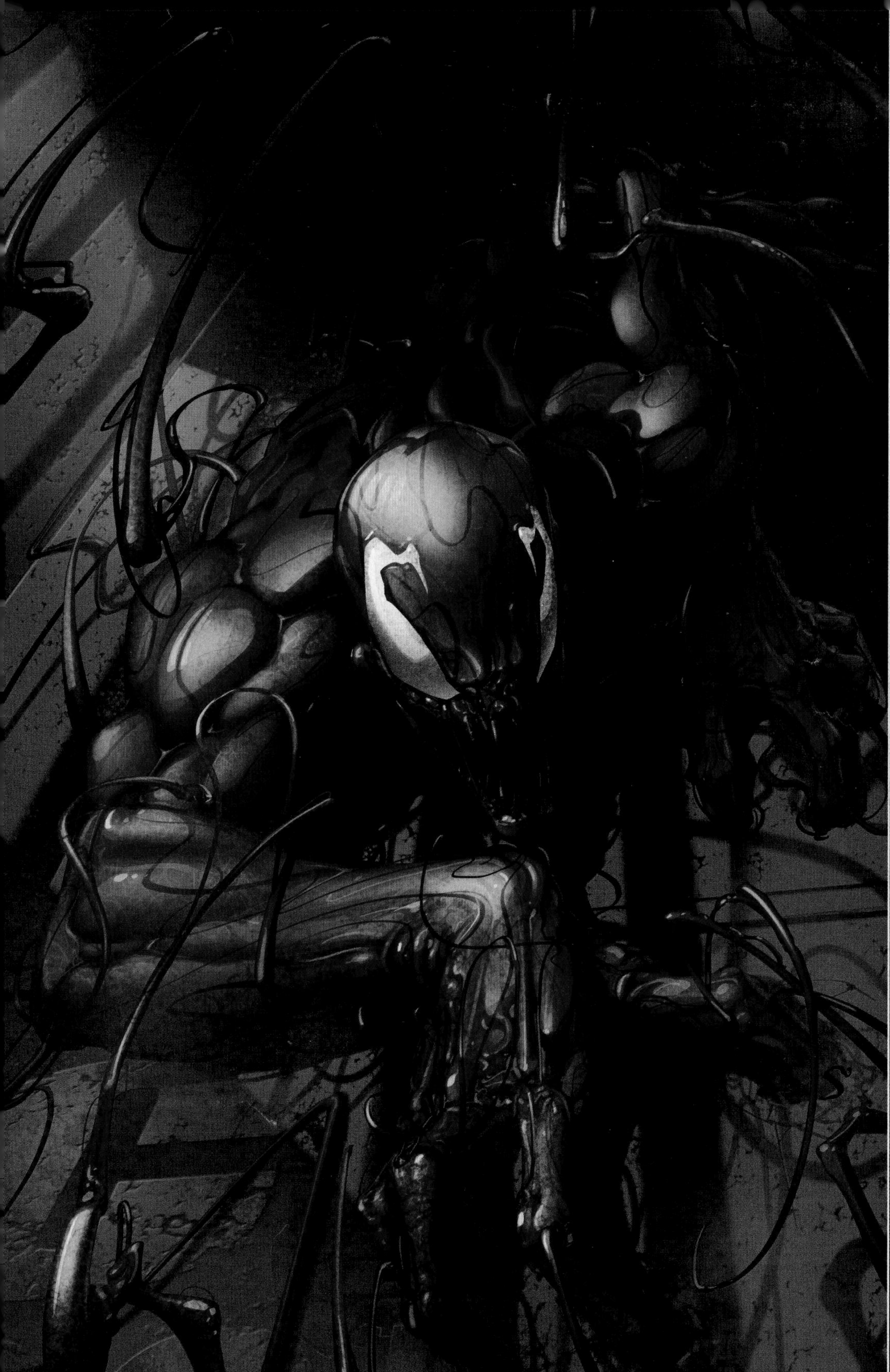

1

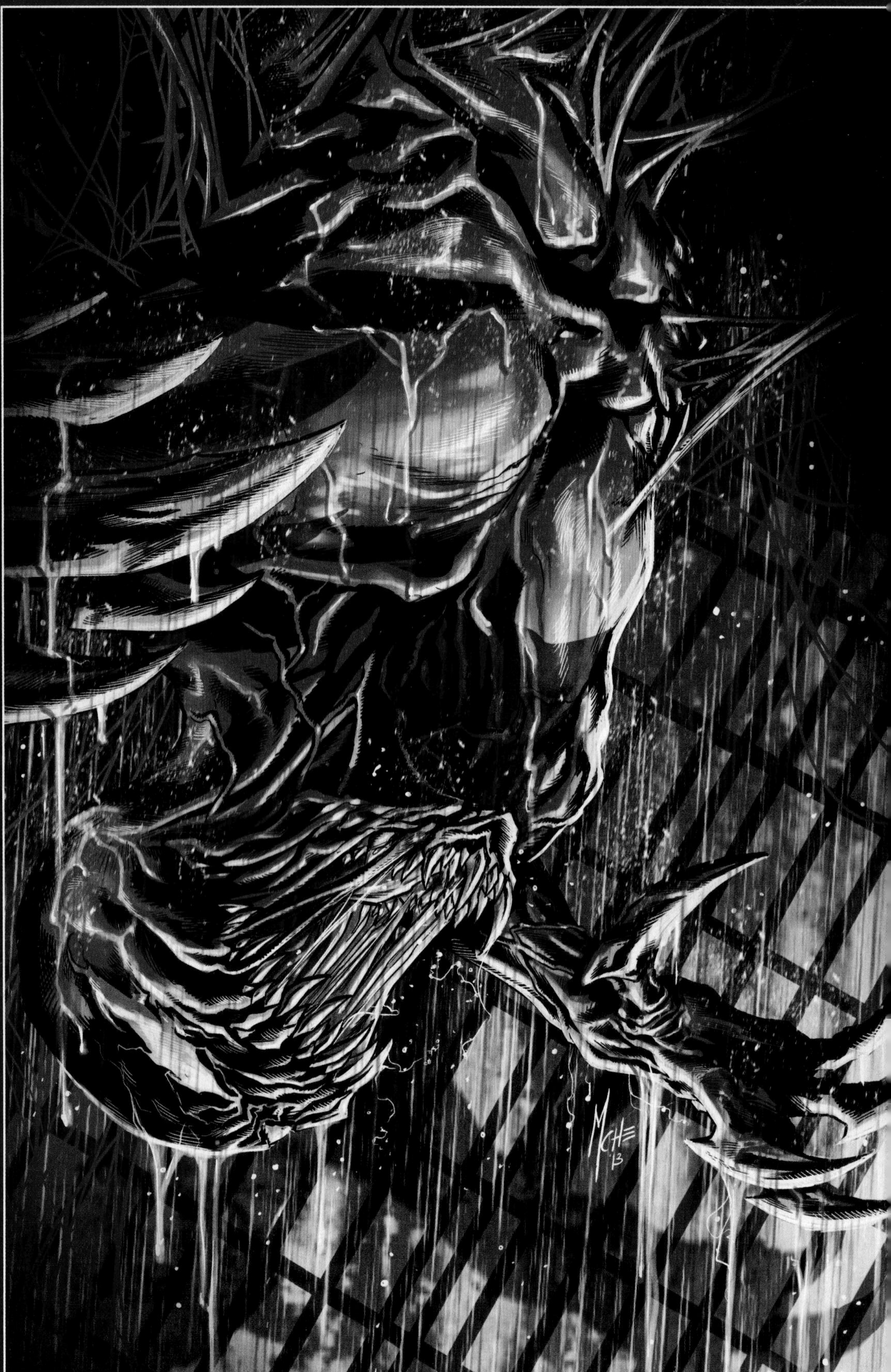

#1 VARIANT BY MARCO CHECCHETTO

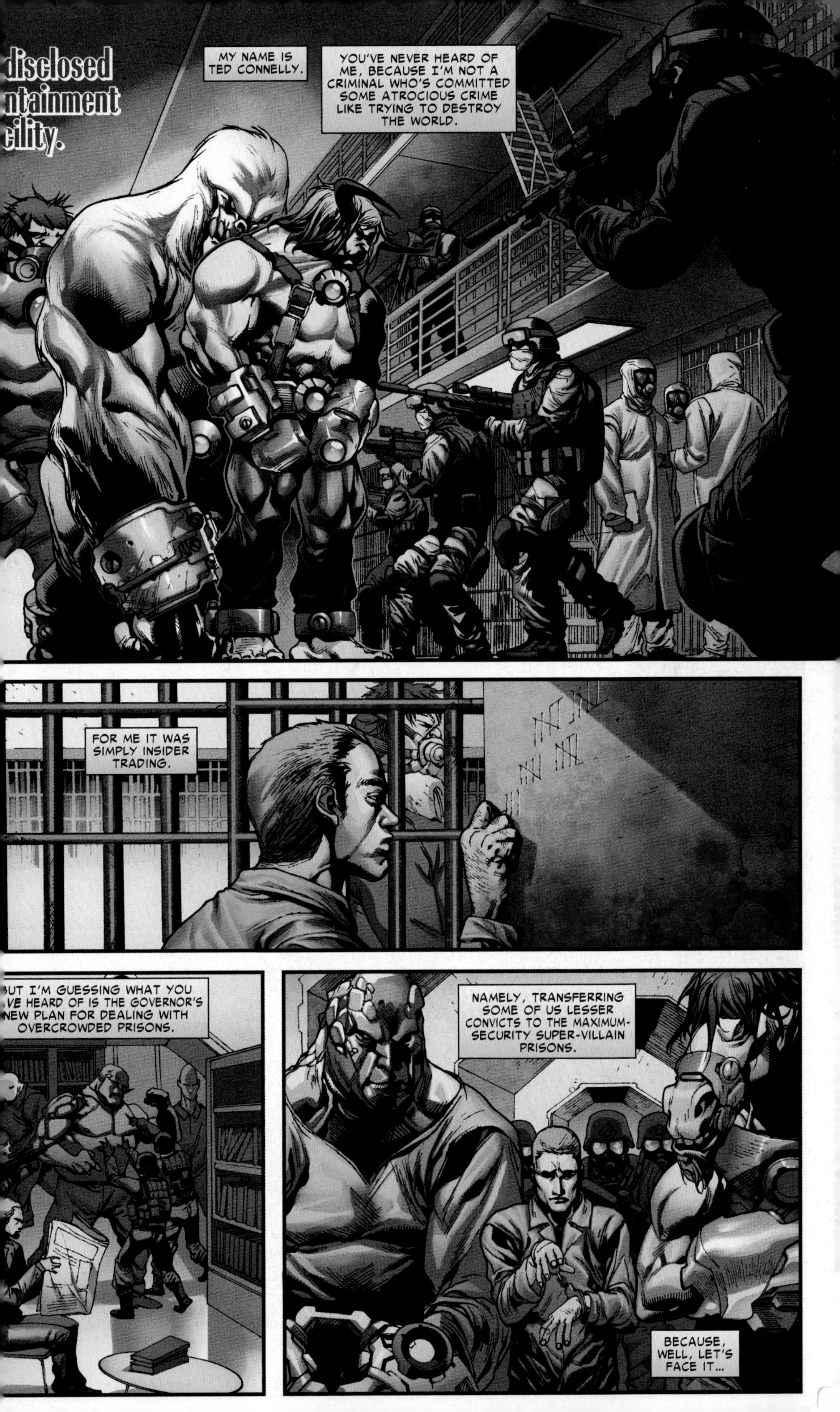
disclosed
ntainment
cility.
MY NAME IS TED CONNELLY.
YOU'VE NEVER HEARD OF ME, BECAUSE I'M NOT A CRIMINAL WHO'S COMMITTED SOME ATROCIOUS CRIME LIKE TRYING TO DESTROY THE WORLD.
FOR ME IT WAS SIMPLY INSIDER TRADING.
UT I'M GUESSING WHAT YOU VE HEARD OF IS THE GOVERNOR'S NEW PLAN FOR DEALING WITH OVERCROWDED PRISONS.
NAMELY, TRANSFERRING SOME OF US LESSER CONVICTS TO THE MAXIMUM-SECURITY SUPER-VILLAIN PRISONS.
BECAUSE, WELL, LET'S FACE IT...

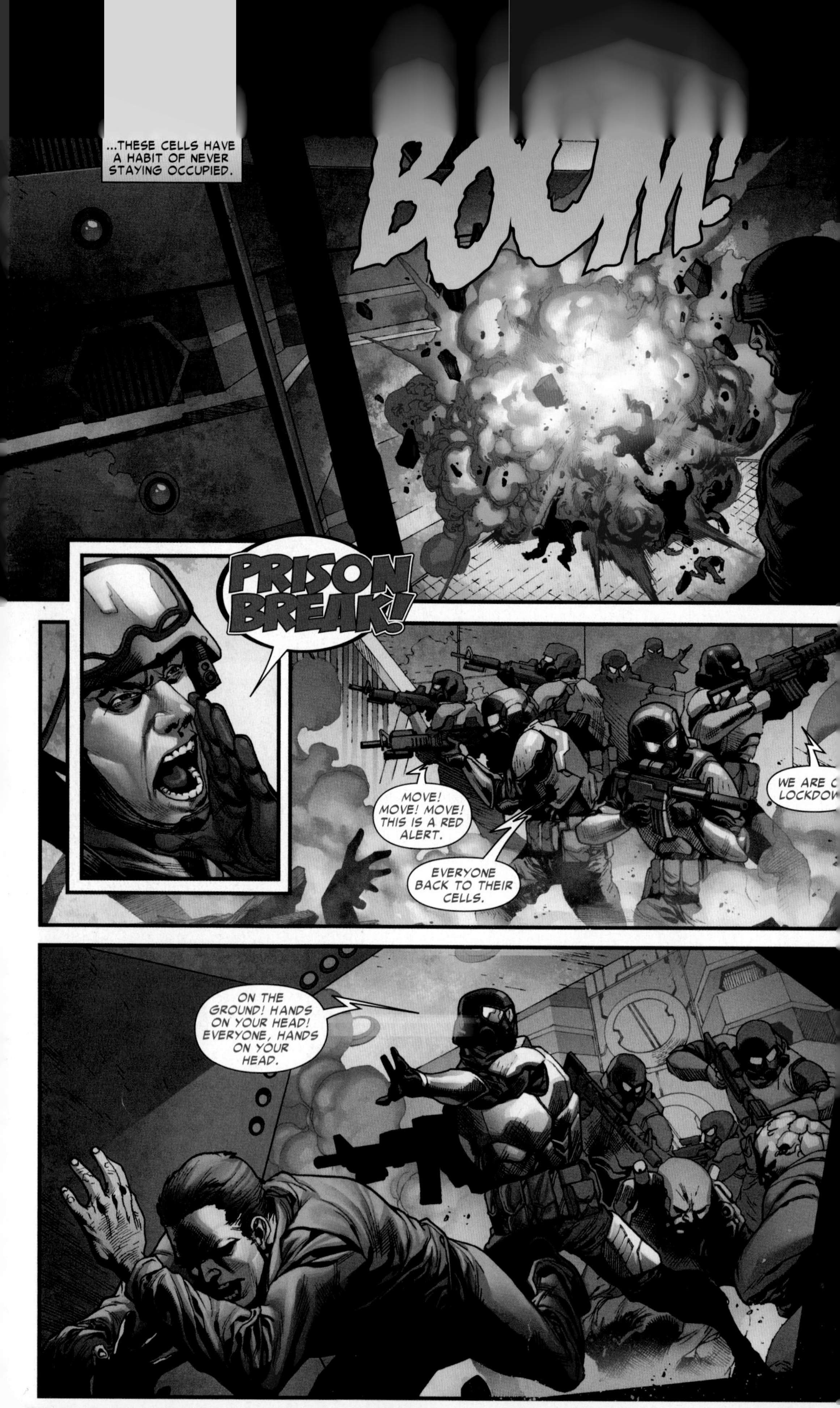
...THESE CELLS HAVE A HABIT OF NEVER STAYING OCCUPIED.
BOOM!
PRISON BREAK!
MOVE! MOVE! MOVE! THIS IS A RED ALERT.
EVERYONE BACK TO THEIR CELLS.
WE ARE C
LOCKDOW
ON THE GROUND! HANDS ON YOUR HEAD! EVERYONE, HANDS ON YOUR HEAD.

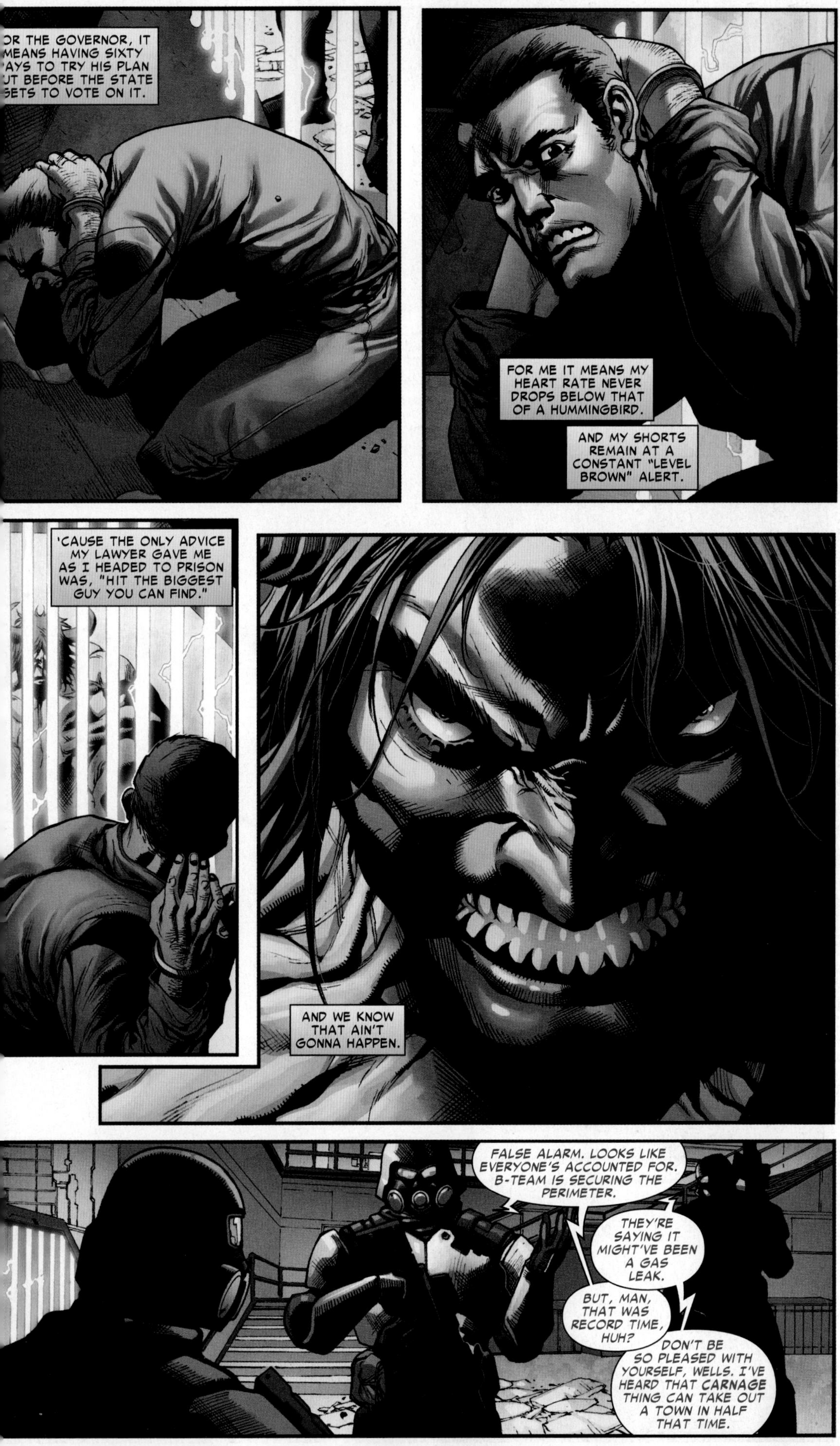

OR THE GOVERNOR, IT MEANS HAVING SIXTY AYS TO TRY HIS PLAN UT BEFORE THE STATE GETS TO VOTE ON IT.
FOR ME IT MEANS MY HEART RATE NEVER DROPS BELOW THAT OF A HUMMINGBIRD.
AND MY SHORTS REMAIN AT A CONSTANT "LEVEL BROWN" ALERT.
'CAUSE THE ONLY ADVICE MY LAWYER GAVE ME AS I HEADED TO PRISON WAS, "HIT THE BIGGEST GUY YOU CAN FIND."
AND WE KNOW THAT AIN'T GONNA HAPPEN.
FALSE ALARM. LOOKS LIKE EVERYONE'S ACCOUNTED FOR. B-TEAM IS SECURING THE PERIMETER.
THEY'RE SAYING IT MIGHT'VE BEEN A GAS LEAK.
BUT, MAN, THAT WAS RECORD TIME, HUH?
DON'T BE SO PLEASED WITH YOURSELF, WELLS. I'VE HEARD THAT CARNAGE THING CAN TAKE OUT A TOWN IN HALF THAT TIME.

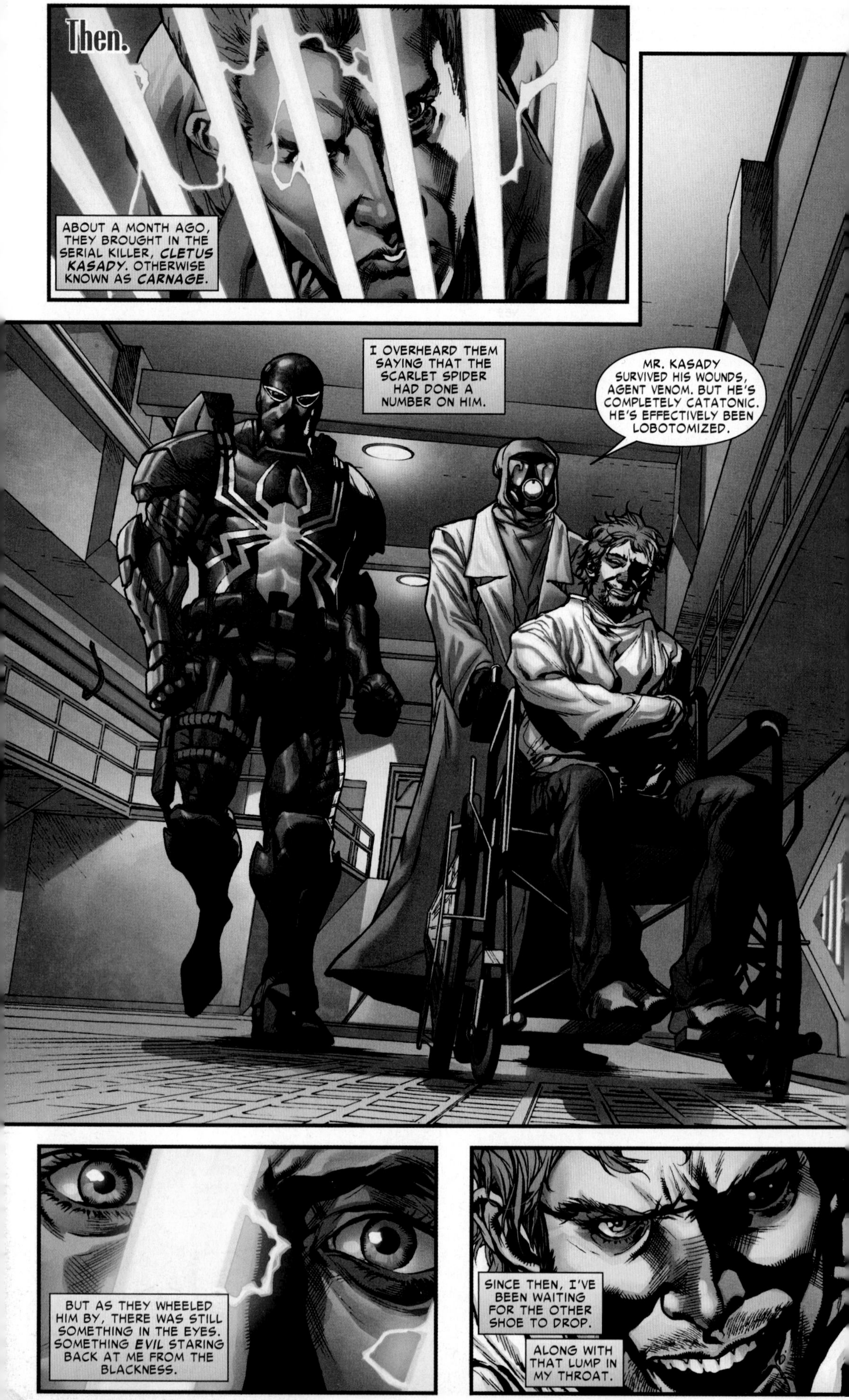
Then.
ABOUT A MONTH AGO, THEY BROUGHT IN THE SERIAL KILLER, CLETUS KASADY. OTHERWISE KNOWN AS CARNAGE.
I OVERHEARD THEM SAYING THAT THE SCARLET SPIDER HAD DONE A NUMBER ON HIM.
MR. KASADY SURVIVED HIS WOUNDS, AGENT VENOM. BUT HE'S COMPLETELY CATATONIC. HE'S EFFECTIVELY BEEN LOBOTOMIZED.
BUT AS THEY WHEELED HIM BY, THERE WAS STILL SOMETHING IN THE EYES. SOMETHING EVIL STARING BACK AT ME FROM THE BLACKNESS.
SINCE THEN, I'VE BEEN WAITING FOR THE OTHER SHOE TO DROP.
ALONG WITH THAT LUMP IN MY THROAT.

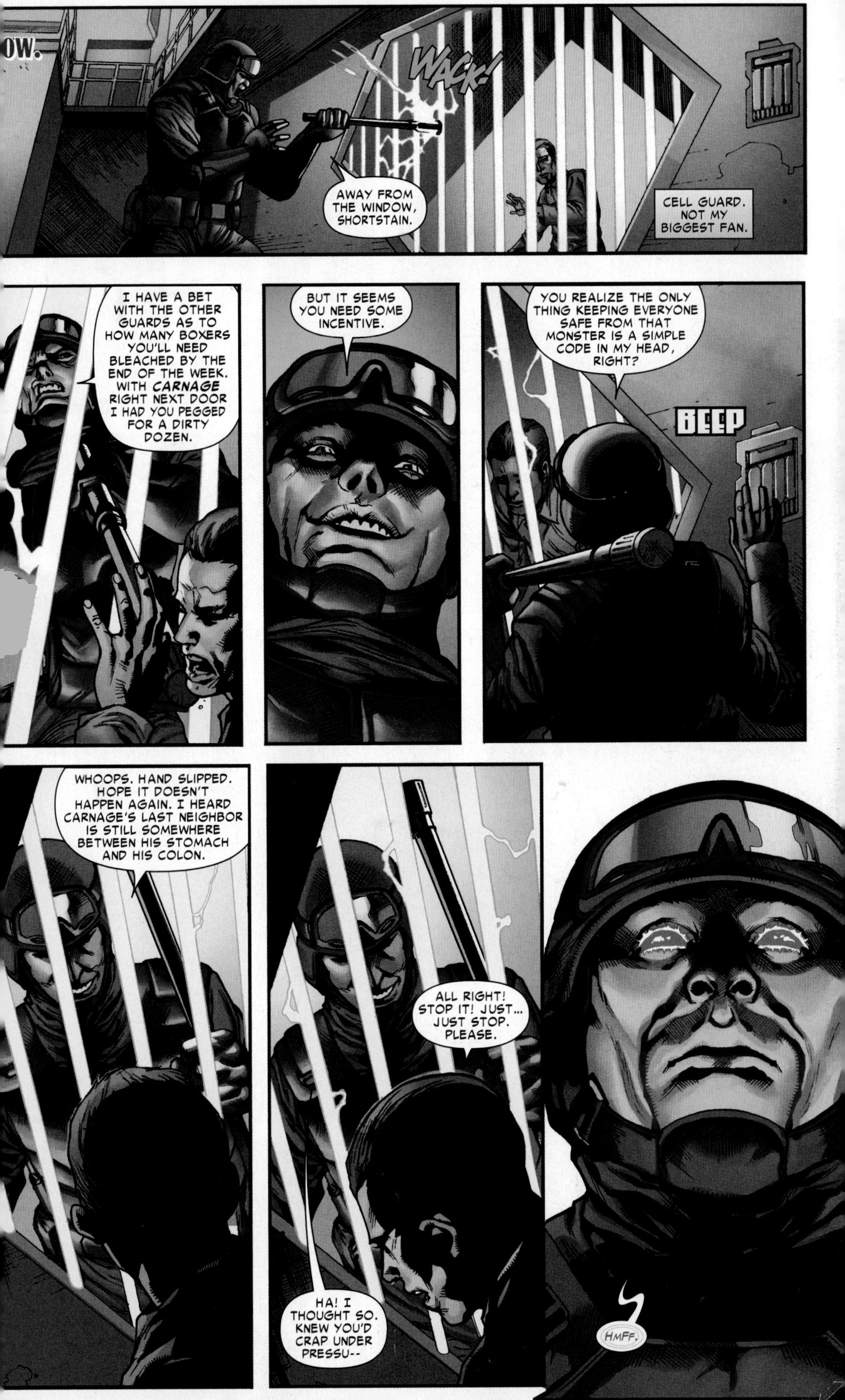
OW.
WACK!
AWAY FROM THE WINDOW, SHORTSTAIN.
CELL GUARD. NOT MY BIGGEST FAN.
I HAVE A BET WITH THE OTHER GUARDS AS TO HOW MANY BOXERS YOU'LL NEED BLEACHED BY THE END OF THE WEEK. WITH CARNAGE RIGHT NEXT DOOR I HAD YOU PEGGED FOR A DIRTY DOZEN.
BUT IT SEEMS YOU NEED SOME INCENTIVE.
YOU REALIZE THE ONLY THING KEEPING EVERYONE SAFE FROM THAT MONSTER IS A SIMPLE CODE IN MY HEAD, RIGHT?
BEEP
WHOOPS. HAND SLIPPED. HOPE IT DOESN'T HAPPEN AGAIN. I HEARD CARNAGE'S LAST NEIGHBOR IS STILL SOMEWHERE BETWEEN HIS STOMACH AND HIS COLON.
ALL RIGHT! STOP IT! JUST... JUST STOP. PLEASE.
HA! I THOUGHT SO. KNEW YOU'D CRAP UNDER PRESSU--
HMFF.

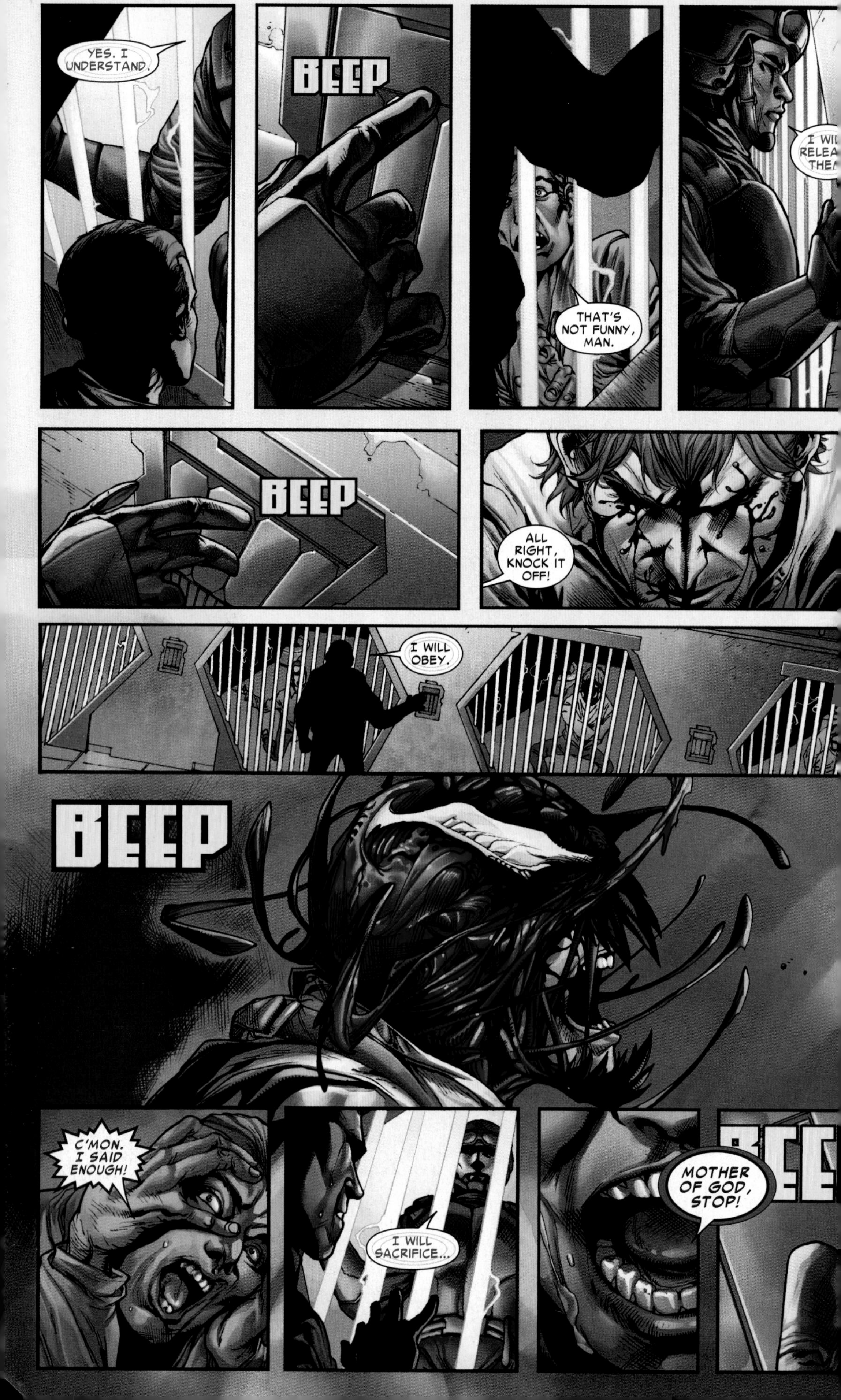

YES. I UNDERSTAND.
BEEP
THAT'S NOT FUNNY, MAN.
BEEP
ALL RIGHT, KNOCK IT OFF!
I WILL OBEY.
BEEP
C'MON. I SAID ENOUGH!
I WILL SACRIFICE...
MOTHER OF GOD, STOP!

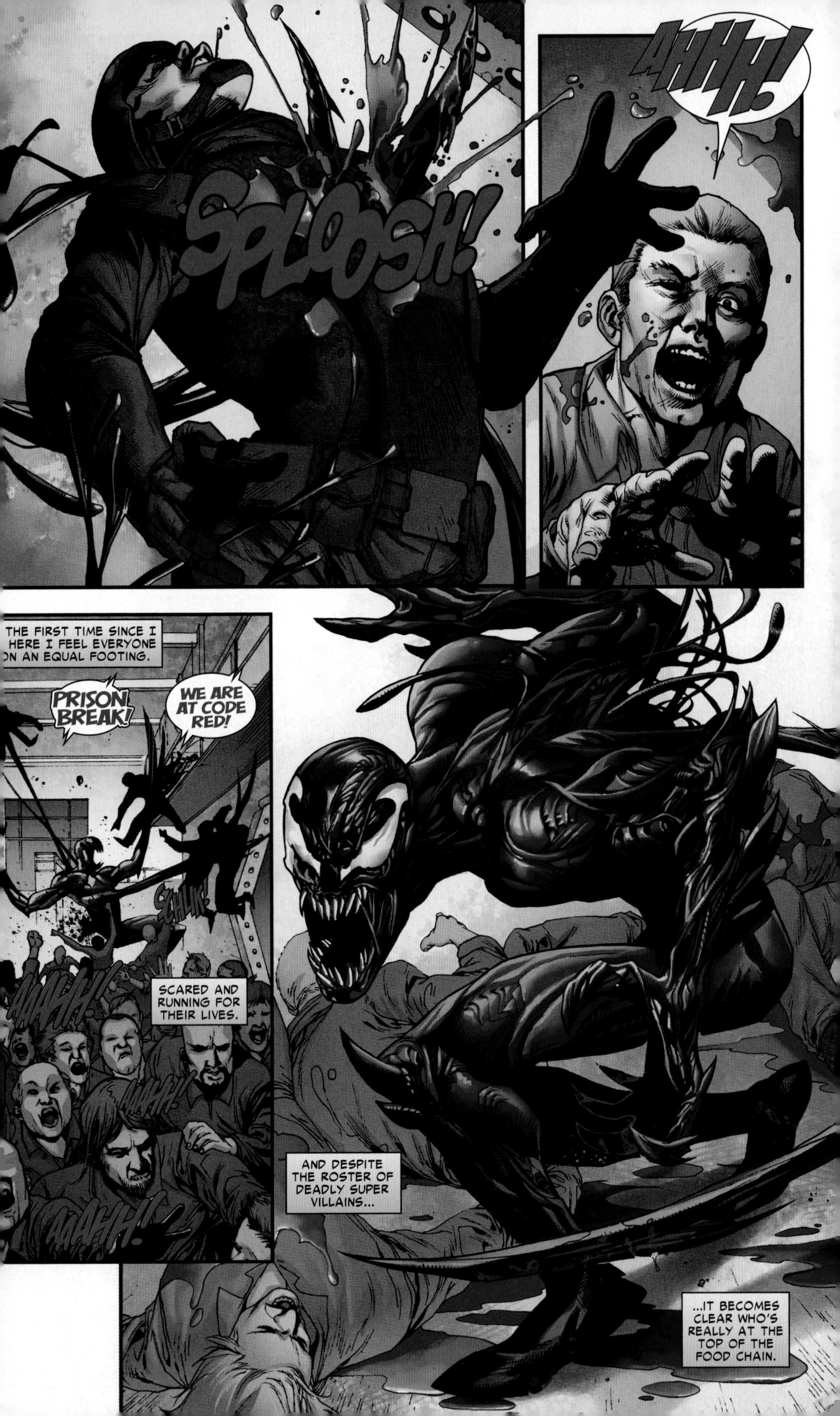
SPLOOSH!
AHHH!
THE FIRST TIME SINCE I
HERE I FEEL EVERYONE
ON AN EQUAL FOOTING.
PRISON BREAK!
WE ARE AT CODE RED!
SCHLUK!
SCARED AND RUNNING FOR THEIR LIVES.
AND DESPITE THE ROSTER OF DEADLY SUPER VILLAINS...
...IT BECOMES CLEAR WHO'S REALLY AT THE TOP OF THE FOOD CHAIN.

MY LEGS BECOME USELESS. IT'S EVERYTHING I FEARED.

I DON'T KNOW HOW IT KILLS SO MANY SO QUICKLY.

I DON'T KNOW HOW IT SEEPS THROUGH THE VENTS AND AIR DUCTS.

BUT WHAT I DO KNOW IS THIS...

WHEN YOU'R ASKED TO VOTE ON TH GOVERNOR "OVERCROWD CELL" PROPOSITIO NEXT MONTH

HiSSSSSSSS

-GASP!-

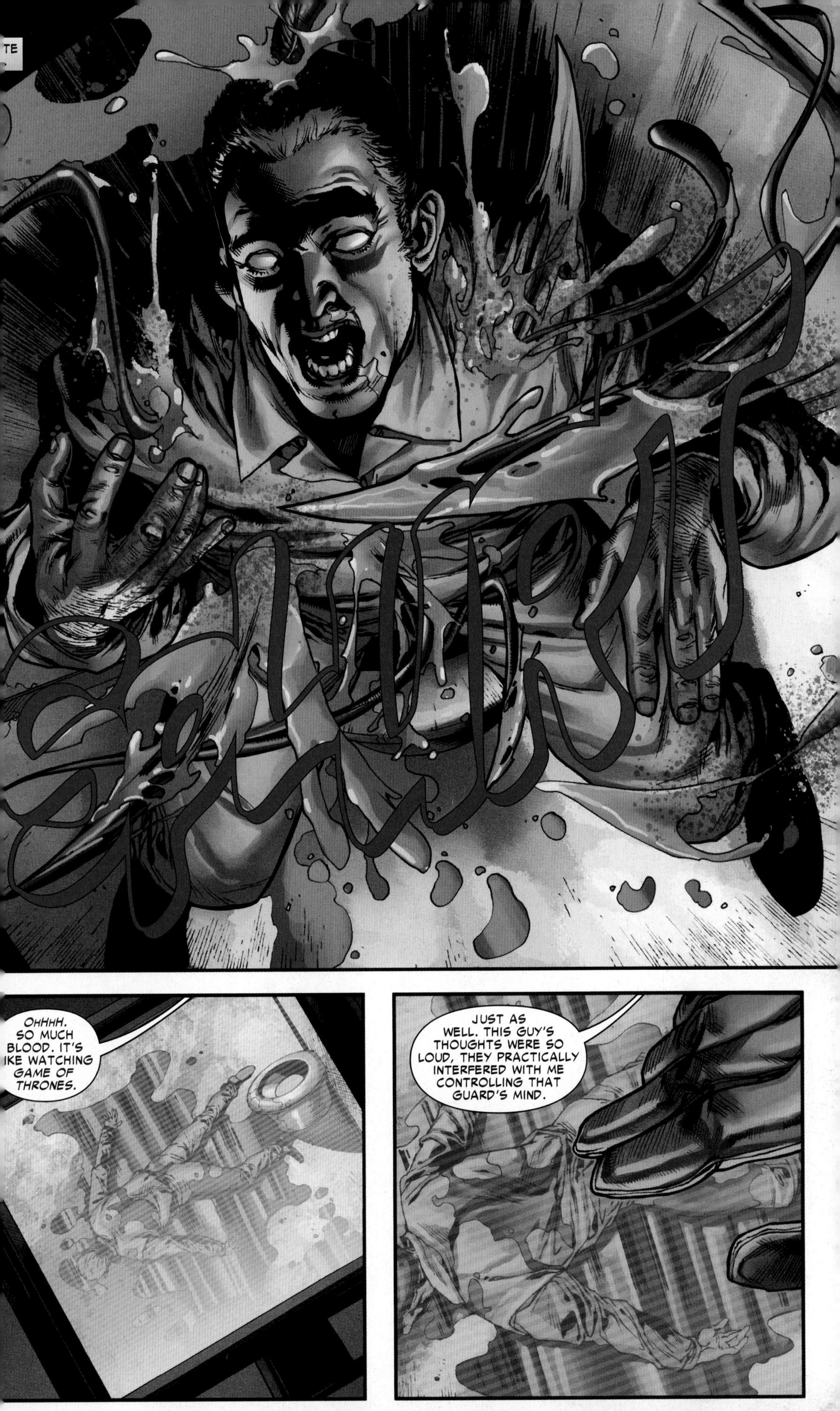
OHHHH. SO MUCH BLOOD. IT'S
IKE WATCHING GAME OF THRONES.
JUST AS WELL. THIS GUY'S THOUGHTS WERE SO LOUD, THEY PRACTICALLY INTERFERED WITH ME CONTROLLING THAT GUARD'S MIND.

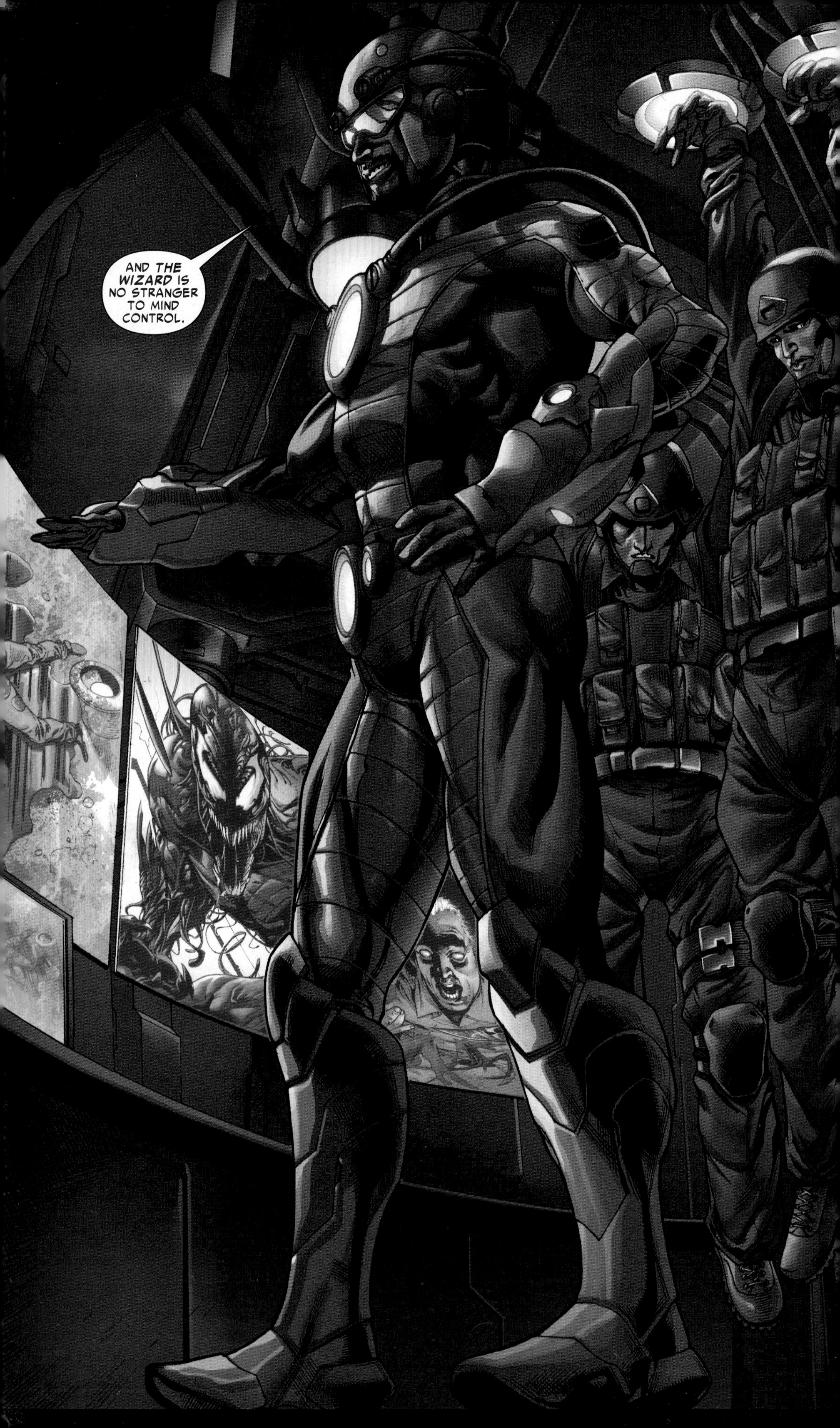
AND THE WIZARD IS NO STRANGER TO MIND CONTROL.

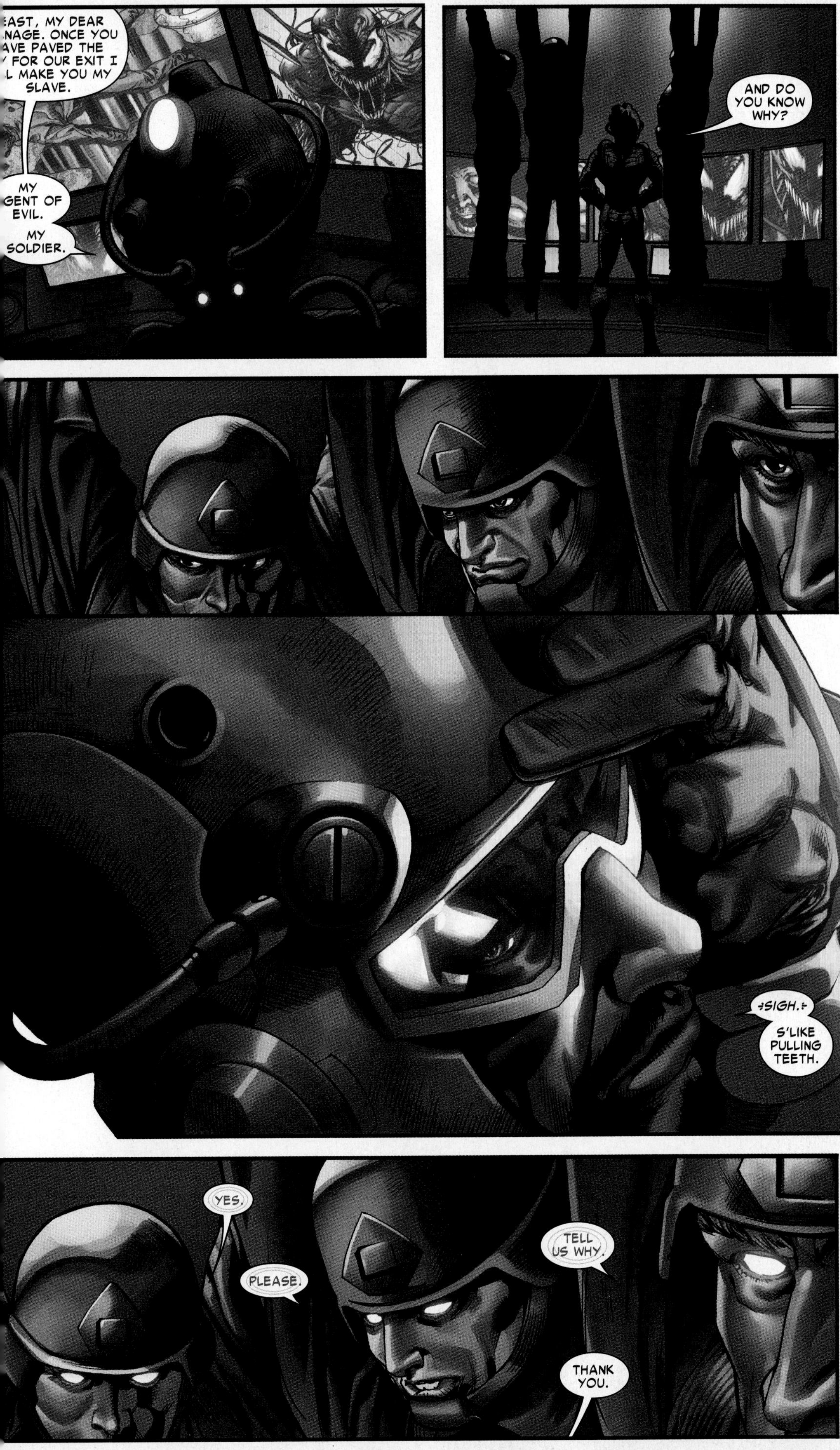
EAST, MY DEAR
NAGE. ONCE YOU
AVE PAVED THE
FOR OUR EXIT I
L MAKE YOU MY
SLAVE.
MY
GENT OF
EVIL.
MY
SOLDIER.
AND DO YOU KNOW WHY?
SIGH.
S'LIKE PULLING TEETH.
YES.
PLEASE.
TELL US WHY.
THANK YOU.

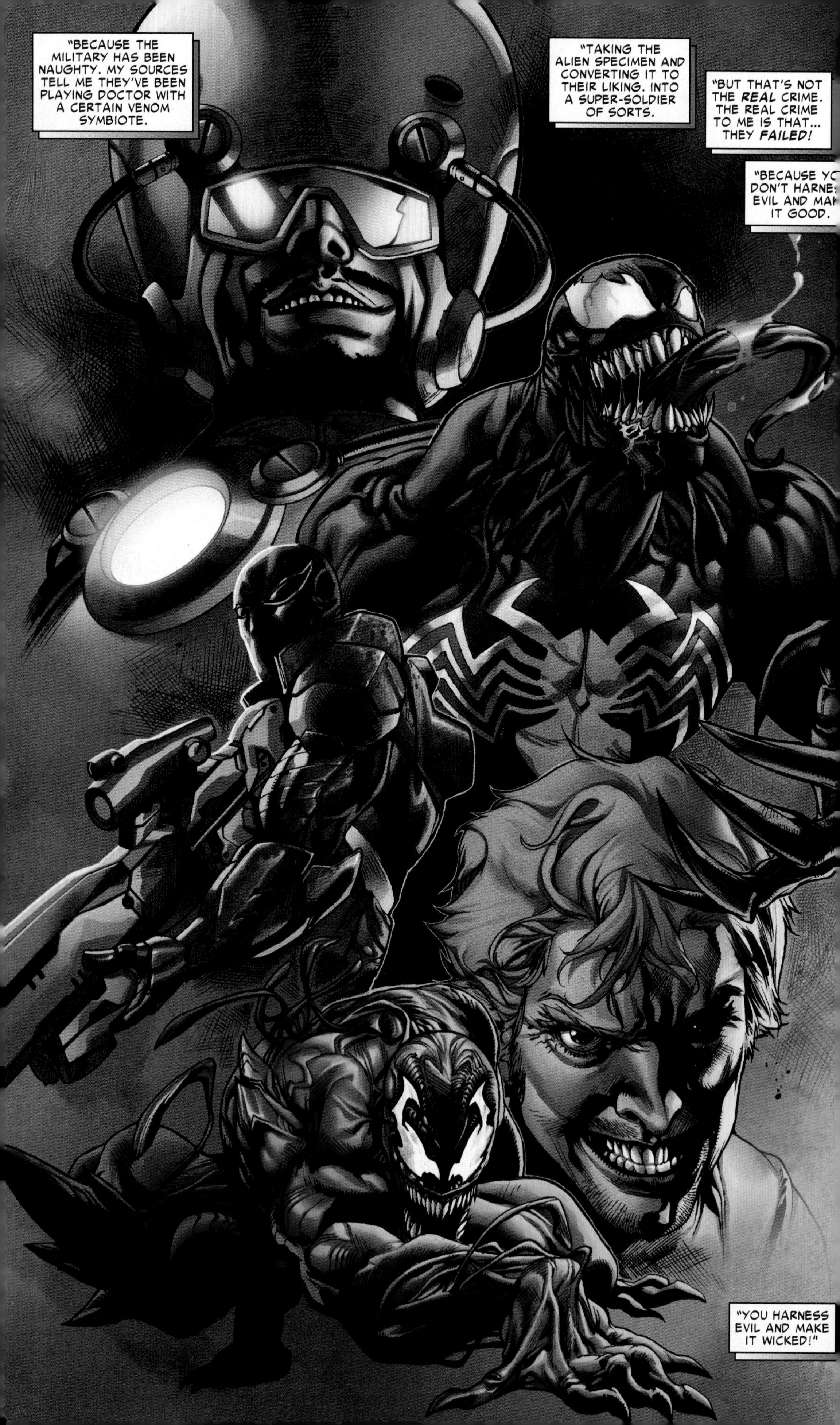
"BECAUSE THE MILITARY HAS BEEN NAUGHTY. MY SOURCES TELL ME THEY'VE BEEN PLAYING DOCTOR WITH A CERTAIN VENOM SYMBIOTE.
"TAKING THE ALIEN SPECIMEN AND CONVERTING IT TO THEIR LIKING. INTO A SUPER-SOLDIER OF SORTS.
"BUT THAT'S NOT THE *REAL* CRIME. THE REAL CRIME TO ME IS THAT... THEY *FAILED!*
"BECAUSE Y DON'T HARNE EVIL AND MA IT GOOD.
"YOU HARNESS EVIL AND MAKE IT WICKED!"

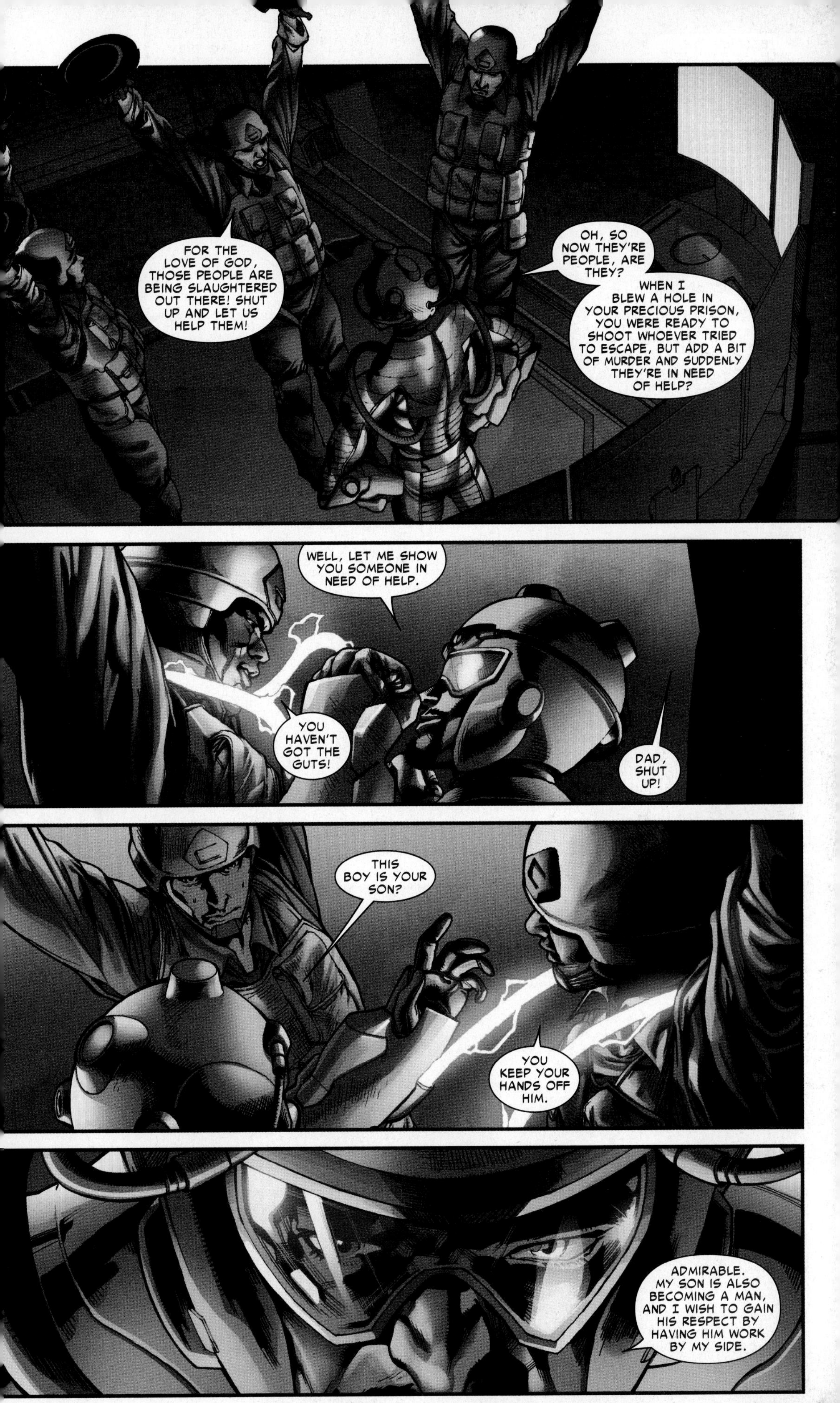
FOR THE LOVE OF GOD, THOSE PEOPLE ARE BEING SLAUGHTERED OUT THERE! SHUT UP AND LET US HELP THEM!
OH, SO NOW THEY'RE PEOPLE, ARE THEY?
WHEN I BLEW A HOLE IN YOUR PRECIOUS PRISON, YOU WERE READY TO SHOOT WHOEVER TRIED TO ESCAPE, BUT ADD A BIT OF MURDER AND SUDDENLY THEY'RE IN NEED OF HELP?
WELL, LET ME SHOW YOU SOMEONE IN NEED OF HELP.
YOU HAVEN'T GOT THE GUTS!
DAD, SHUT UP!
THIS BOY IS YOUR SON?
YOU KEEP YOUR HANDS OFF HIM.
ADMIRABLE. MY SON IS ALSO BECOMING A MAN, AND I WISH TO GAIN HIS RESPECT BY HAVING HIM WORK BY MY SIDE.

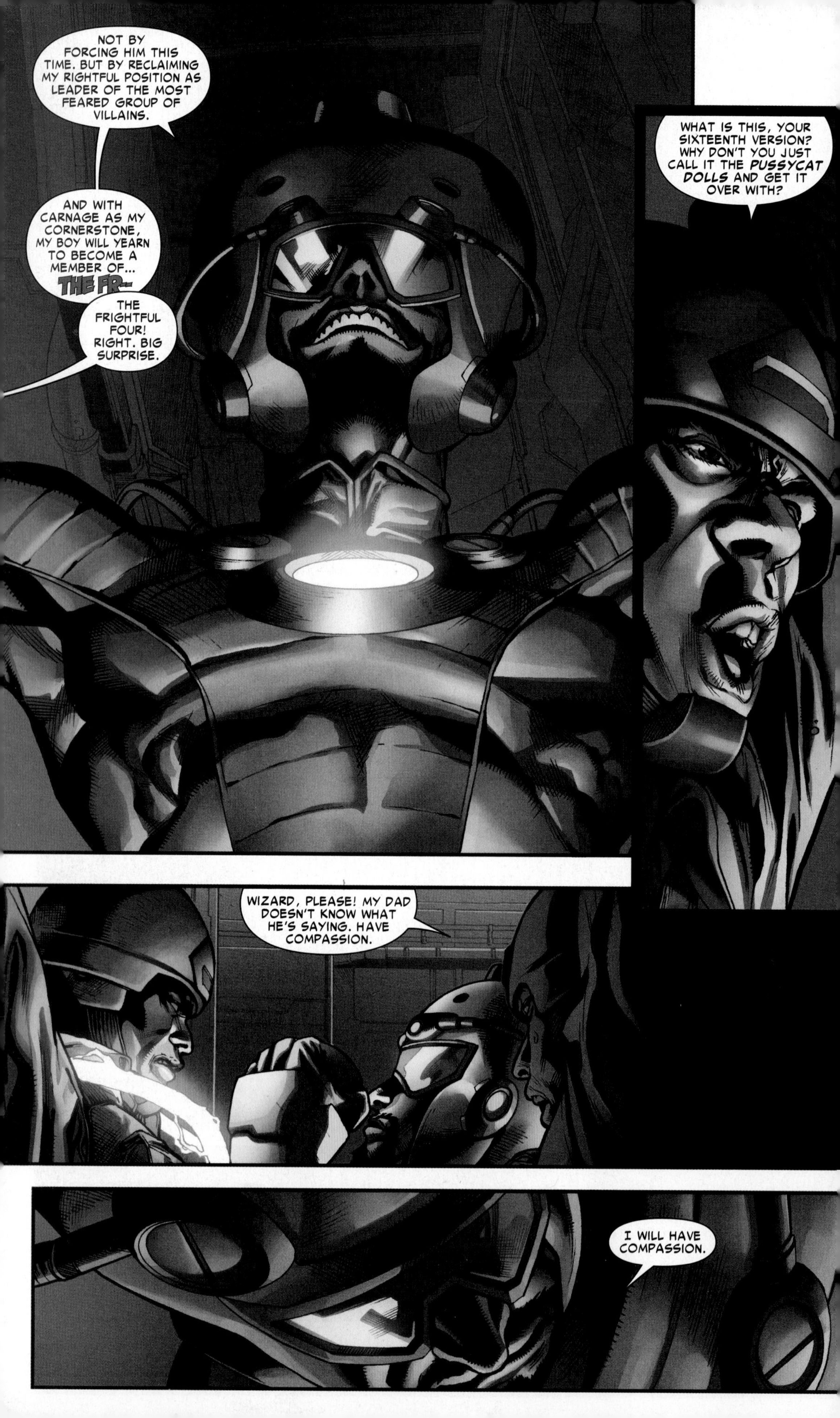
NOT BY FORCING HIM THIS TIME. BUT BY RECLAIMING MY RIGHTFUL POSITION AS LEADER OF THE MOST FEARED GROUP OF VILLAINS.
AND WITH CARNAGE AS MY CORNERSTONE, MY BOY WILL YEARN TO BECOME A MEMBER OF... THE FR--
THE FRIGHTFUL FOUR! RIGHT. BIG SURPRISE.
WHAT IS THIS, YOUR SIXTEENTH VERSION? WHY DON'T YOU JUST CALL IT THE PUSSYCAT DOLLS AND GET IT OVER WITH?
WIZARD, PLEASE! MY DAD DOESN'T KNOW WHAT HE'S SAYING. HAVE COMPASSION.
I WILL HAVE COMPASSION.

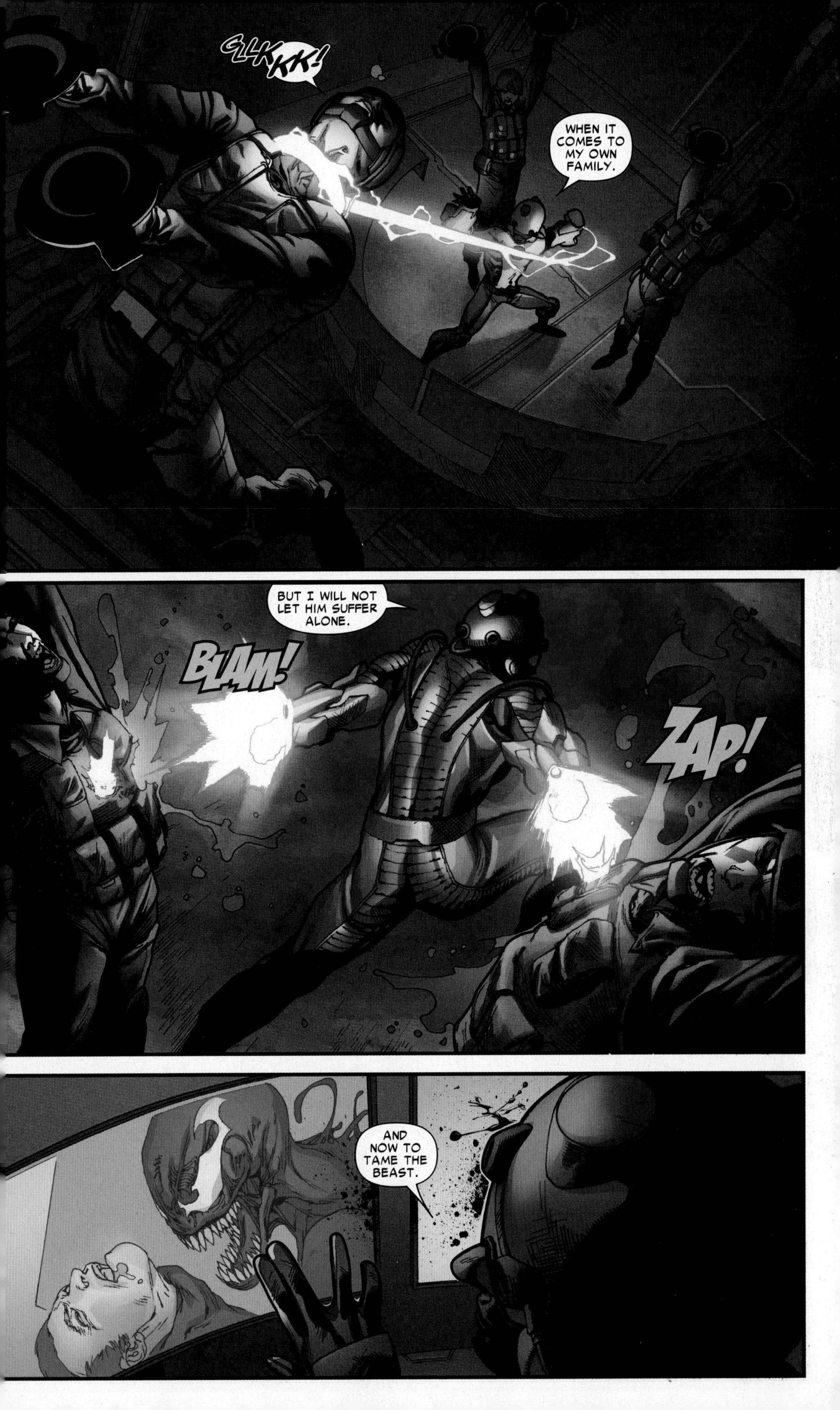
GLLKKK!
WHEN IT COMES TO MY OWN FAMILY.
BUT I WILL NOT LET HIM SUFFER ALONE.
BLAM!
ZAP!
AND NOW TO TAME THE BEAST.

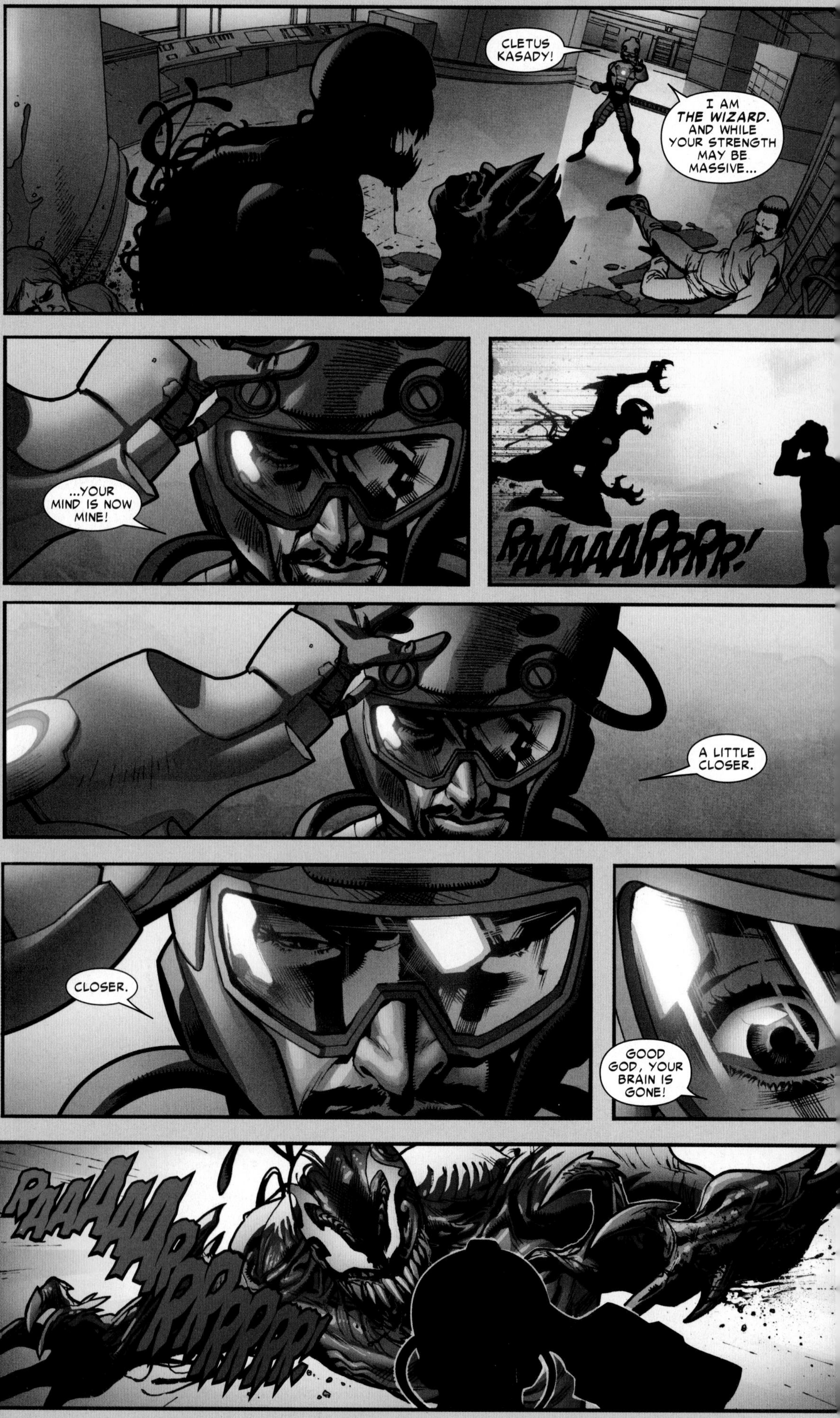

CLETUS KASADY!
I AM THE WIZARD. AND WHILE YOUR STRENGTH MAY BE MASSIVE...
...YOUR MIND IS NOW MINE!
RAAAAAARRRRR!
A LITTLE CLOSER.
CLOSER.
GOOD GOD, YOUR BRAIN IS GONE!
RAAAAARRRRRRRR

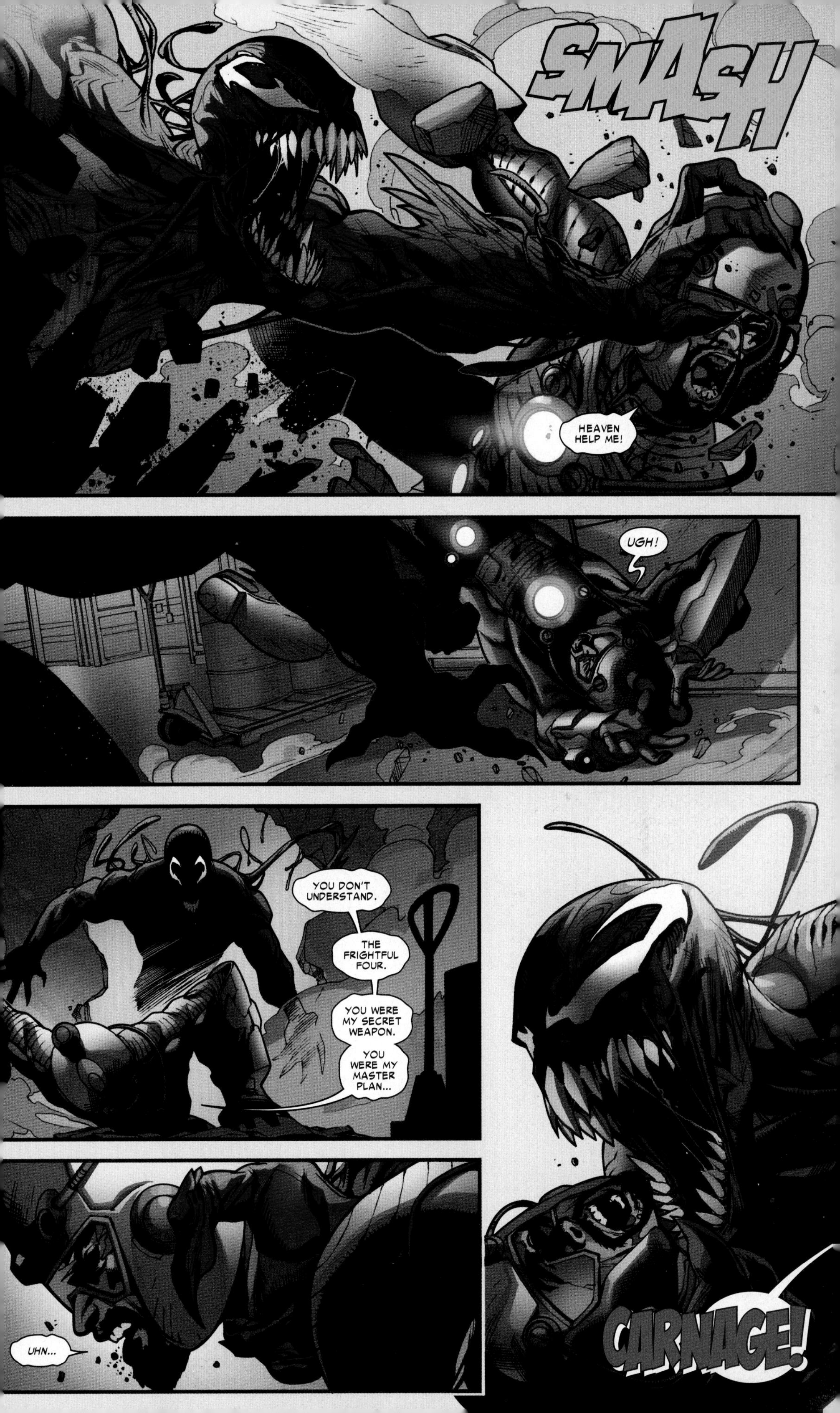
SMASH
HEAVEN HELP ME!
UGH!
YOU DON'T UNDERSTAND.
THE FRIGHTFUL FOUR.
YOU WERE MY SECRET WEAPON.
YOU WERE MY MASTER PLAN...
UHN...
CARNAGE!

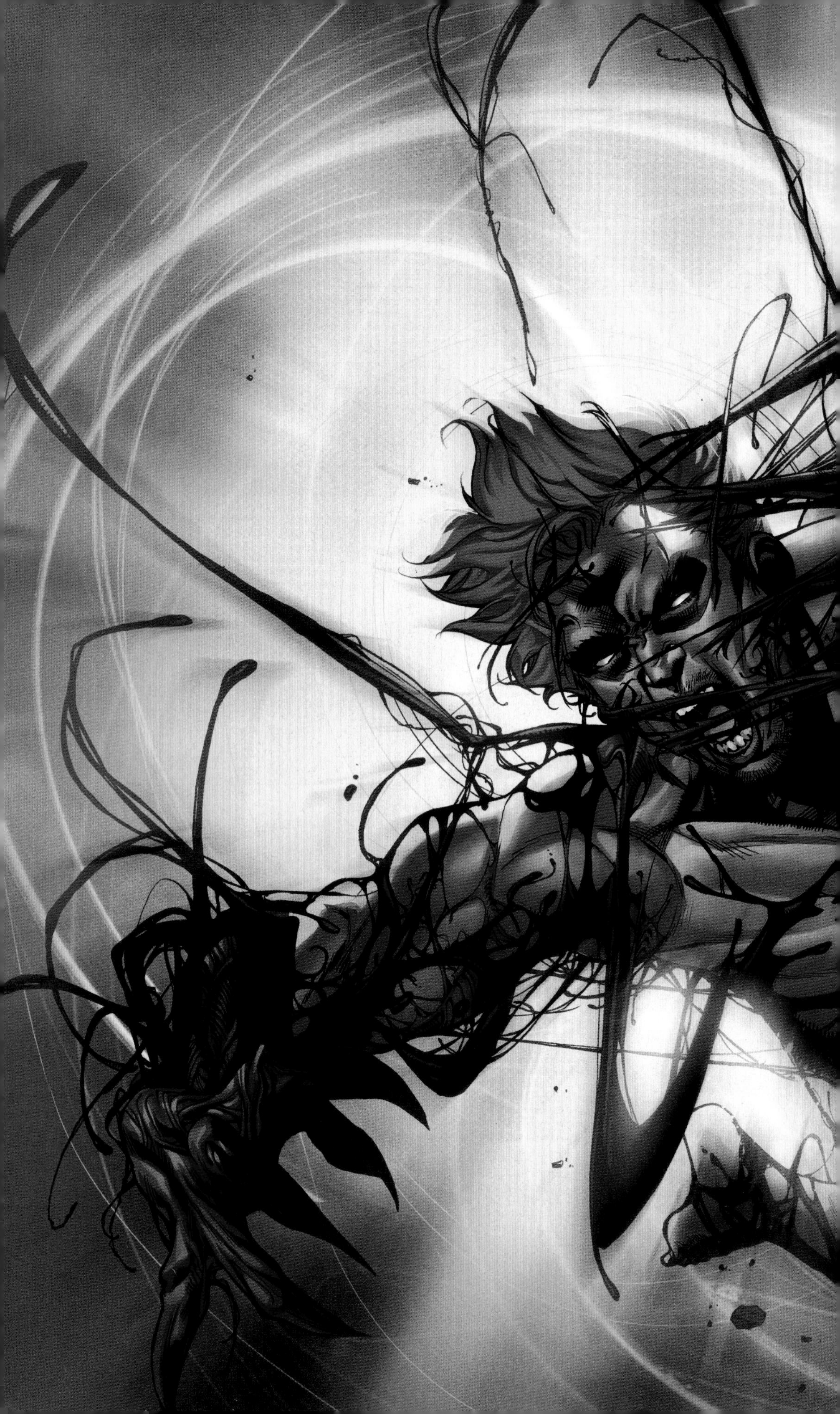

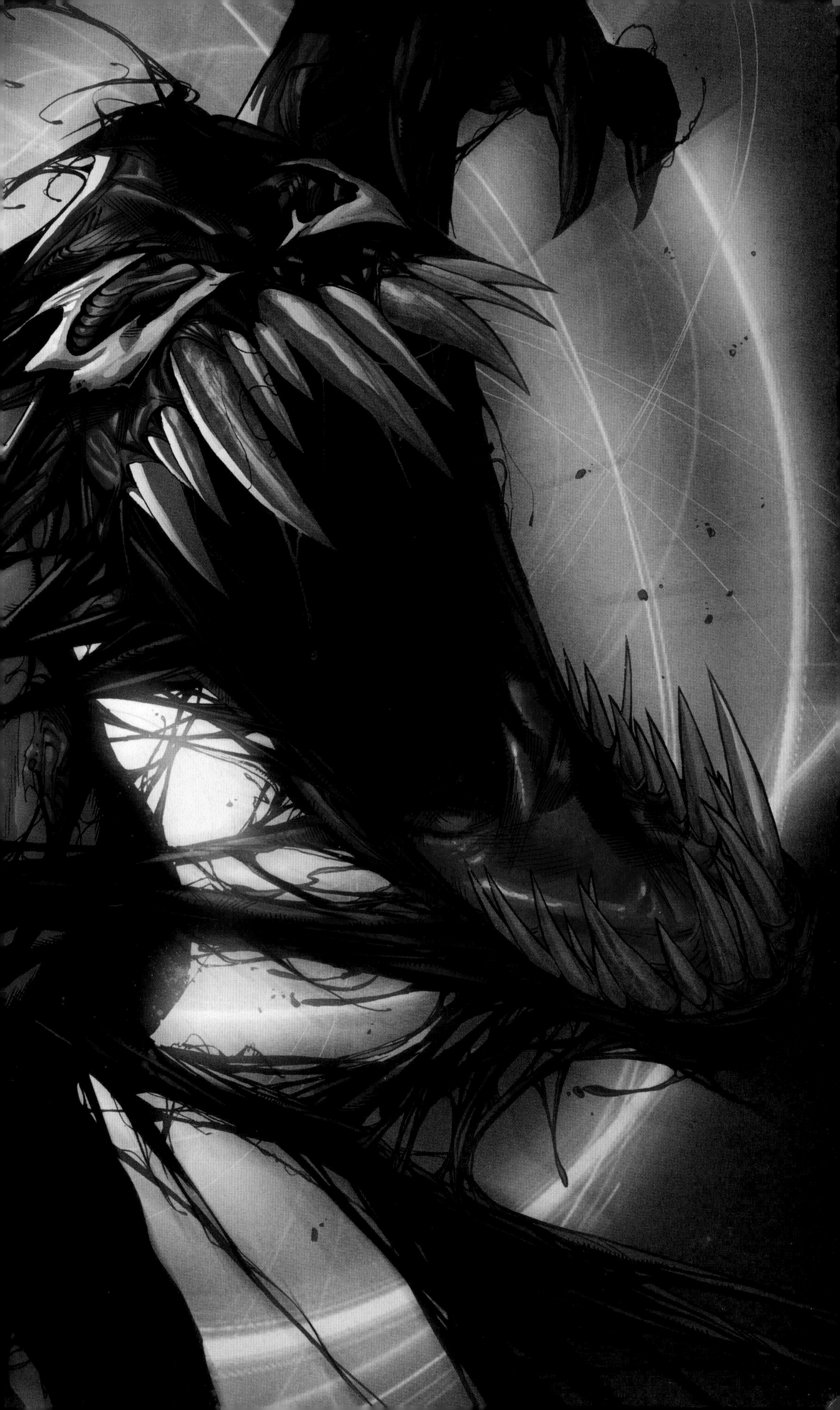

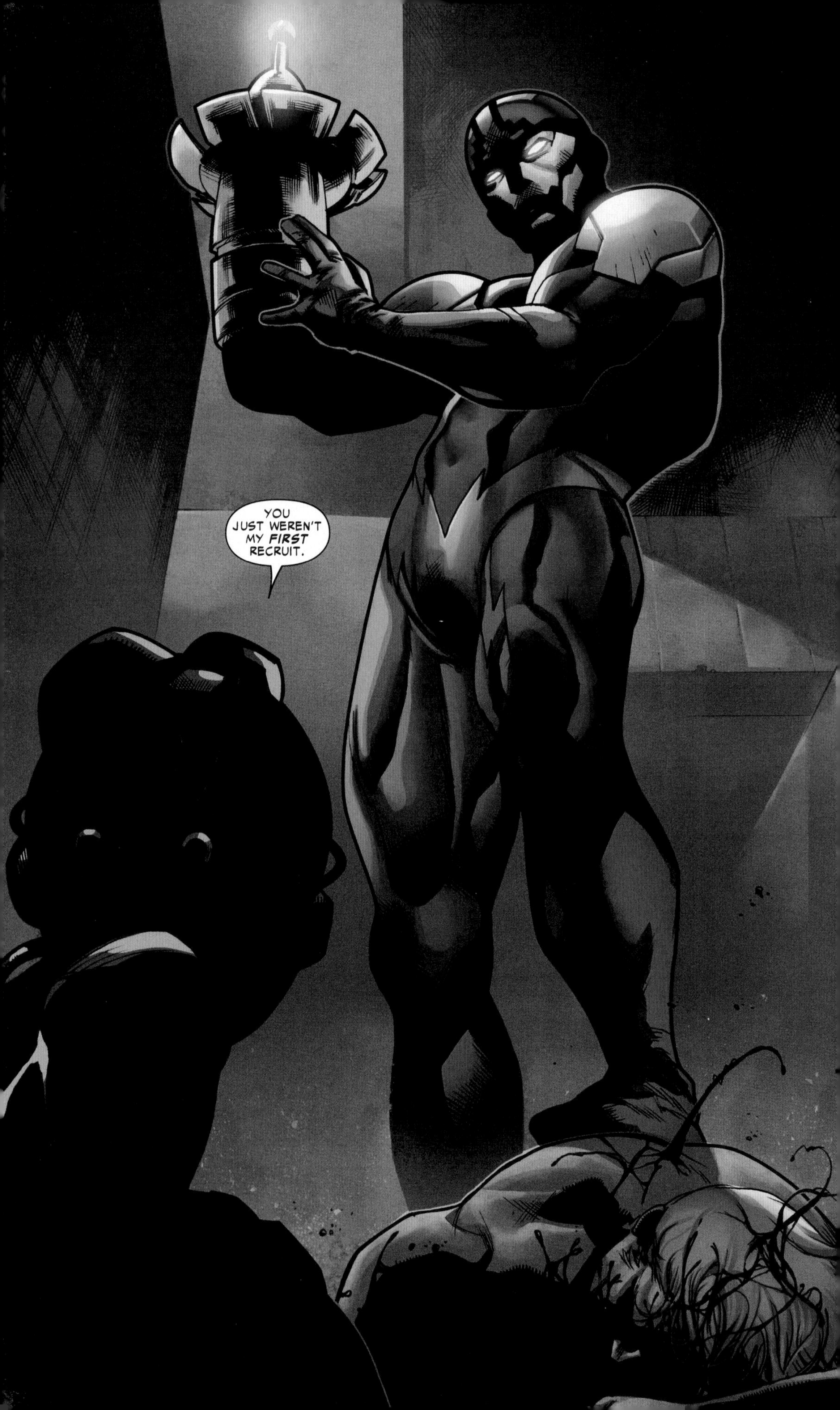
YOU JUST WEREN'T MY FIRST RECRUIT.

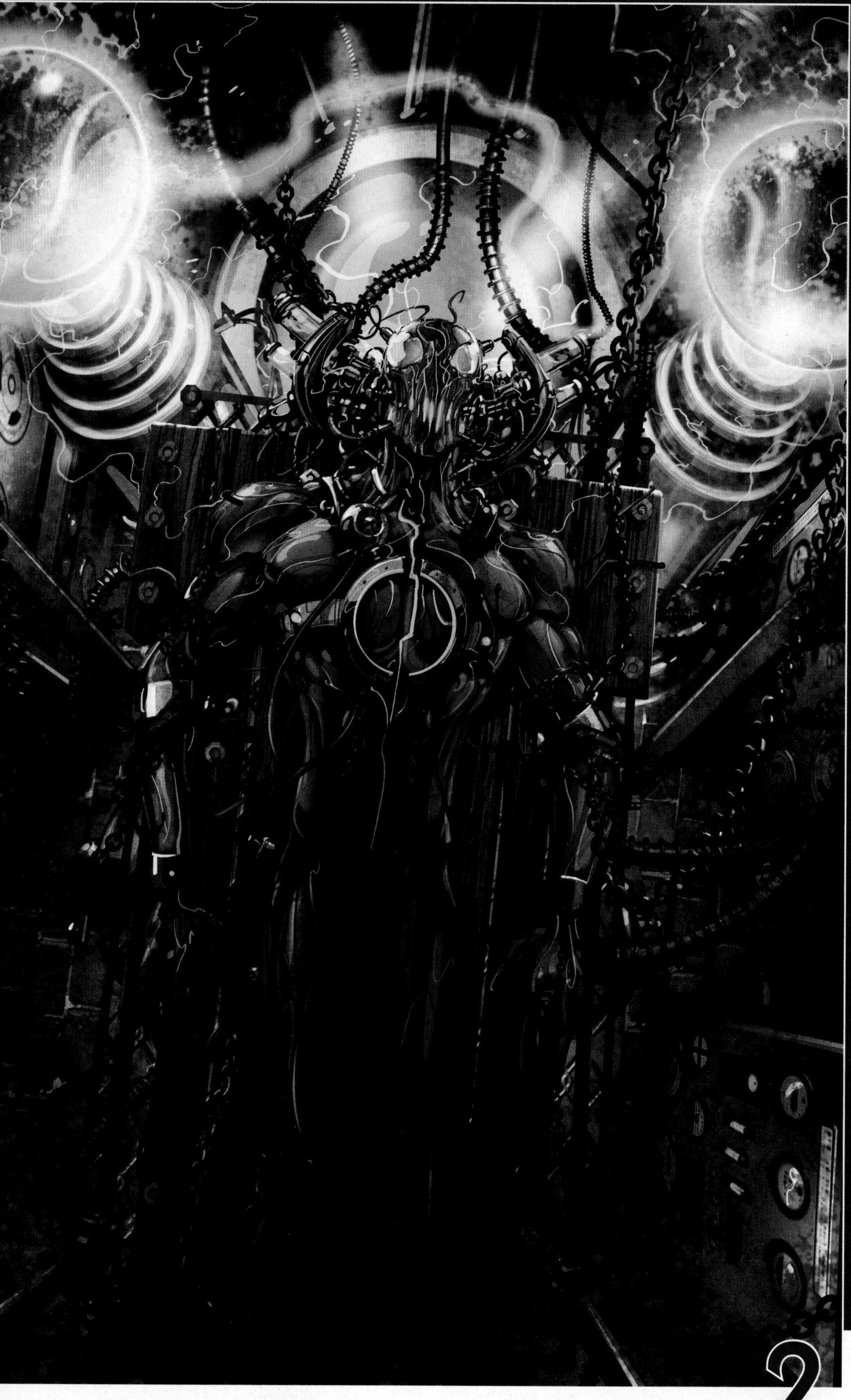

2

FORTUNATELY, CARNAGE IS NO STRANGER TO PAIN.

HE'S JUST USUALLY ON THE OTHER SIDE OF IT IS ALL.

HOW WILL YOU KEEP HIM AT BAY IF HE HAS NO MIND LEFT TO CONTROL?

EVERYTHING HAS A MIND, DEAR KLAW. I WAS JUST FOCUSING ON THE WRONG ONE.

THIS NEW HELMET OF MINE CAN ACCESS ANYONE OR ANYTHING. I JUST NEED TO CALIBRATE FOR THE SYMBIOTE'S BRAIN AND NOT KASADY'S.

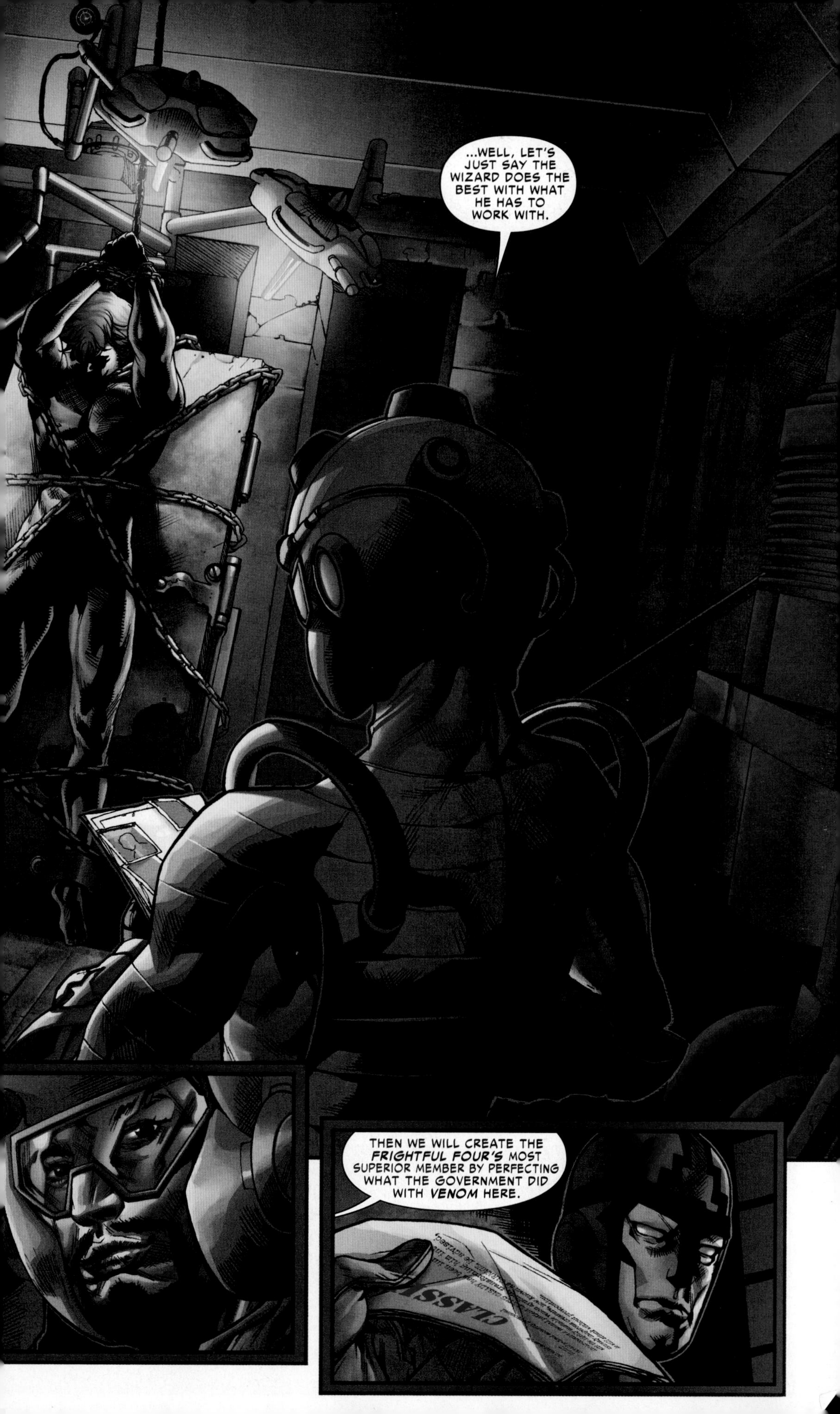
...WELL, LET'S JUST SAY THE WIZARD DOES THE BEST WITH WHAT HE HAS TO WORK WITH.
THEN WE WILL CREATE THE *FRIGHTFUL FOUR'S* MOST SUPERIOR MEMBER BY PERFECTING WHAT THE GOVERNMENT DID WITH *VENOM* HERE.

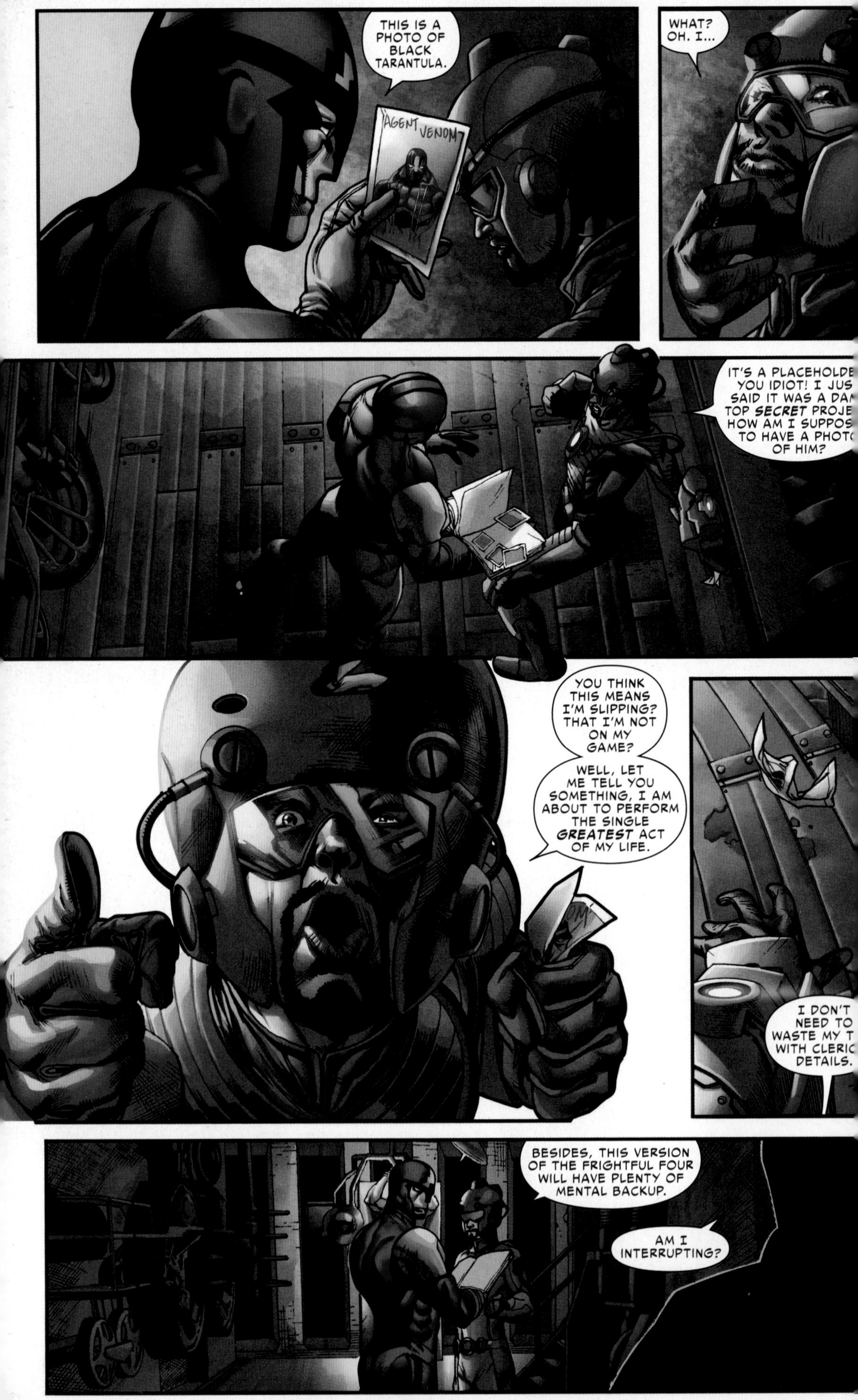
THIS IS A PHOTO OF BLACK TARANTULA.
AGENT VENOM
WHAT? OH. I...
IT'S A PLACEHOLDE YOU IDIOT! I JUS SAID IT WAS A DAM TOP *SECRET* PROJE HOW AM I SUPPOS TO HAVE A PHOTO OF HIM?
YOU THINK THIS MEANS I'M SLIPPING? THAT I'M NOT ON MY GAME?
WELL, LET ME TELL YOU SOMETHING, I AM ABOUT TO PERFORM THE SINGLE *GREATEST* ACT OF MY LIFE.
I DON'T NEED TO WASTE MY T WITH CLERIC DETAILS.
BESIDES, THIS VERSION OF THE FRIGHTFUL FOUR WILL HAVE PLENTY OF MENTAL BACKUP.
AM I INTERRUPTING?

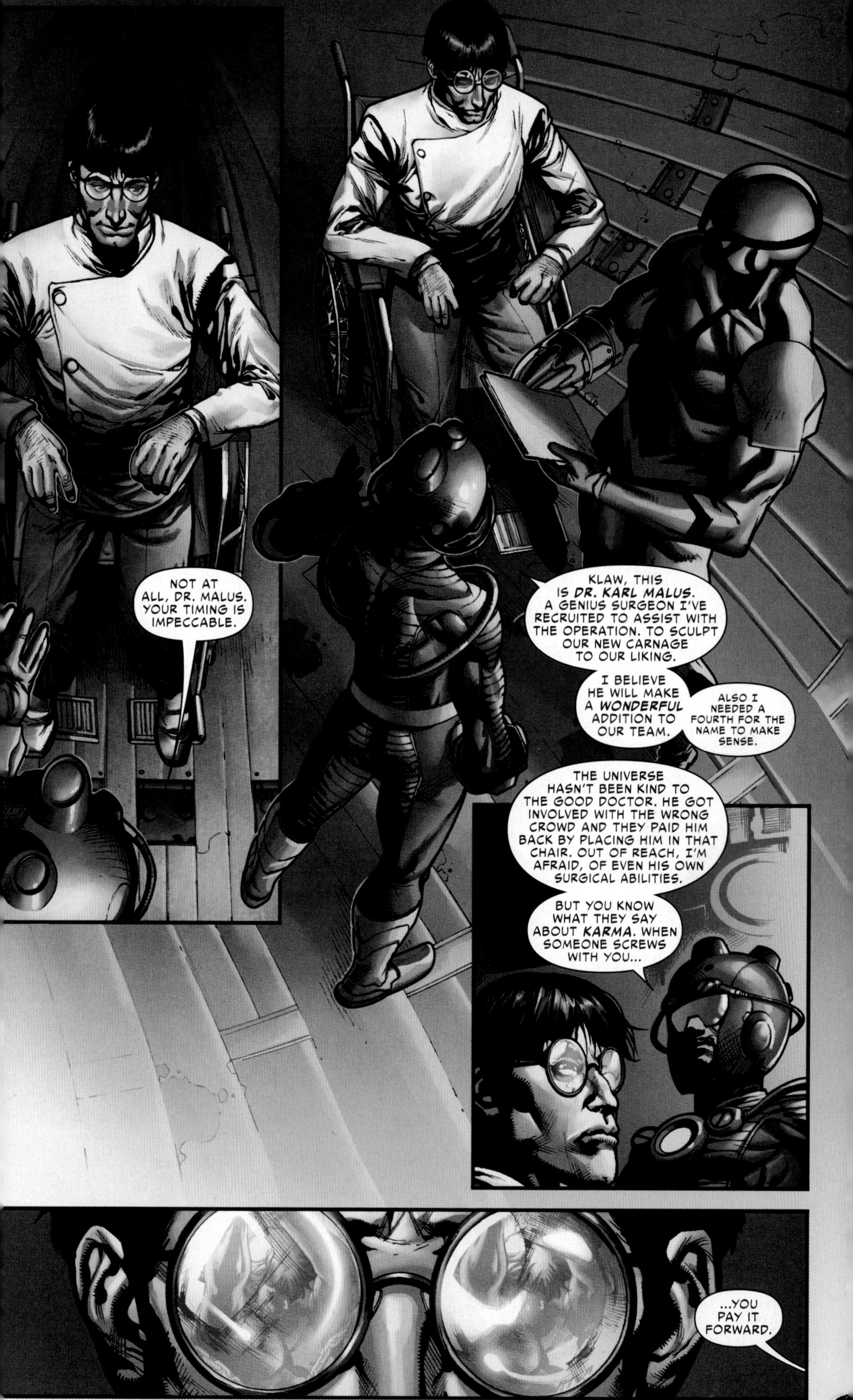
NOT AT ALL, DR. MALUS. YOUR TIMING IS IMPECCABLE.
KLAW, THIS IS DR. KARL MALUS. A GENIUS SURGEON I'VE RECRUITED TO ASSIST WITH THE OPERATION. TO SCULPT OUR NEW CARNAGE TO OUR LIKING.
I BELIEVE HE WILL MAKE A WONDERFUL ADDITION TO OUR TEAM.
ALSO I NEEDED A FOURTH FOR THE NAME TO MAKE SENSE.
THE UNIVERSE HASN'T BEEN KIND TO THE GOOD DOCTOR. HE GOT INVOLVED WITH THE WRONG CROWD AND THEY PAID HIM BACK BY PLACING HIM IN THAT CHAIR. OUT OF REACH, I'M AFRAID, OF EVEN HIS OWN SURGICAL ABILITIES.
BUT YOU KNOW WHAT THEY SAY ABOUT KARMA. WHEN SOMEONE SCREWS WITH YOU...
...YOU PAY IT FORWARD.

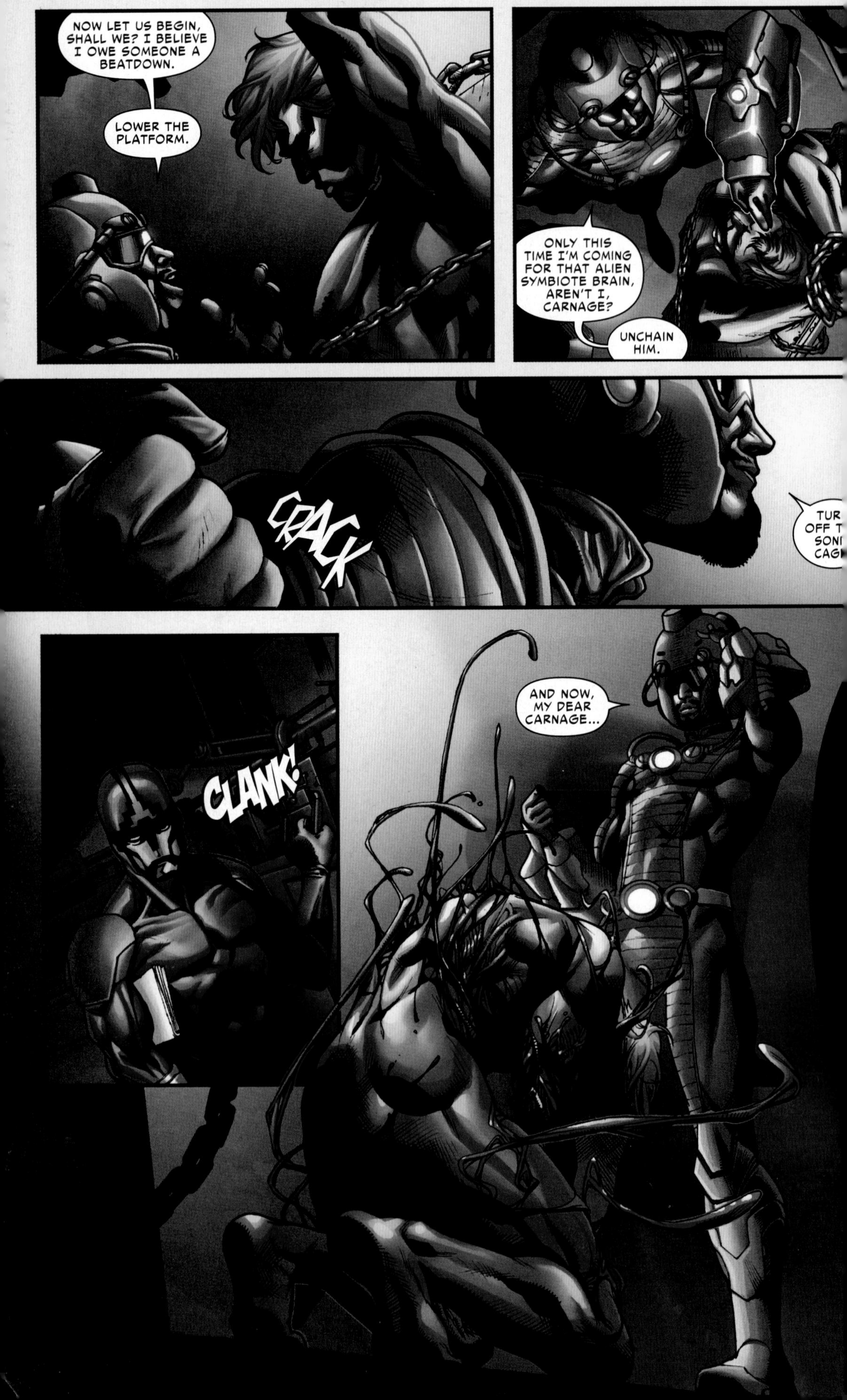
NOW LET US BEGIN, SHALL WE? I BELIEVE I OWE SOMEONE A BEATDOWN.
LOWER THE PLATFORM.
ONLY THIS TIME I'M COMING FOR THAT ALIEN SYMBIOTE BRAIN, AREN'T I, CARNAGE?
UNCHAIN HIM.
CRACK
TUR OFF T SONI CAG
CLANK!
AND NOW, MY DEAR CARNAGE...

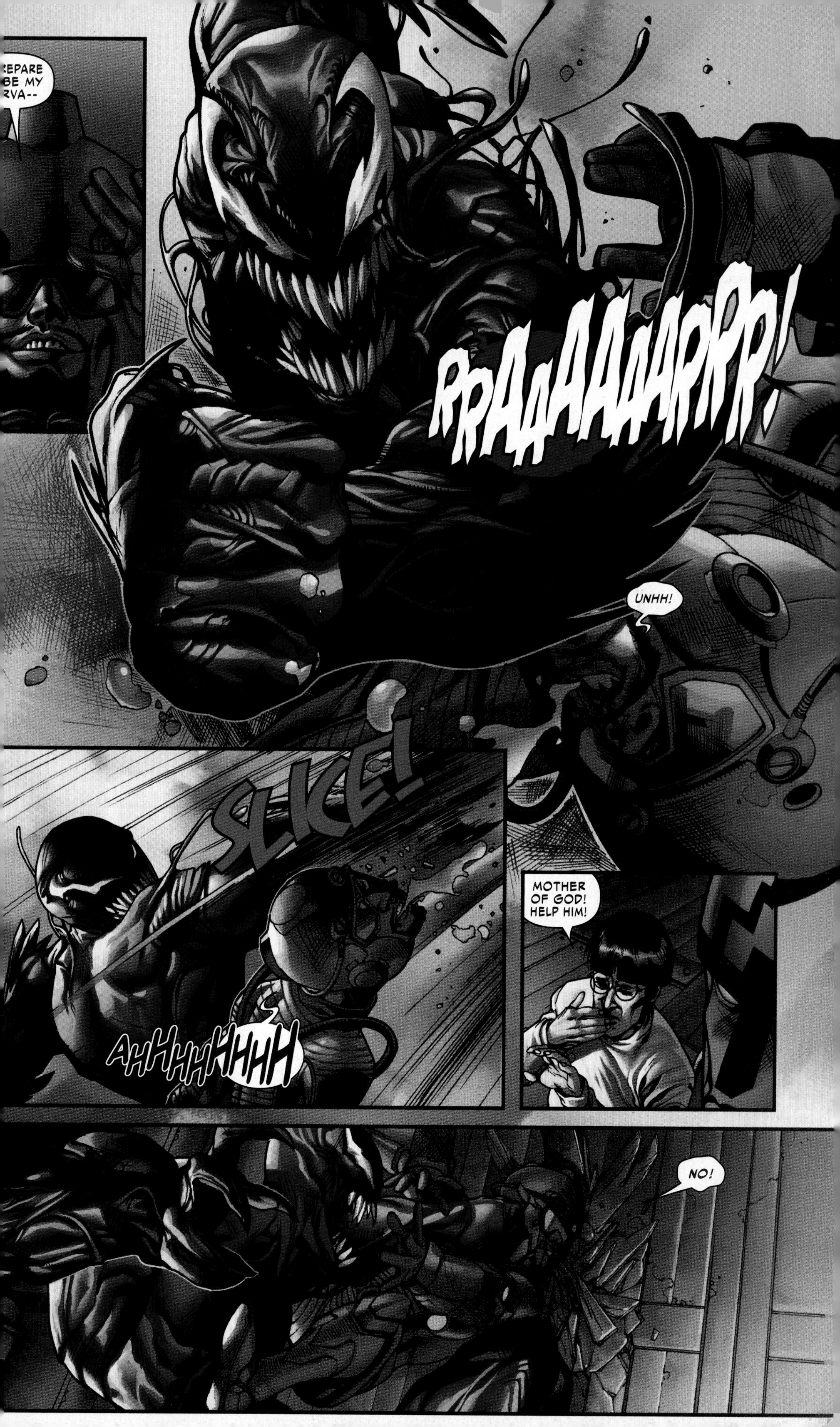

REPARE
BE MY
RVA--
RRAAAAAARRR!
UNHH!
SLICE!
AHHHHHHHH
MOTHER OF GOD! HELP HIM!
NO!

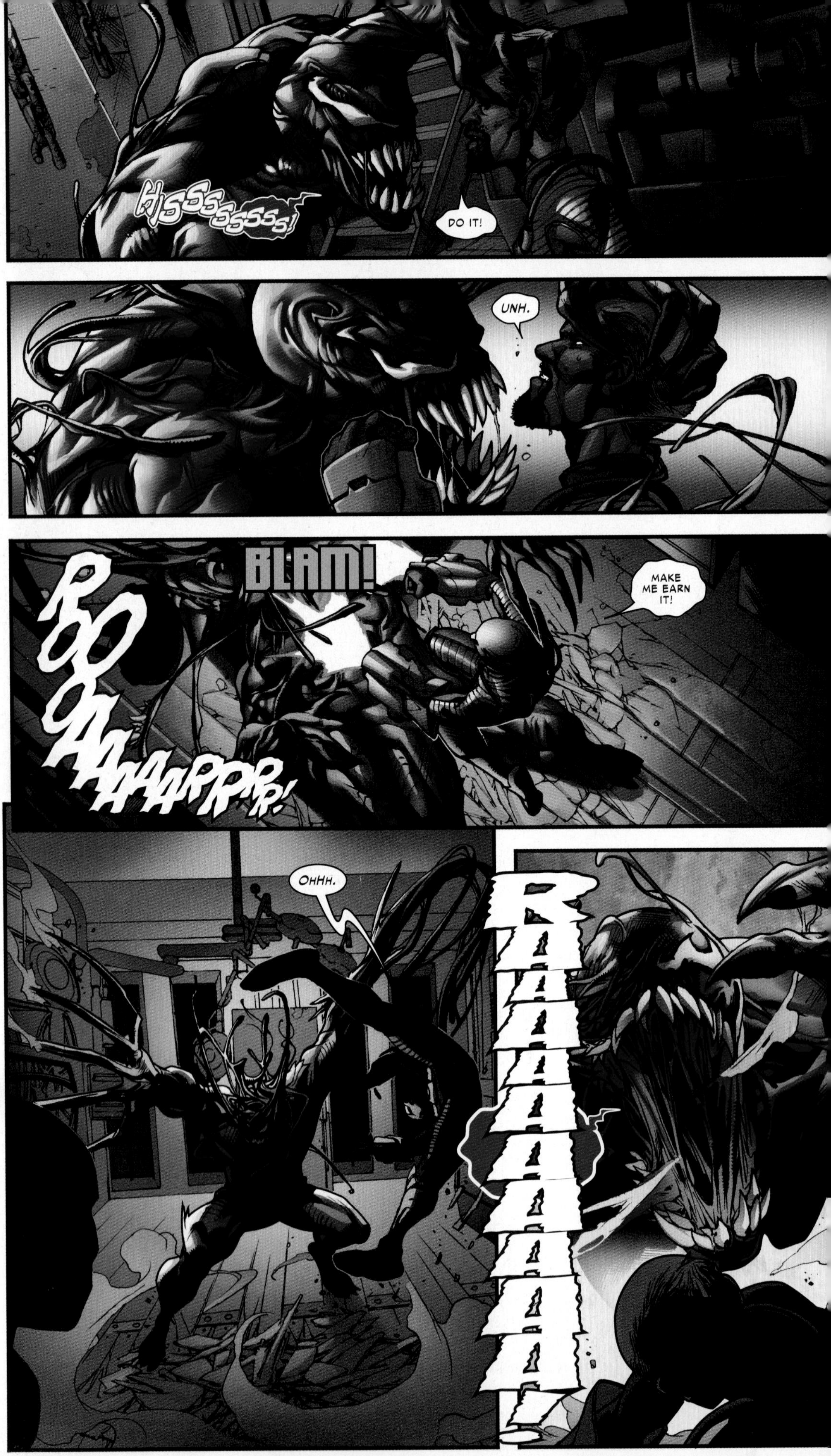
HISSSSSSSSS!
DO IT!
UNH.
BLAM!
ROOOAAAAAARRRR!
MAKE ME EARN IT!
OHHH.
RAAAAAAAAAAA

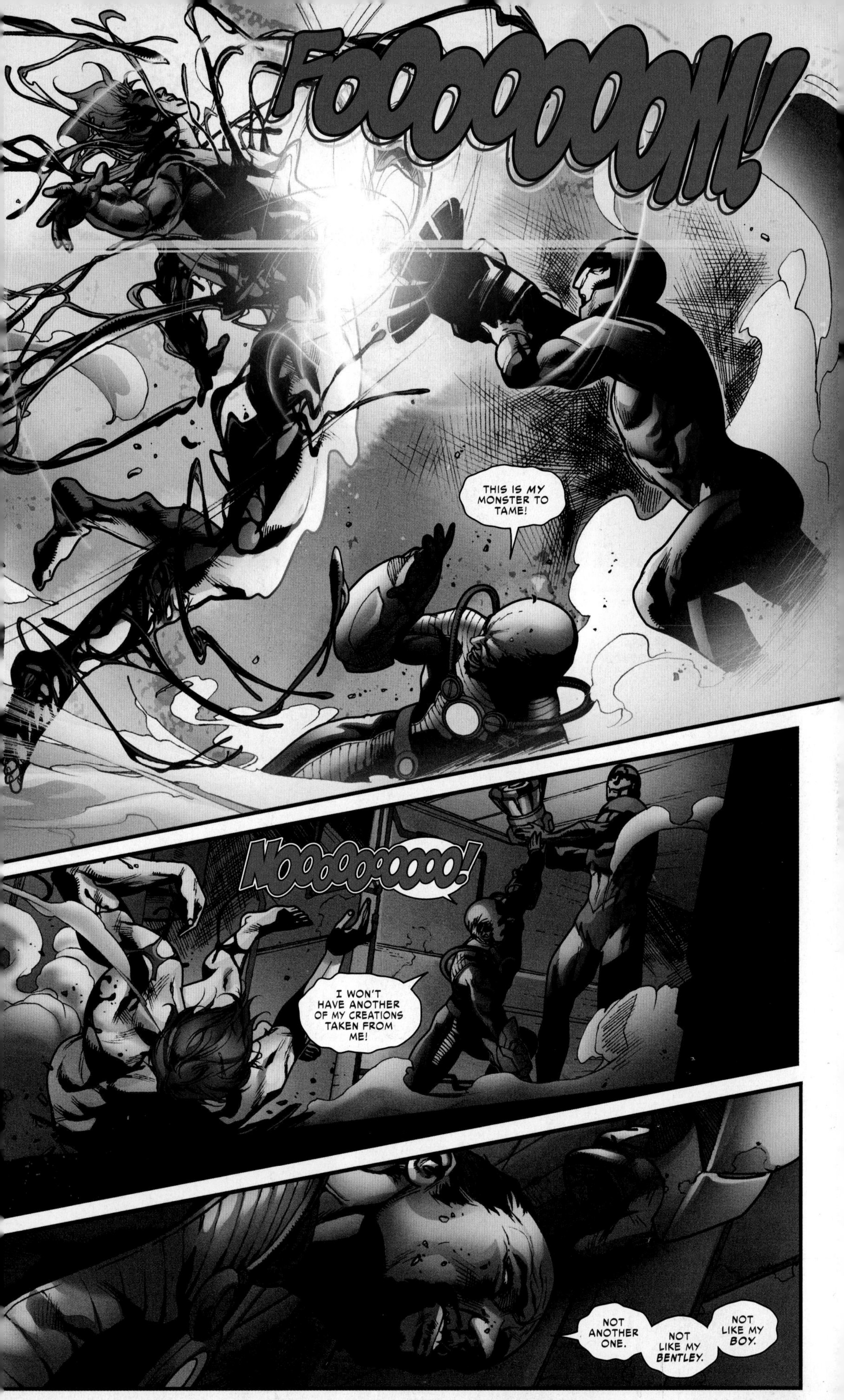
FOOOOOOOM!
THIS IS MY MONSTER TO TAME!
NOOOOOOOO!
I WON'T HAVE ANOTHER OF MY CREATIONS TAKEN FROM ME!
NOT ANOTHER ONE.
NOT LIKE MY BENTLEY.
NOT LIKE MY BOY.

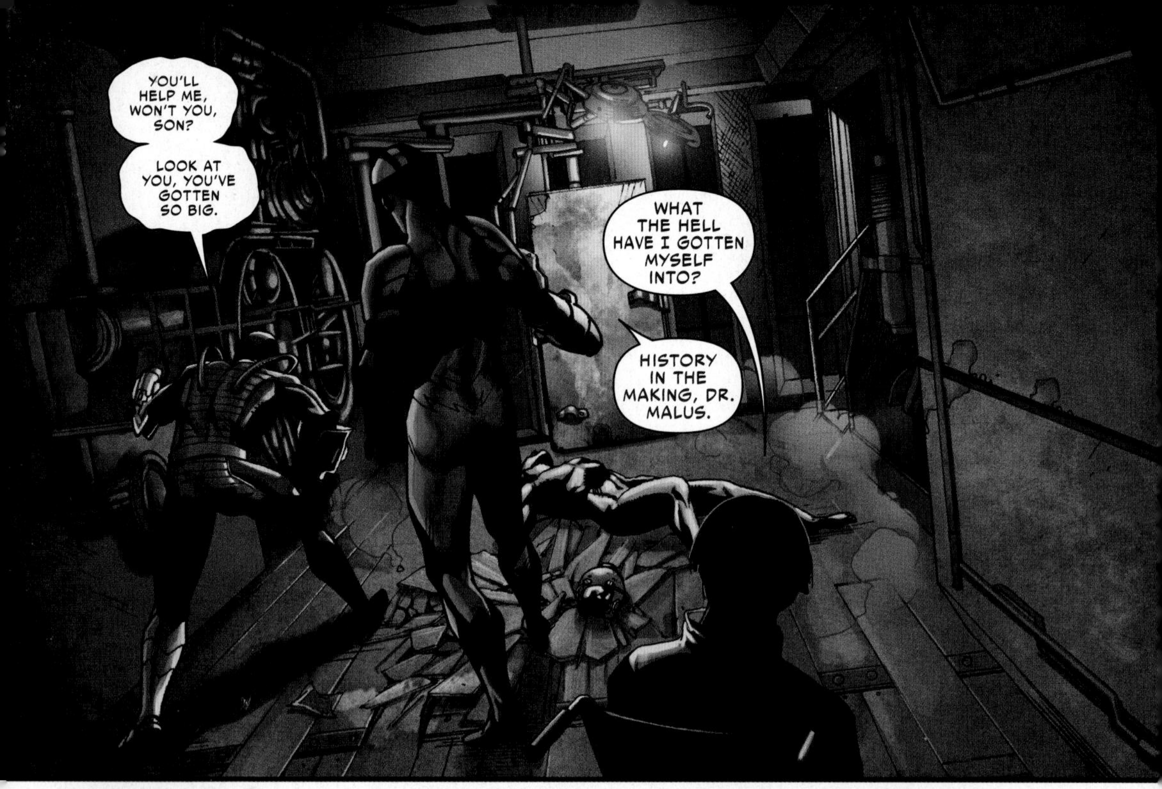
YOU'LL HELP ME, WON'T YOU, SON?
LOOK AT YOU, YOU'VE GOTTEN SO BIG.
WHAT THE HELL HAVE I GOTTEN MYSELF INTO?
HISTORY IN THE MAKING, DR. MALUS.

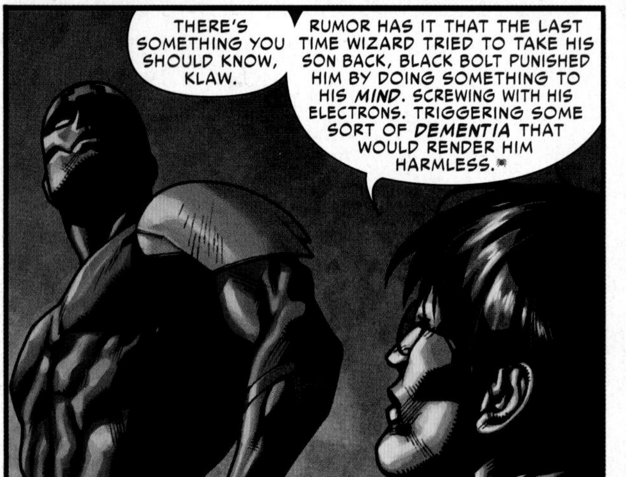
THERE'S SOMETHING YOU SHOULD KNOW, KLAW.
RUMOR HAS IT THAT THE LAST TIME WIZARD TRIED TO TAKE HIS SON BACK, BLACK BOLT PUNISHED HIM BY DOING SOMETHING TO HIS MIND. SCREWING WITH HIS ELECTRONS. TRIGGERING SOME SORT OF DEMENTIA THAT WOULD RENDER HIM HARMLESS.
THIS HAPPENED IN FF #7! CRAZY STUFF! --SLIGHTLY SANE SANA.

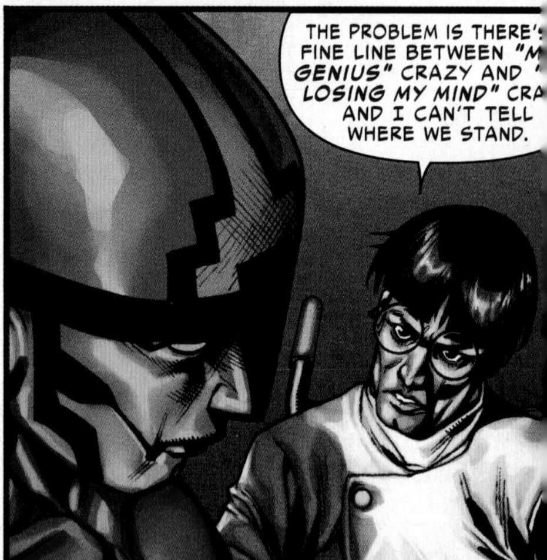
THE PROBLEM IS THERE'S FINE LINE BETWEEN "M GENIUS" CRAZY AND " LOSING MY MIND" CRA AND I CAN'T TELL WHERE WE STAND.

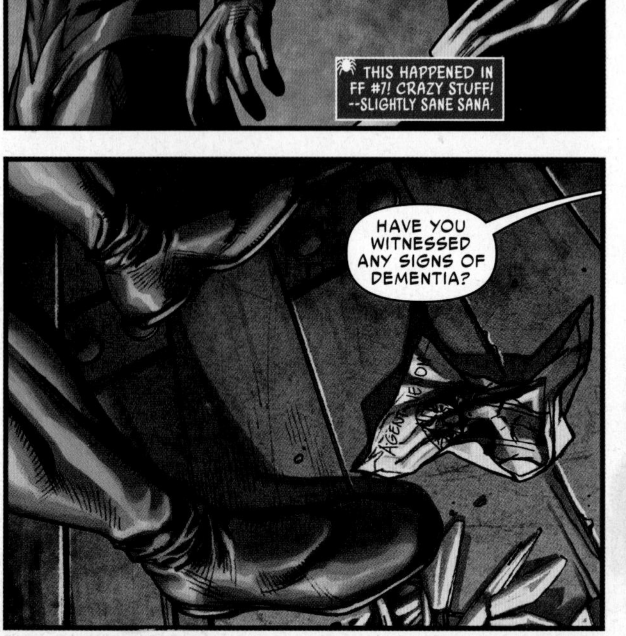
HAVE YOU WITNESSED ANY SIGNS OF DEMENTIA?

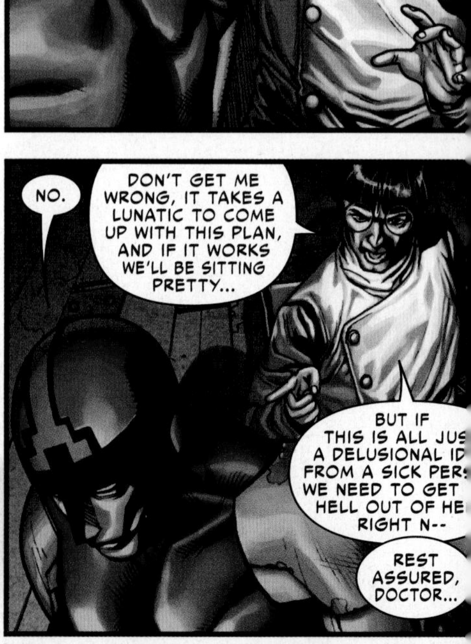
NO.
DON'T GET ME WRONG, IT TAKES A LUNATIC TO COME UP WITH THIS PLAN, AND IF IT WORKS WE'LL BE SITTING PRETTY...
BUT IF THIS IS ALL JUS A DELUSIONAL ID FROM A SICK PER WE NEED TO GET HELL OUT OF HE RIGHT N--
REST ASSURED, DOCTOR...

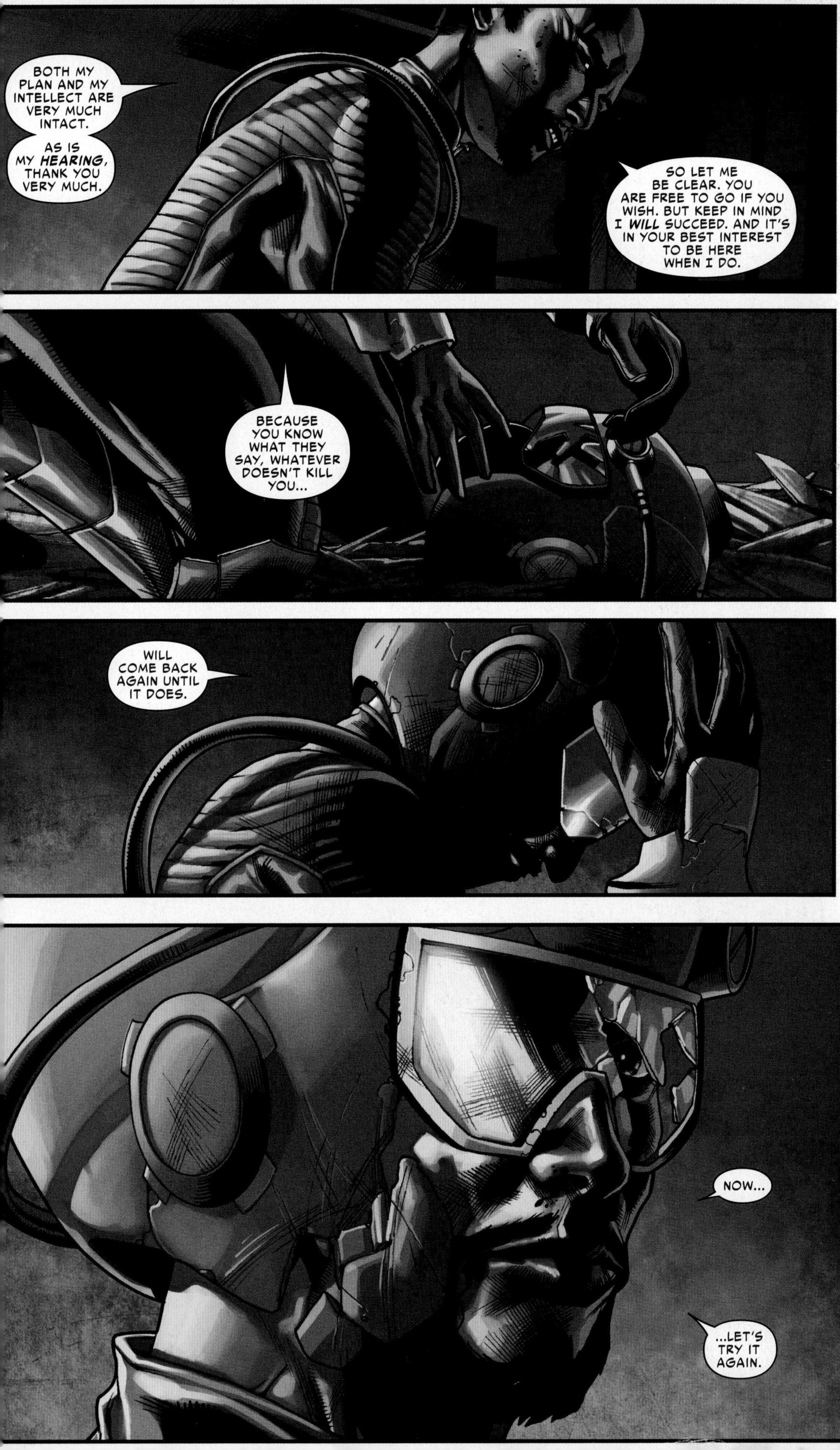
BOTH MY PLAN AND MY INTELLECT ARE VERY MUCH INTACT.
AS IS MY ***HEARING***, THANK YOU VERY MUCH.
SO LET ME BE CLEAR. YOU ARE FREE TO GO IF YOU WISH. BUT KEEP IN MIND I ***WILL*** SUCCEED. AND IT'S IN YOUR BEST INTEREST TO BE HERE WHEN I DO.
BECAUSE YOU KNOW WHAT THEY SAY, WHATEVER DOESN'T KILL YOU...
WILL COME BACK AGAIN UNTIL IT DOES.
NOW...
...LET'S TRY IT AGAIN.

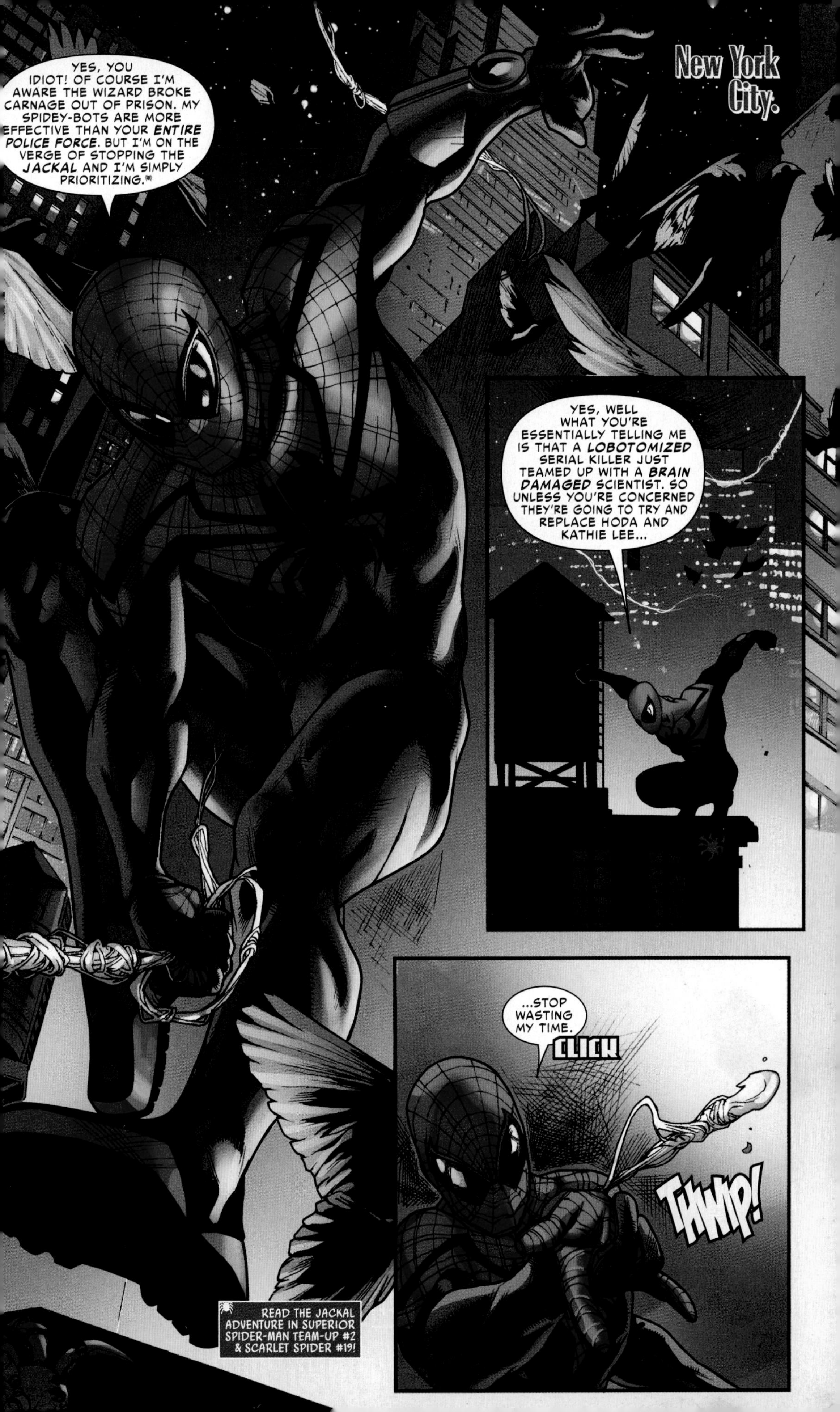
New York City.
YES, YOU IDIOT! OF COURSE I'M AWARE THE WIZARD BROKE CARNAGE OUT OF PRISON. MY SPIDEY-BOTS ARE MORE EFFECTIVE THAN YOUR ENTIRE POLICE FORCE. BUT I'M ON THE VERGE OF STOPPING THE JACKAL AND I'M SIMPLY PRIORITIZING.*
YES, WELL WHAT YOU'RE ESSENTIALLY TELLING ME IS THAT A LOBOTOMIZED SERIAL KILLER JUST TEAMED UP WITH A BRAIN DAMAGED SCIENTIST. SO UNLESS YOU'RE CONCERNED THEY'RE GOING TO TRY AND REPLACE HODA AND KATHIE LEE...
...STOP WASTING MY TIME.
CLICK
THWIP!
READ THE JACKAL ADVENTURE IN SUPERIOR SPIDER-MAN TEAM-UP #2 & SCARLET SPIDER #19!

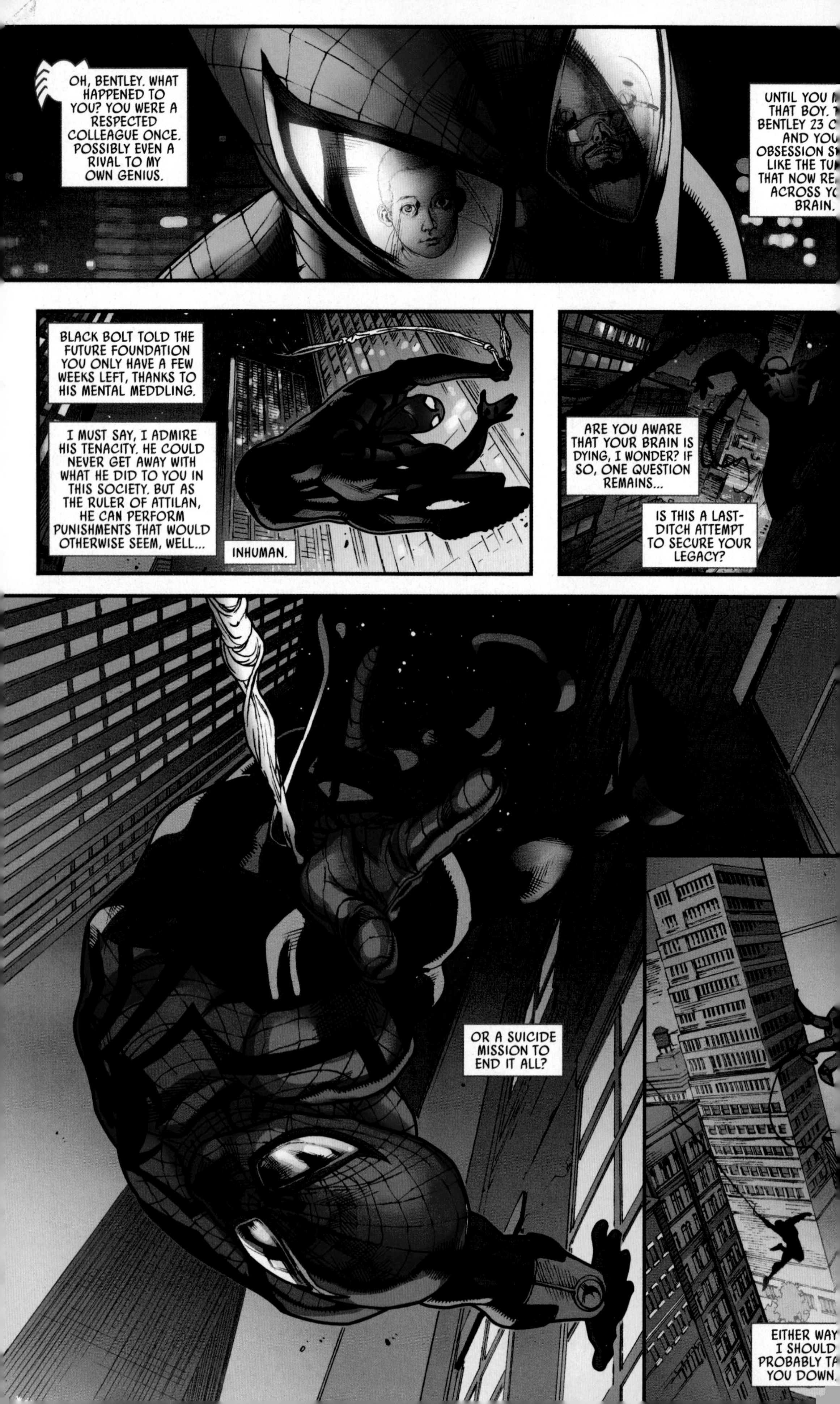
OH, BENTLEY. WHAT HAPPENED TO YOU? YOU WERE A RESPECTED COLLEAGUE ONCE. POSSIBLY EVEN A RIVAL TO MY OWN GENIUS.
UNTIL YOU M THAT BOY. T BENTLEY 23 C AND YOU OBSESSION S LIKE THE TU THAT NOW RE ACROSS YO BRAIN.
BLACK BOLT TOLD THE FUTURE FOUNDATION YOU ONLY HAVE A FEW WEEKS LEFT, THANKS TO HIS MENTAL MEDDLING.
I MUST SAY, I ADMIRE HIS TENACITY. HE COULD NEVER GET AWAY WITH WHAT HE DID TO YOU IN THIS SOCIETY. BUT AS THE RULER OF ATTILAN, HE CAN PERFORM PUNISHMENTS THAT WOULD OTHERWISE SEEM, WELL...
INHUMAN.
ARE YOU AWARE THAT YOUR BRAIN IS DYING, I WONDER? IF SO, ONE QUESTION REMAINS...
IS THIS A LAST-DITCH ATTEMPT TO SECURE YOUR LEGACY?
OR A SUICIDE MISSION TO END IT ALL?
EITHER WAY I SHOULD PROBABLY TA YOU DOWN.

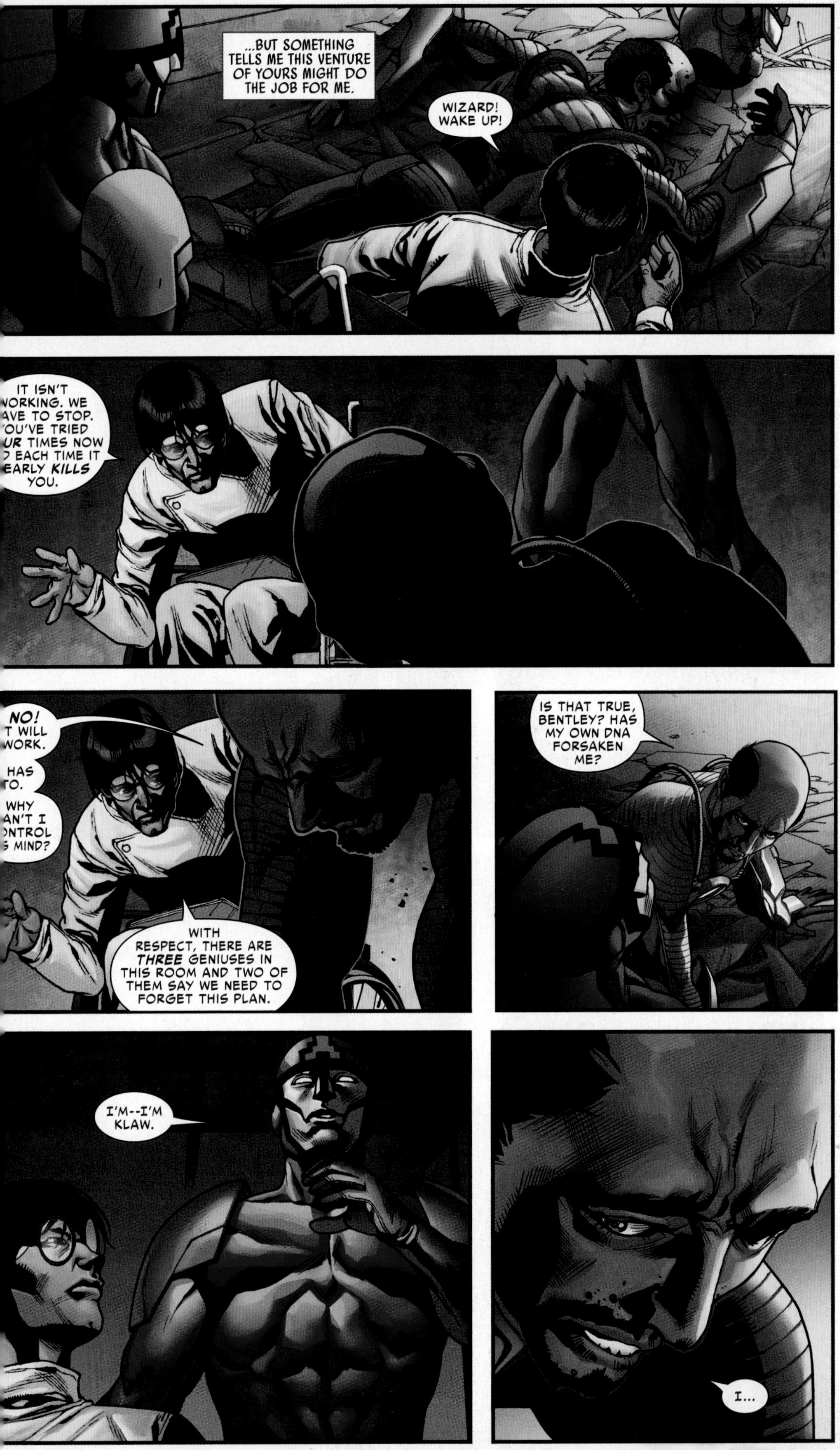
...BUT SOMETHING TELLS ME THIS VENTURE OF YOURS MIGHT DO THE JOB FOR ME.
WIZARD! WAKE UP!
IT ISN'T VORKING. WE AVE TO STOP. 'OU'VE TRIED UR TIMES NOW D EACH TIME IT EARLY KILLS YOU.
NO! T WILL VORK.
HAS TO.
WHY AN'T I ONTROL S MIND?
WITH RESPECT, THERE ARE THREE GENIUSES IN THIS ROOM AND TWO OF THEM SAY WE NEED TO FORGET THIS PLAN.
IS THAT TRUE, BENTLEY? HAS MY OWN DNA FORSAKEN ME?
I'M--I'M KLAW.
I...

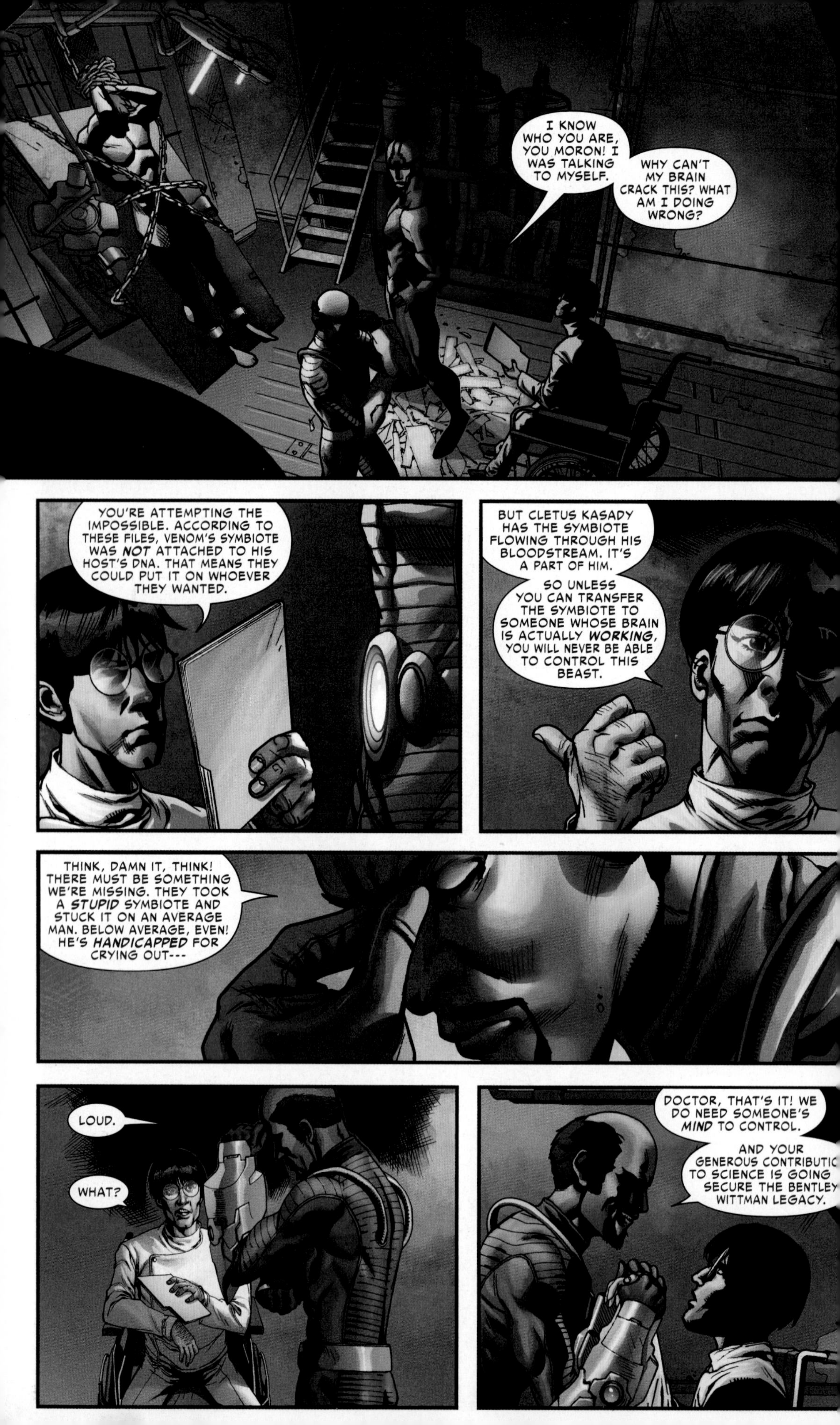

I KNOW WHO YOU ARE, YOU MORON! I WAS TALKING TO MYSELF.
WHY CAN'T MY BRAIN CRACK THIS? WHAT AM I DOING WRONG?
YOU'RE ATTEMPTING THE IMPOSSIBLE. ACCORDING TO THESE FILES, VENOM'S SYMBIOTE WAS *NOT* ATTACHED TO HIS HOST'S DNA. THAT MEANS THEY COULD PUT IT ON WHOEVER THEY WANTED.
BUT CLETUS KASADY HAS THE SYMBIOTE FLOWING THROUGH HIS BLOODSTREAM. IT'S A PART OF HIM.
SO UNLESS YOU CAN TRANSFER THE SYMBIOTE TO SOMEONE WHOSE BRAIN IS ACTUALLY *WORKING*, YOU WILL NEVER BE ABLE TO CONTROL THIS BEAST.
THINK, DAMN IT, THINK! THERE MUST BE SOMETHING WE'RE MISSING. THEY TOOK A *STUPID* SYMBIOTE AND STUCK IT ON AN AVERAGE MAN. BELOW AVERAGE, EVEN! HE'S *HANDICAPPED* FOR CRYING OUT---
LOUD.
WHAT?
DOCTOR, THAT'S IT! WE DO NEED SOMEONE'S *MIND* TO CONTROL.
AND YOUR GENEROUS CONTRIBUTIC TO SCIENCE IS GOING SECURE THE BENTLEY WITTMAN LEGACY.

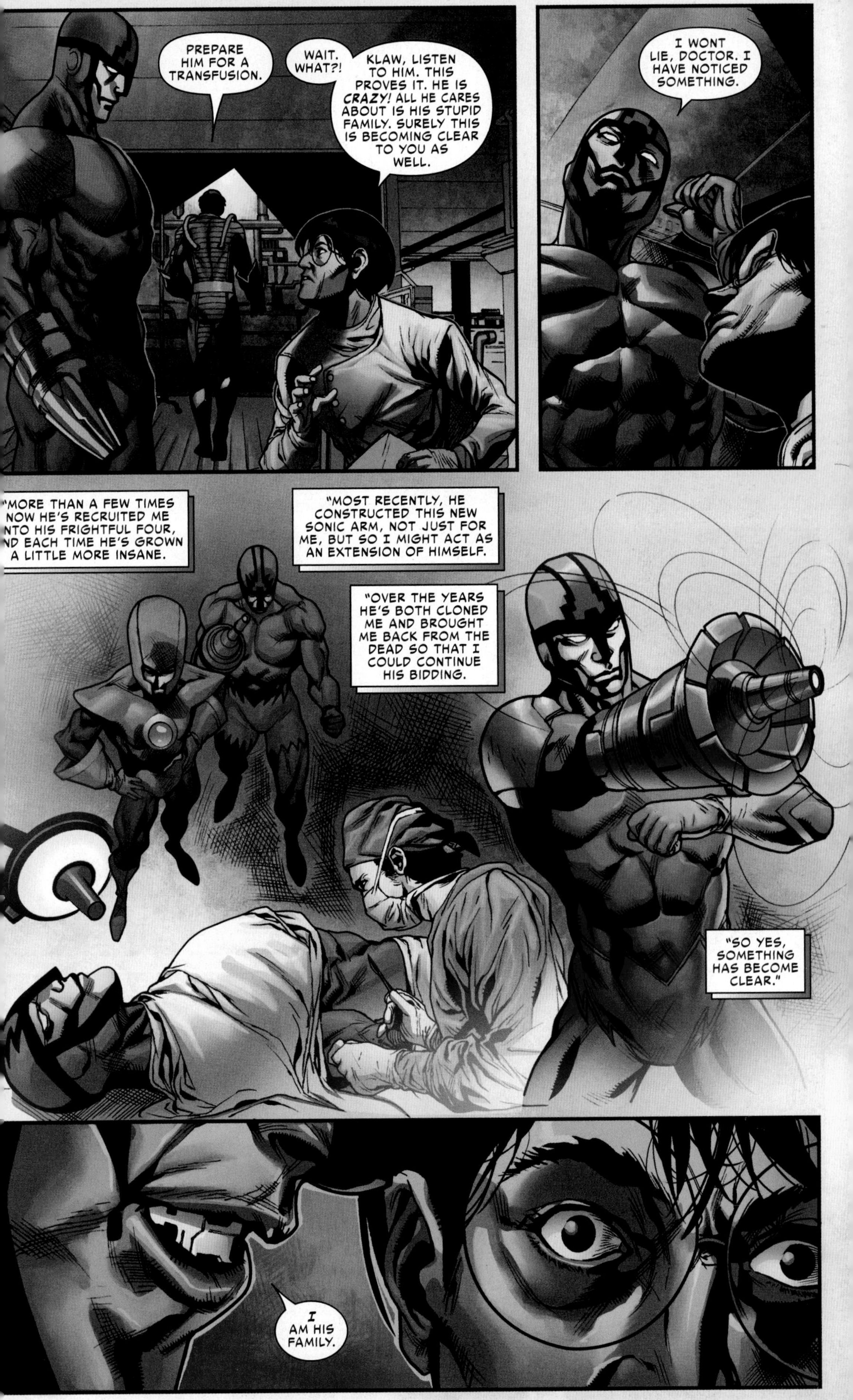
PREPARE HIM FOR A TRANSFUSION.
WAIT. WHAT?!
KLAW, LISTEN TO HIM. THIS PROVES IT. HE IS *CRAZY!* ALL HE CARES ABOUT IS HIS STUPID FAMILY. SURELY THIS IS BECOMING CLEAR TO YOU AS WELL.
I WONT LIE, DOCTOR. I HAVE NOTICED SOMETHING.
"MORE THAN A FEW TIMES NOW HE'S RECRUITED ME INTO HIS FRIGHTFUL FOUR, AND EACH TIME HE'S GROWN A LITTLE MORE INSANE.
"MOST RECENTLY, HE CONSTRUCTED THIS NEW SONIC ARM, NOT JUST FOR ME, BUT SO I MIGHT ACT AS AN EXTENSION OF HIMSELF.
"OVER THE YEARS HE'S BOTH CLONED ME AND BROUGHT ME BACK FROM THE DEAD SO THAT I COULD CONTINUE HIS BIDDING.
"SO YES, SOMETHING HAS BECOME CLEAR."
I AM HIS FAMILY.

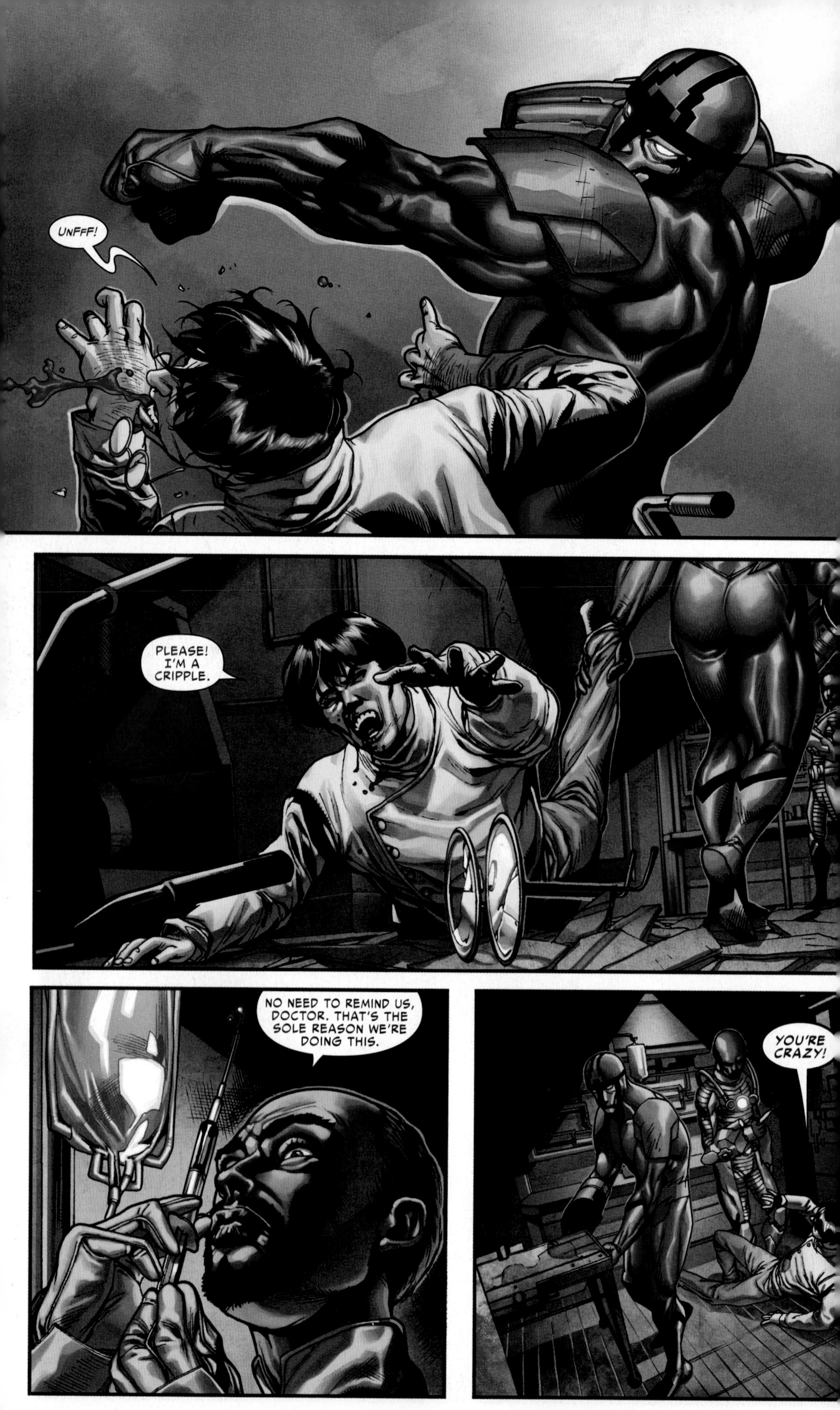
UNFFF!
PLEASE! I'M A CRIPPLE.
NO NEED TO REMIND US, DOCTOR. THAT'S THE SOLE REASON WE'RE DOING THIS.
YOU'RE CRAZY!

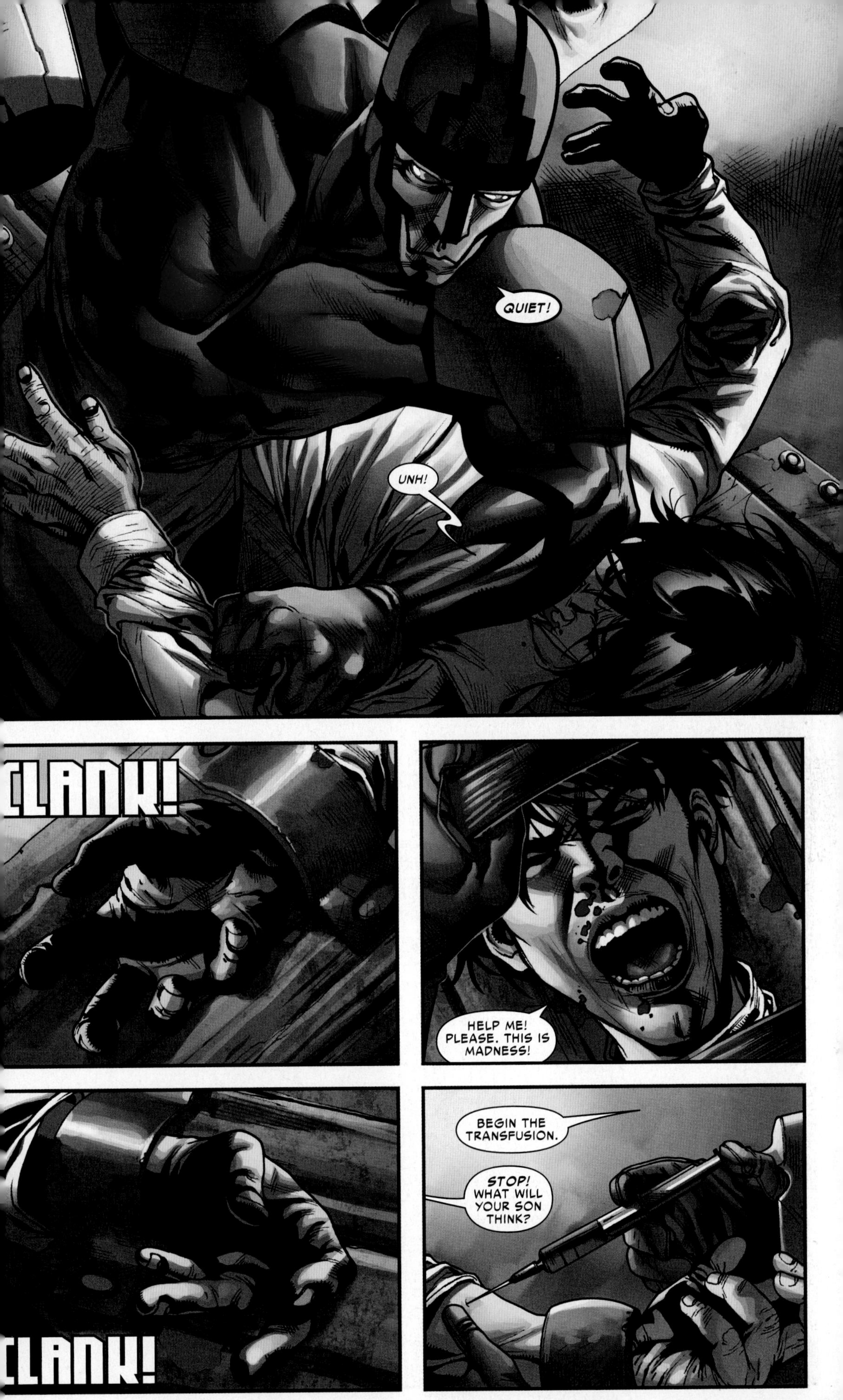
QUIET!
UNH!
CLANK!
HELP ME! PLEASE. THIS IS MADNESS!
CLANK!
BEGIN THE TRANSFUSION.
STOP! WHAT WILL YOUR SON THINK?

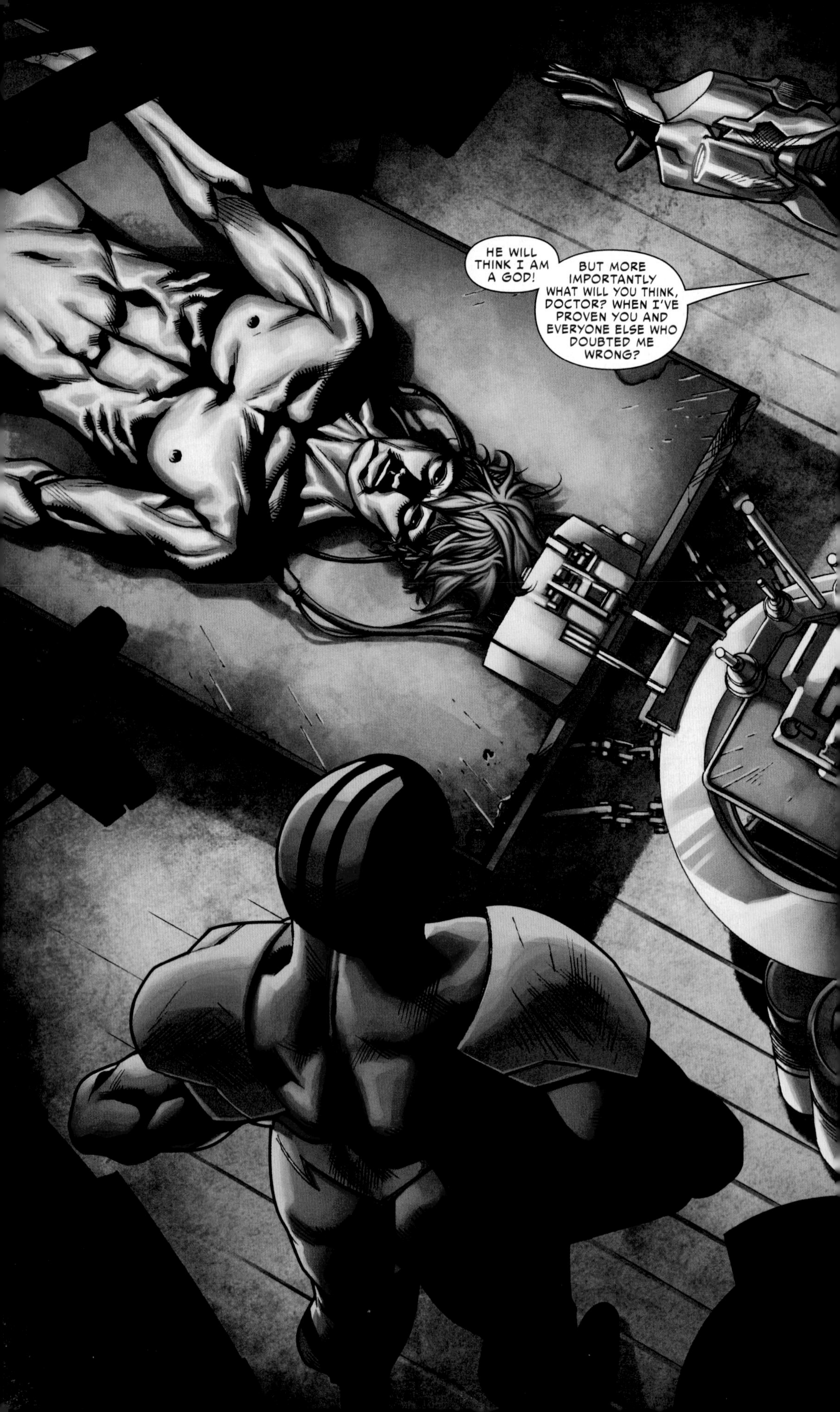
HE WILL THINK I AM A GOD!
BUT MORE IMPORTANTLY WHAT WILL YOU THINK, DOCTOR? WHEN I'VE PROVEN YOU AND EVERYONE ELSE WHO DOUBTED ME WRONG?

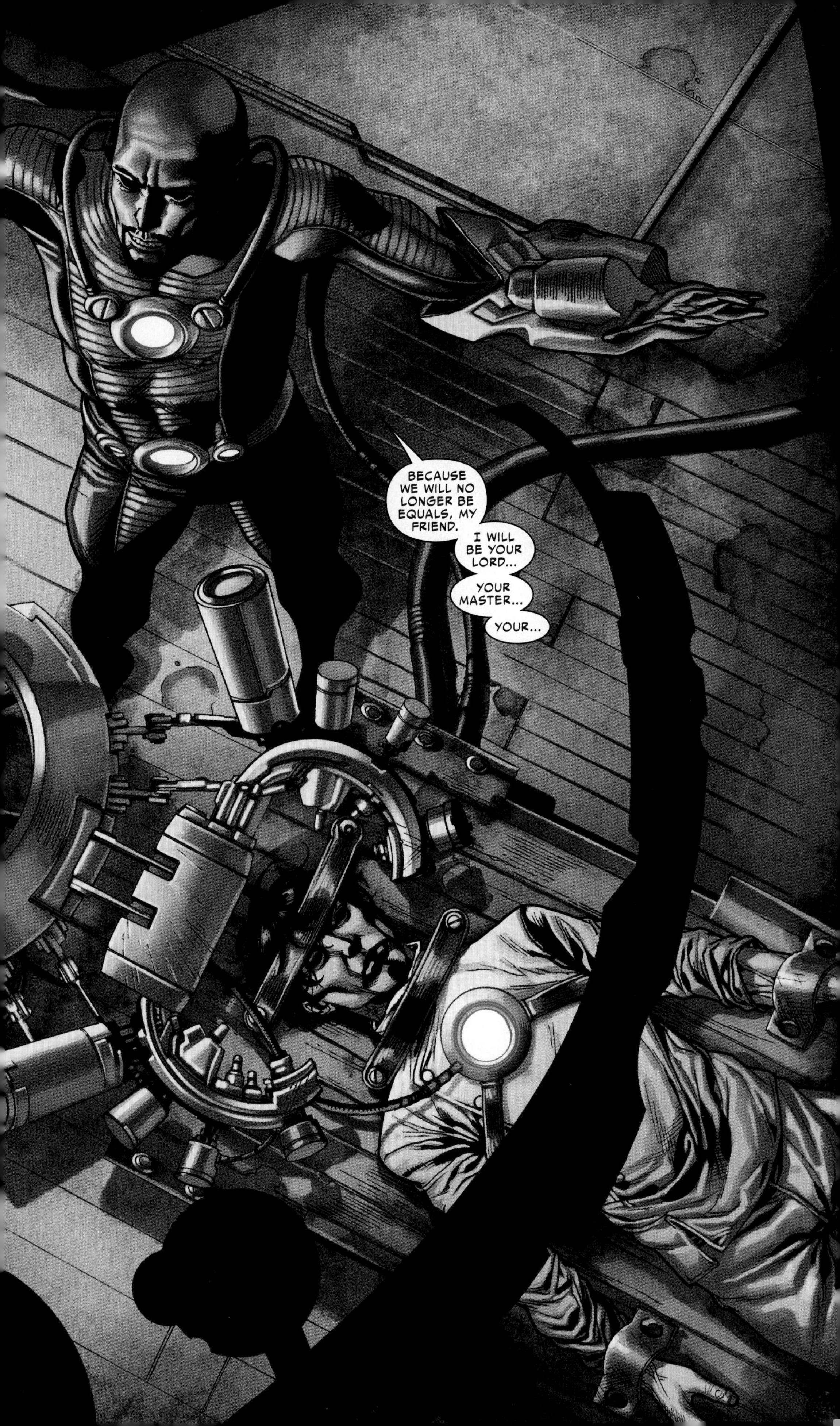
BECAUSE WE WILL NO LONGER BE EQUALS, MY FRIEND.
I WILL BE YOUR LORD...
YOUR MASTER...
YOUR...

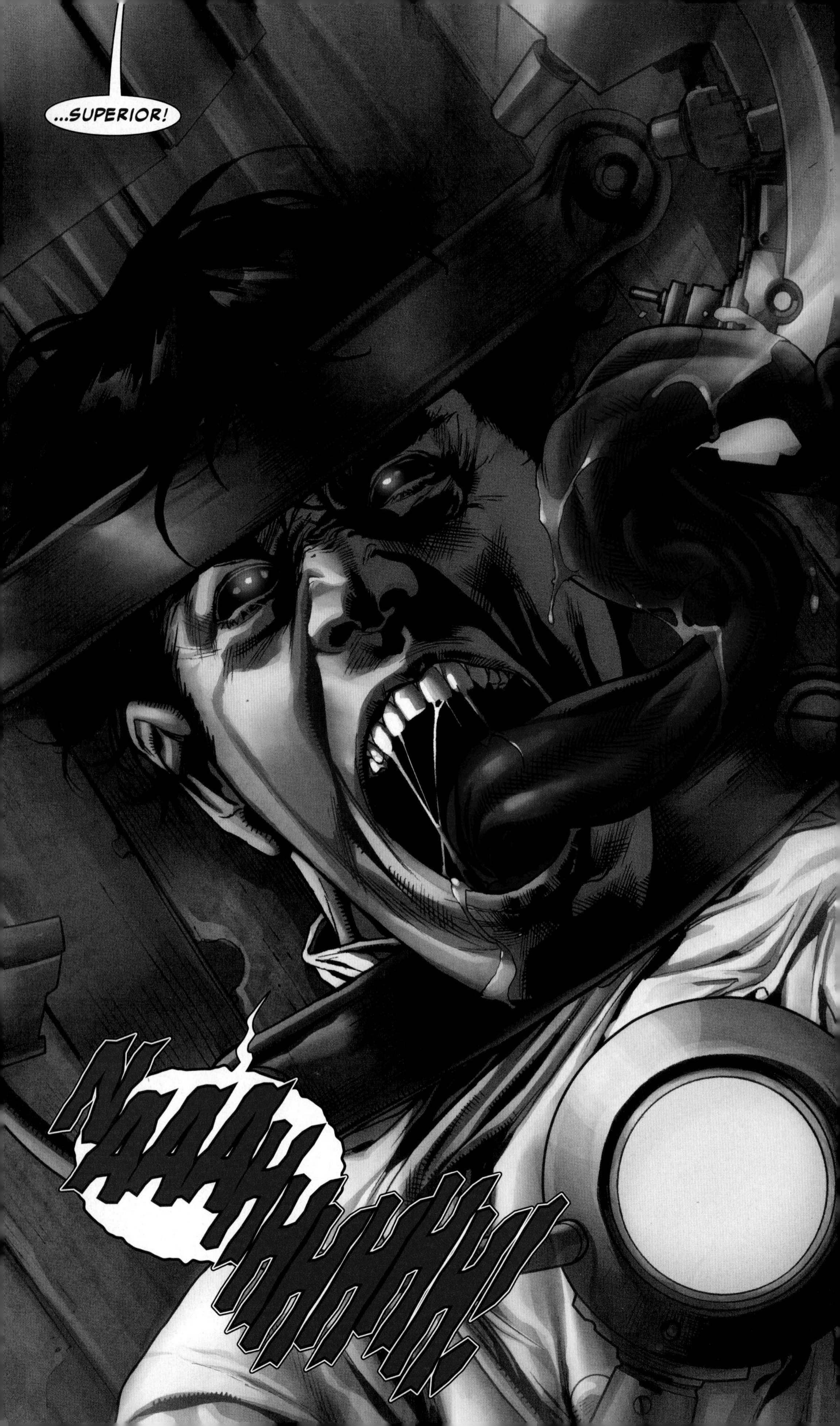
...SUPERIOR!
NAAAHHHHHH!

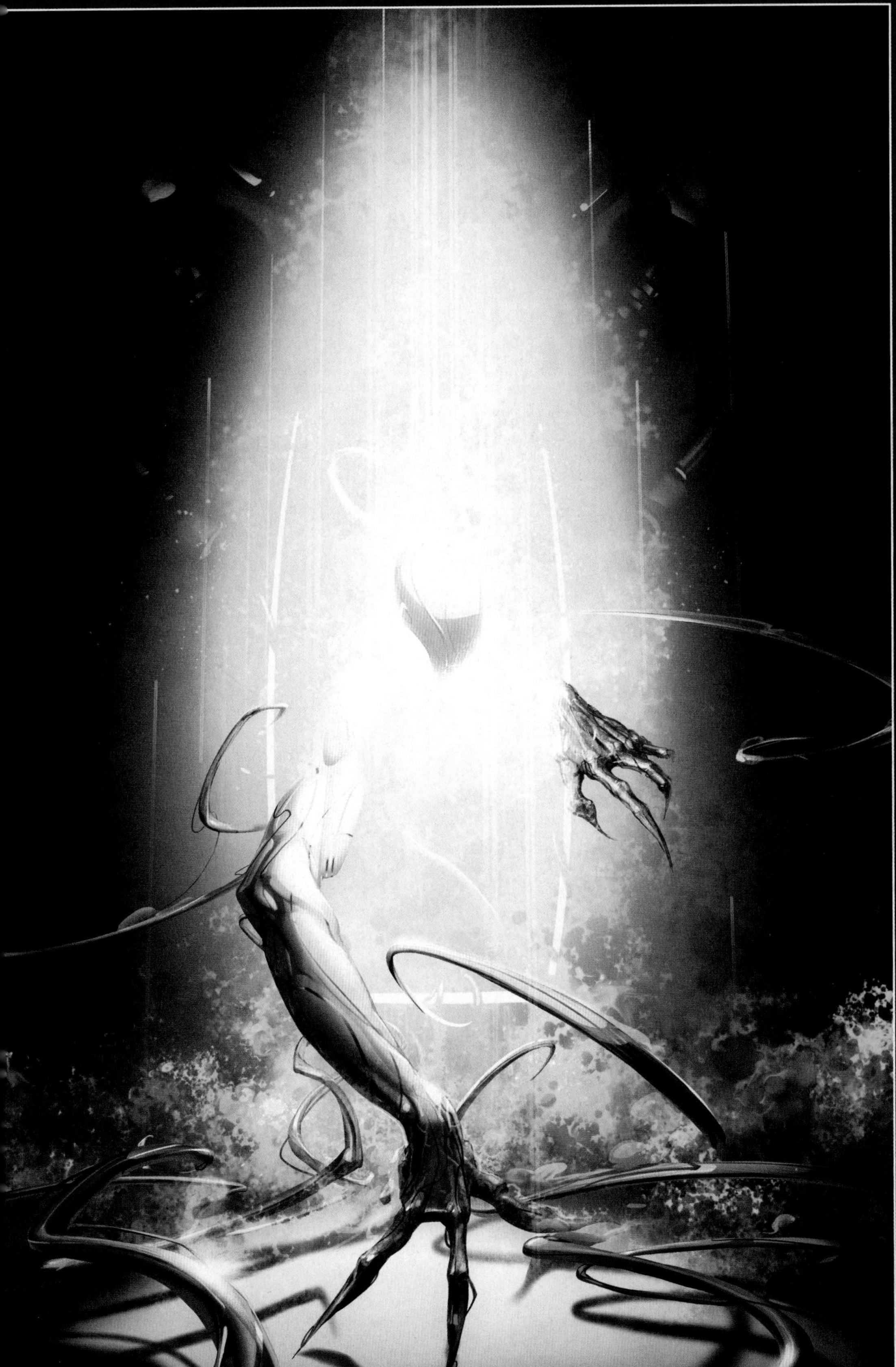

3

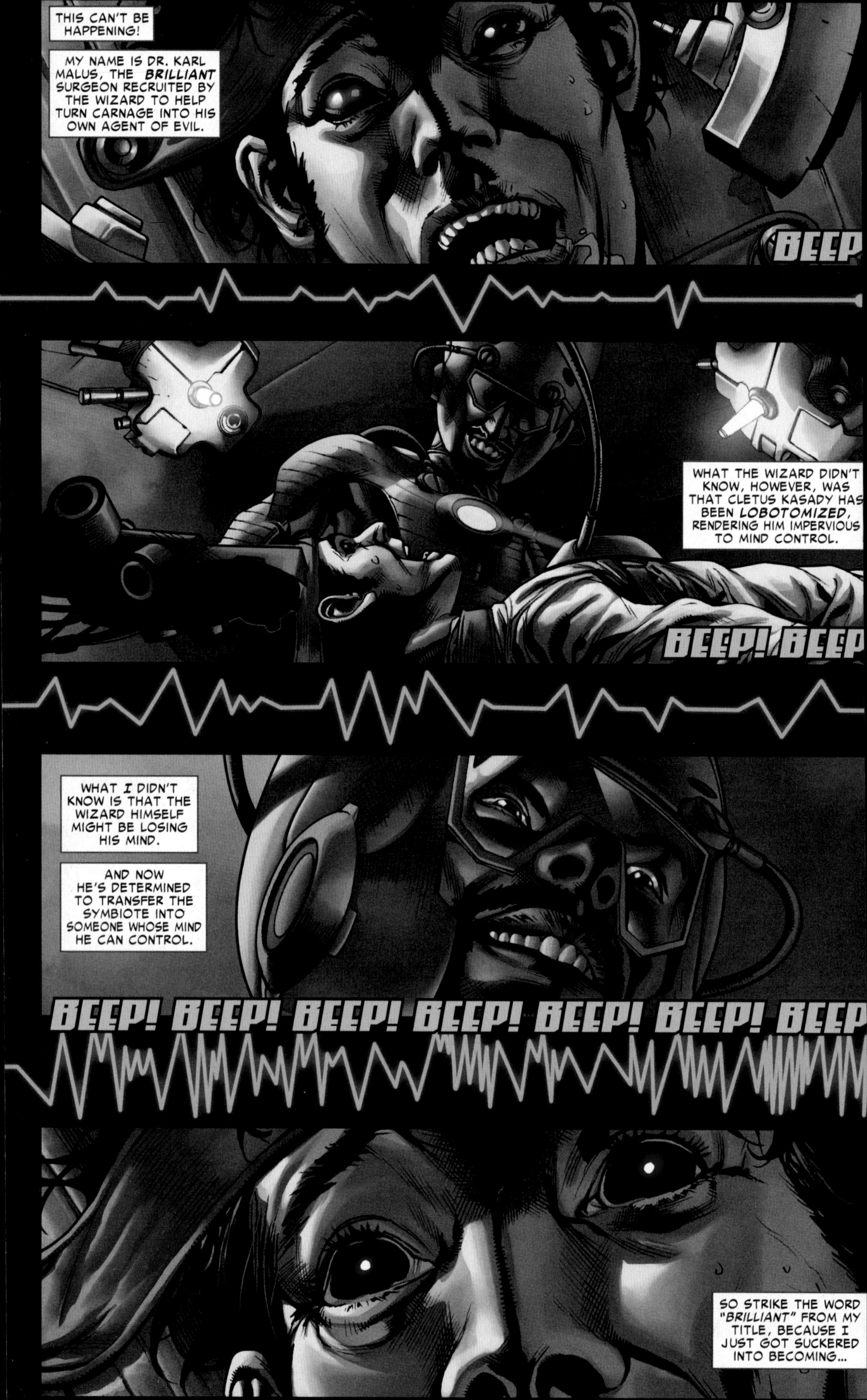

THIS CAN'T BE HAPPENING!
MY NAME IS DR. KARL MALUS, THE BRILLIANT SURGEON RECRUITED BY THE WIZARD TO HELP TURN CARNAGE INTO HIS OWN AGENT OF EVIL.
BEEP
WHAT THE WIZARD DIDN'T KNOW, HOWEVER, WAS THAT CLETUS KASADY HAS BEEN LOBOTOMIZED, RENDERING HIM IMPERVIOUS TO MIND CONTROL.
BEEP! BEEP
WHAT I DIDN'T KNOW IS THAT THE WIZARD HIMSELF MIGHT BE LOSING HIS MIND.
AND NOW HE'S DETERMINED TO TRANSFER THE SYMBIOTE INTO SOMEONE WHOSE MIND HE CAN CONTROL.
BEEP! BEEP! BEEP! BEEP! BEEP! BEEP! BEEP
SO STRIKE THE WORD "BRILLIANT" FROM MY TITLE, BECAUSE I JUST GOT SUCKERED INTO BECOMING...

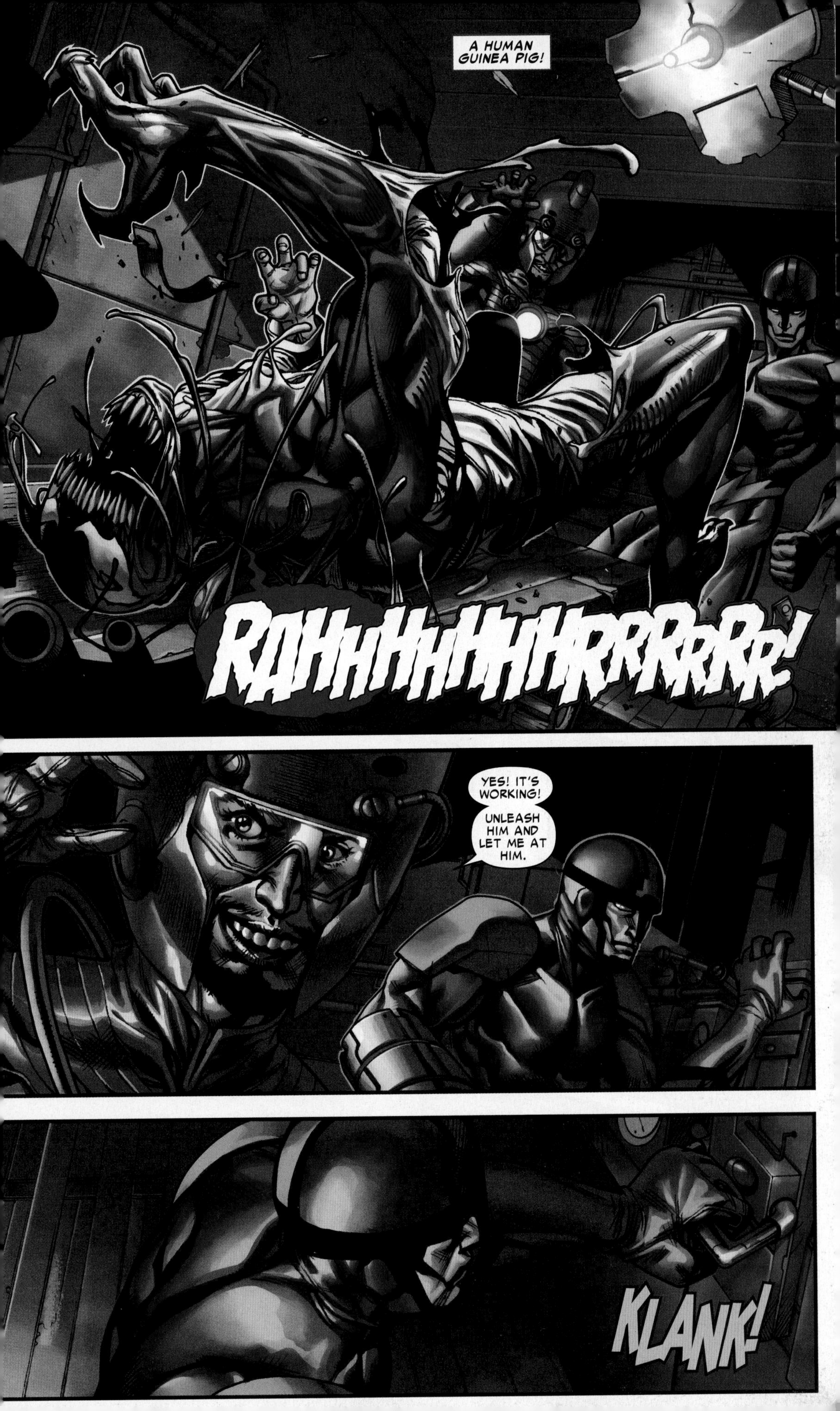
A HUMAN GUINEA PIG!
RAHHHHHHHRRRRRR!
YES! IT'S WORKING!
UNLEASH HIM AND LET ME AT HIM.
KLANK!

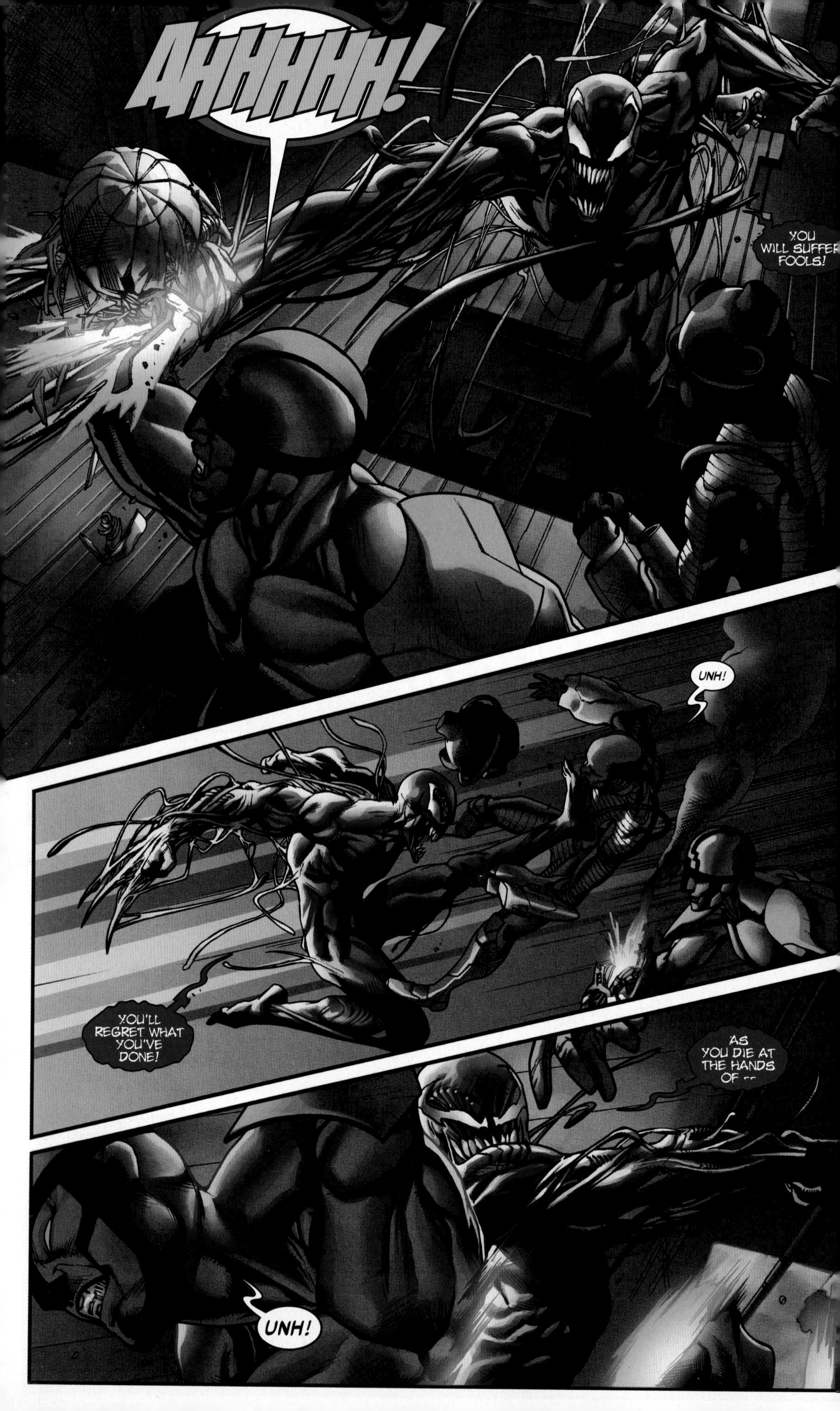
AHHHHH!
YOU WILL SUFFER FOOLS!
UNH!
YOU'LL REGRET WHAT YOU'VE DONE!
AS YOU DIE AT THE HANDS OF --
UNH!

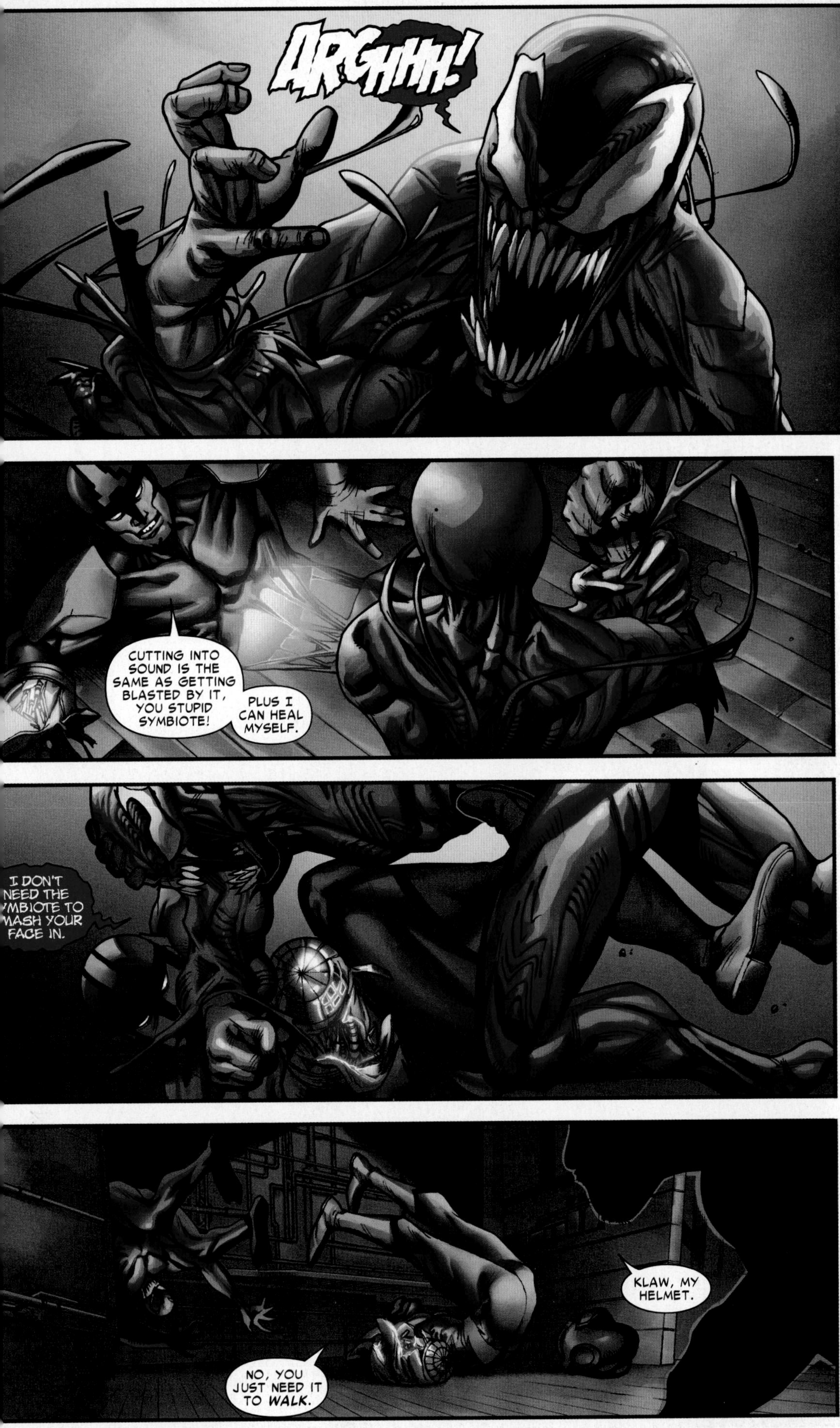
ARGHHH!
CUTTING INTO SOUND IS THE SAME AS GETTING BLASTED BY IT, YOU STUPID SYMBIOTE!
PLUS I CAN HEAL MYSELF.
I DON'T NEED THE YMBIOTE TO MASH YOUR FACE IN.
KLAW, MY HELMET.
NO, YOU JUST NEED IT TO WALK.

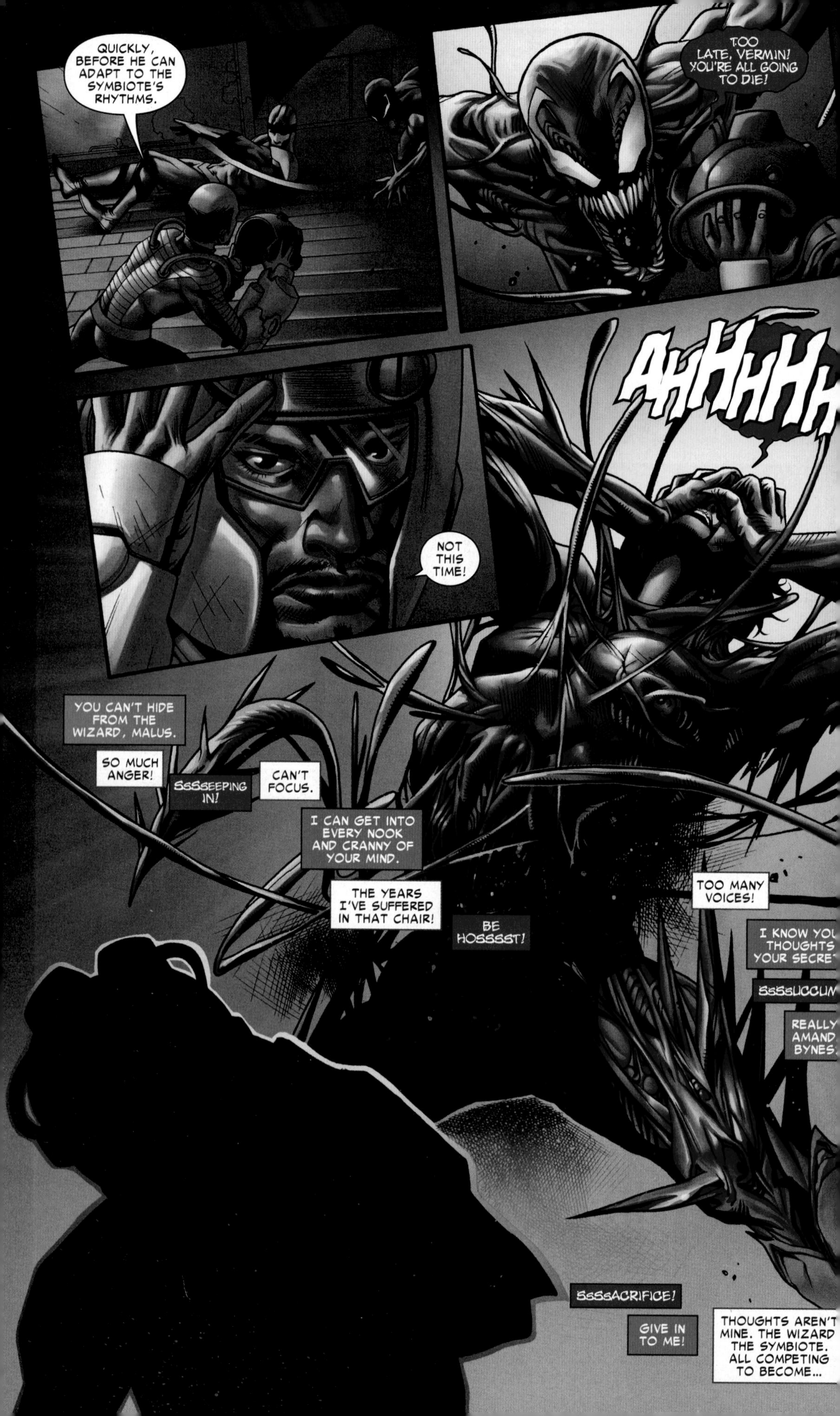
QUICKLY, BEFORE HE CAN ADAPT TO THE SYMBIOTE'S RHYTHMS.
TOO LATE, VERMIN! YOU'RE ALL GOING TO DIE!
AHHHHH
NOT THIS TIME!
YOU CAN'T HIDE FROM THE WIZARD, MALUS.
SO MUCH ANGER!
SSSSEEPING IN!
CAN'T FOCUS.
I CAN GET INTO EVERY NOOK AND CRANNY OF YOUR MIND.
THE YEARS I'VE SUFFERED IN THAT CHAIR!
BE HOSSSST!
TOO MANY VOICES!
I KNOW YOU THOUGHTS YOUR SECRE
SSSSUCCUM
REALLY AMAND BYNES.
SSSSACRIFICE!
GIVE IN TO ME!
THOUGHTS AREN'T MINE. THE WIZARD THE SYMBIOTE. ALL COMPETING TO BECOME...

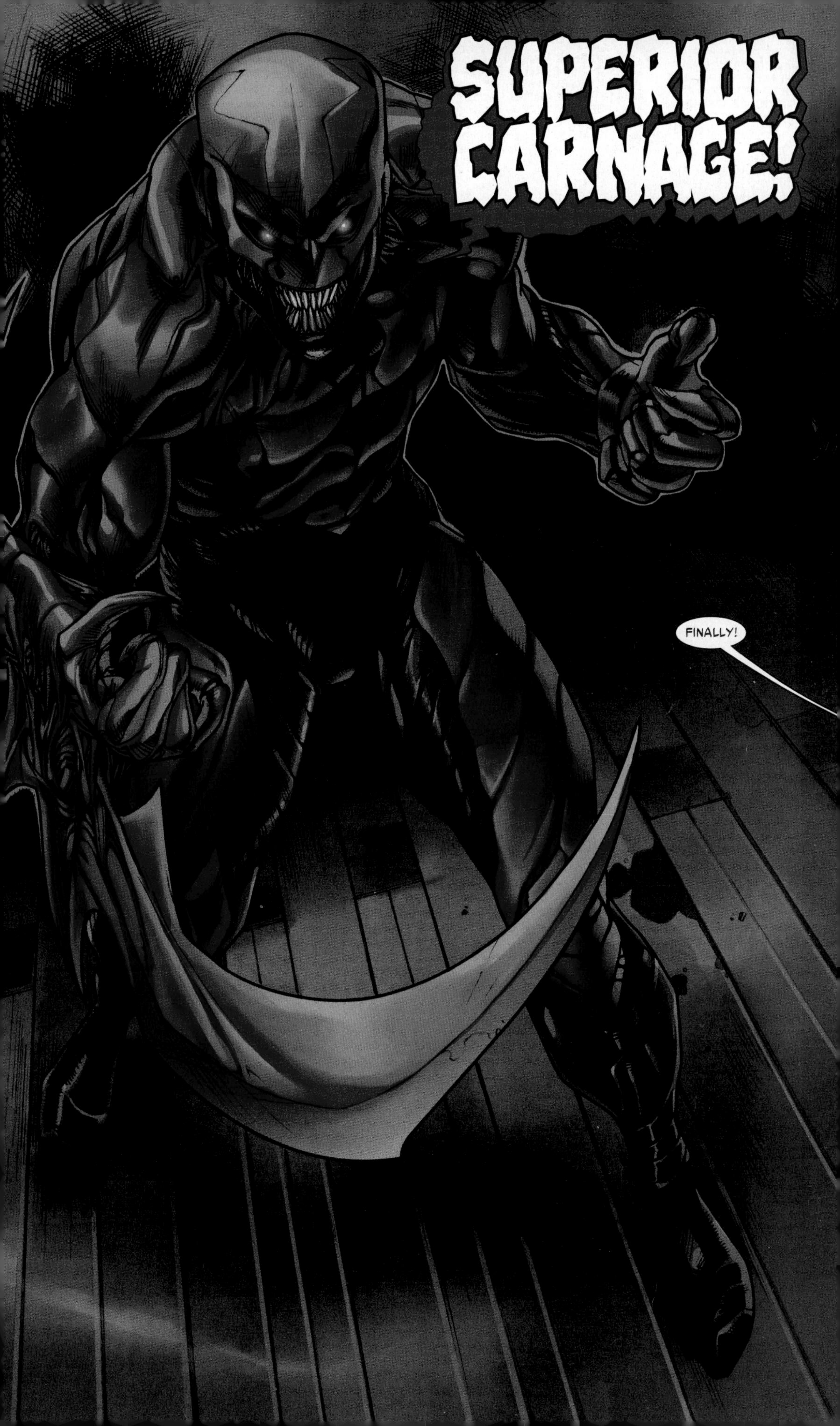
SUPERIOR CARNAGE!
FINALLY!

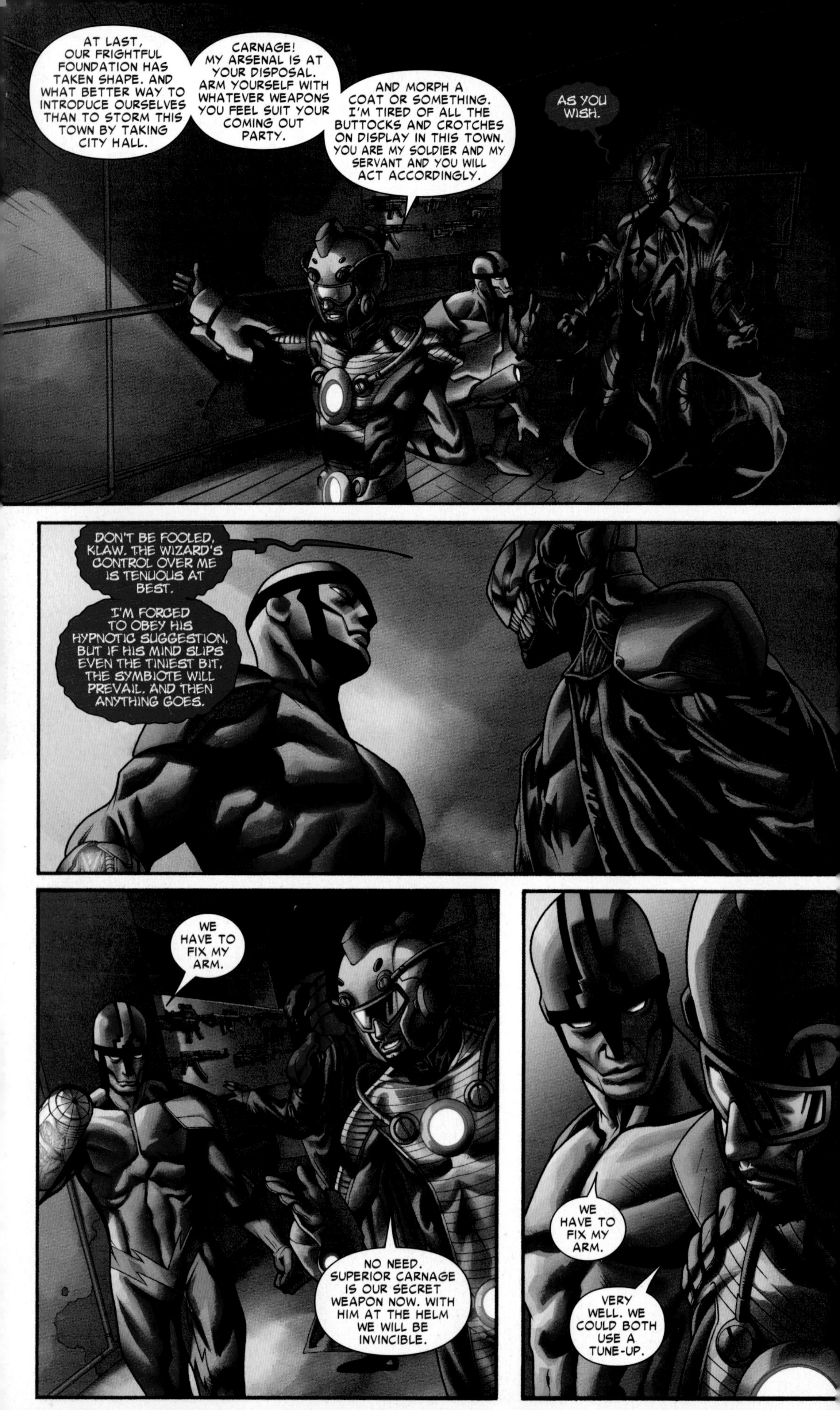
AT LAST, OUR FRIGHTFUL FOUNDATION HAS TAKEN SHAPE. AND WHAT BETTER WAY TO INTRODUCE OURSELVES THAN TO STORM THIS TOWN BY TAKING CITY HALL.
CARNAGE! MY ARSENAL IS AT YOUR DISPOSAL. ARM YOURSELF WITH WHATEVER WEAPONS YOU FEEL SUIT YOUR COMING OUT PARTY.
AND MORPH A COAT OR SOMETHING. I'M TIRED OF ALL THE BUTTOCKS AND CROTCHES ON DISPLAY IN THIS TOWN. YOU ARE MY SOLDIER AND MY SERVANT AND YOU WILL ACT ACCORDINGLY.
AS YOU WISH.
DON'T BE FOOLED, KLAW. THE WIZARD'S CONTROL OVER ME IS TENUOUS AT BEST.
I'M FORCED TO OBEY HIS HYPNOTIC SUGGESTION, BUT IF HIS MIND SLIPS EVEN THE TINIEST BIT, THE SYMBIOTE WILL PREVAIL. AND THEN ANYTHING GOES.
WE HAVE TO FIX MY ARM.
NO NEED. SUPERIOR CARNAGE IS OUR SECRET WEAPON NOW. WITH HIM AT THE HELM WE WILL BE INVINCIBLE.
WE HAVE TO FIX MY ARM.
VERY WELL. WE COULD BOTH USE A TUNE-UP.

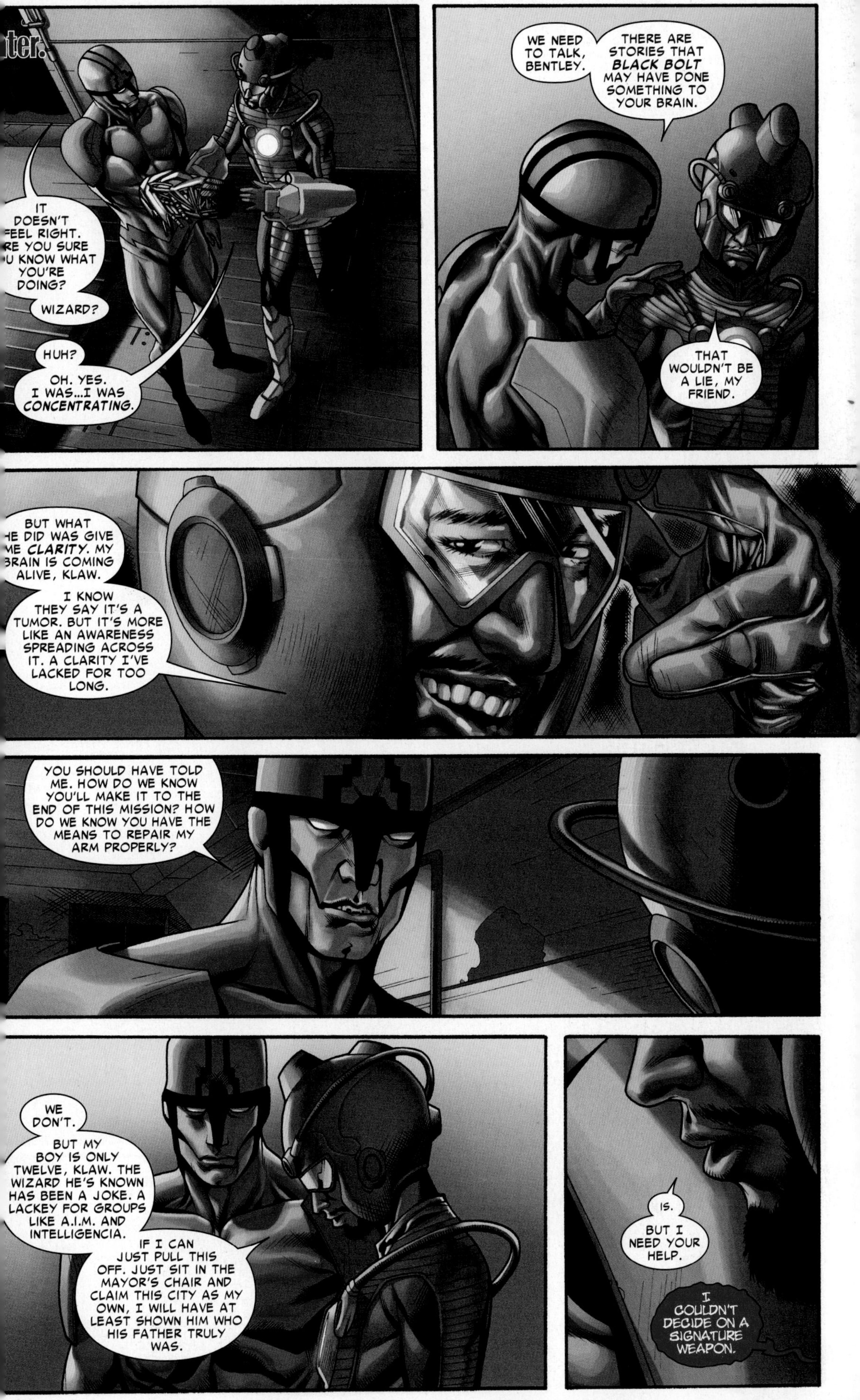

IT DOESN'T FEEL RIGHT. ARE YOU SURE YOU KNOW WHAT YOU'RE DOING?
WIZARD?
HUH?
OH. YES. I WAS...I WAS CONCENTRATING.
WE NEED TO TALK, BENTLEY.
THERE ARE STORIES THAT BLACK BOLT MAY HAVE DONE SOMETHING TO YOUR BRAIN.
THAT WOULDN'T BE A LIE, MY FRIEND.
BUT WHAT HE DID WAS GIVE ME CLARITY. MY BRAIN IS COMING ALIVE, KLAW.
I KNOW THEY SAY IT'S A TUMOR. BUT IT'S MORE LIKE AN AWARENESS SPREADING ACROSS IT. A CLARITY I'VE LACKED FOR TOO LONG.
YOU SHOULD HAVE TOLD ME. HOW DO WE KNOW YOU'LL MAKE IT TO THE END OF THIS MISSION? HOW DO WE KNOW YOU HAVE THE MEANS TO REPAIR MY ARM PROPERLY?
WE DON'T.
BUT MY BOY IS ONLY TWELVE, KLAW. THE WIZARD HE'S KNOWN HAS BEEN A JOKE. A LACKEY FOR GROUPS LIKE A.I.M. AND INTELLIGENCIA.
IF I CAN JUST PULL THIS OFF. JUST SIT IN THE MAYOR'S CHAIR AND CLAIM THIS CITY AS MY OWN, I WILL HAVE AT LEAST SHOWN HIM WHO HIS FATHER TRULY WAS.
IS.
BUT I NEED YOUR HELP.
I COULDN'T DECIDE ON A SIGNATURE WEAPON.

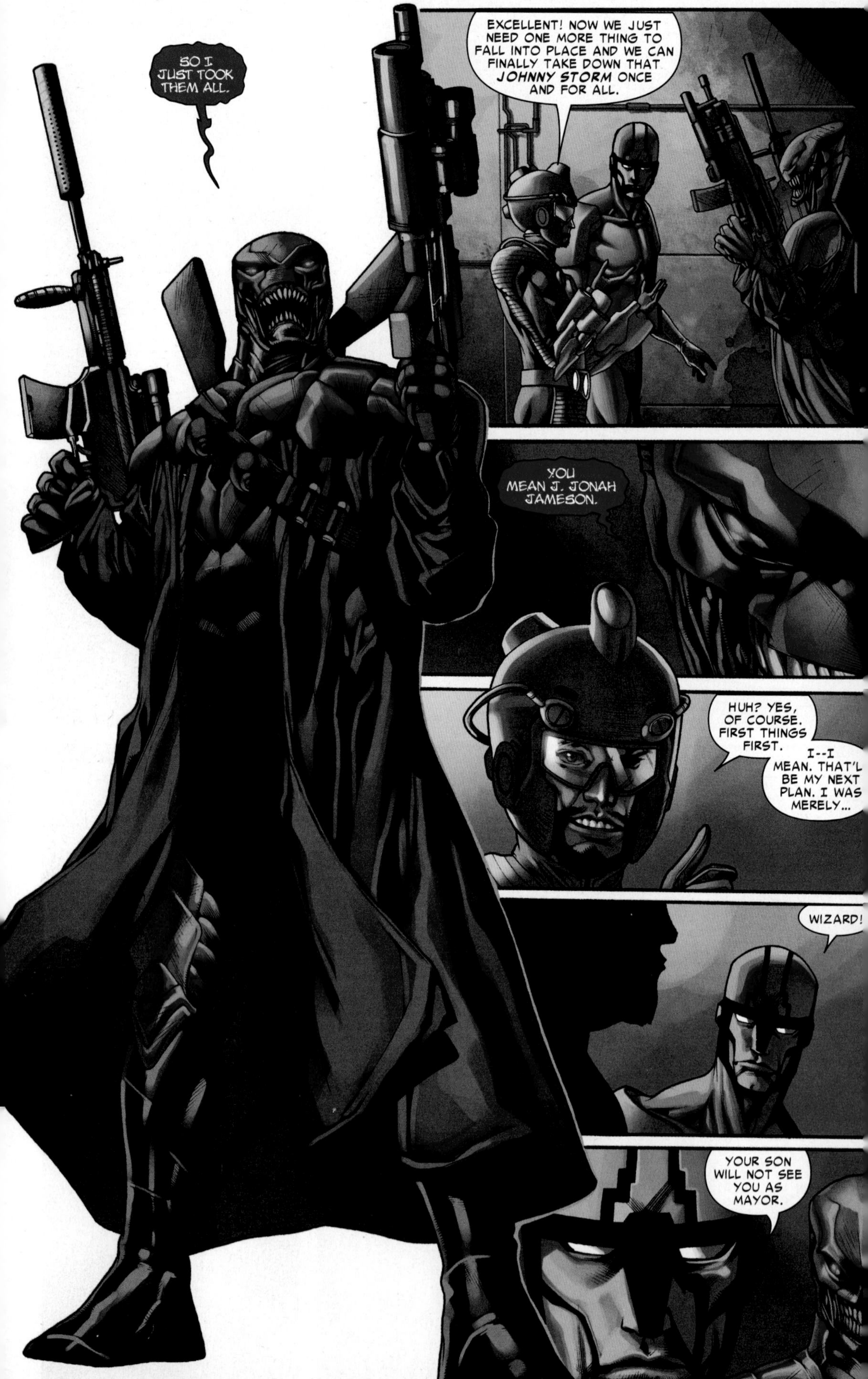
SO I JUST TOOK THEM ALL.
EXCELLENT! NOW WE JUST NEED ONE MORE THING TO FALL INTO PLACE AND WE CAN FINALLY TAKE DOWN THAT JOHNNY STORM ONCE AND FOR ALL.
YOU MEAN J. JONAH JAMESON.
HUH? YES, OF COURSE. FIRST THINGS FIRST.
I--I MEAN. THAT'L BE MY NEXT PLAN. I WAS MERELY...
WIZARD!
YOUR SON WILL NOT SEE YOU AS MAYOR.

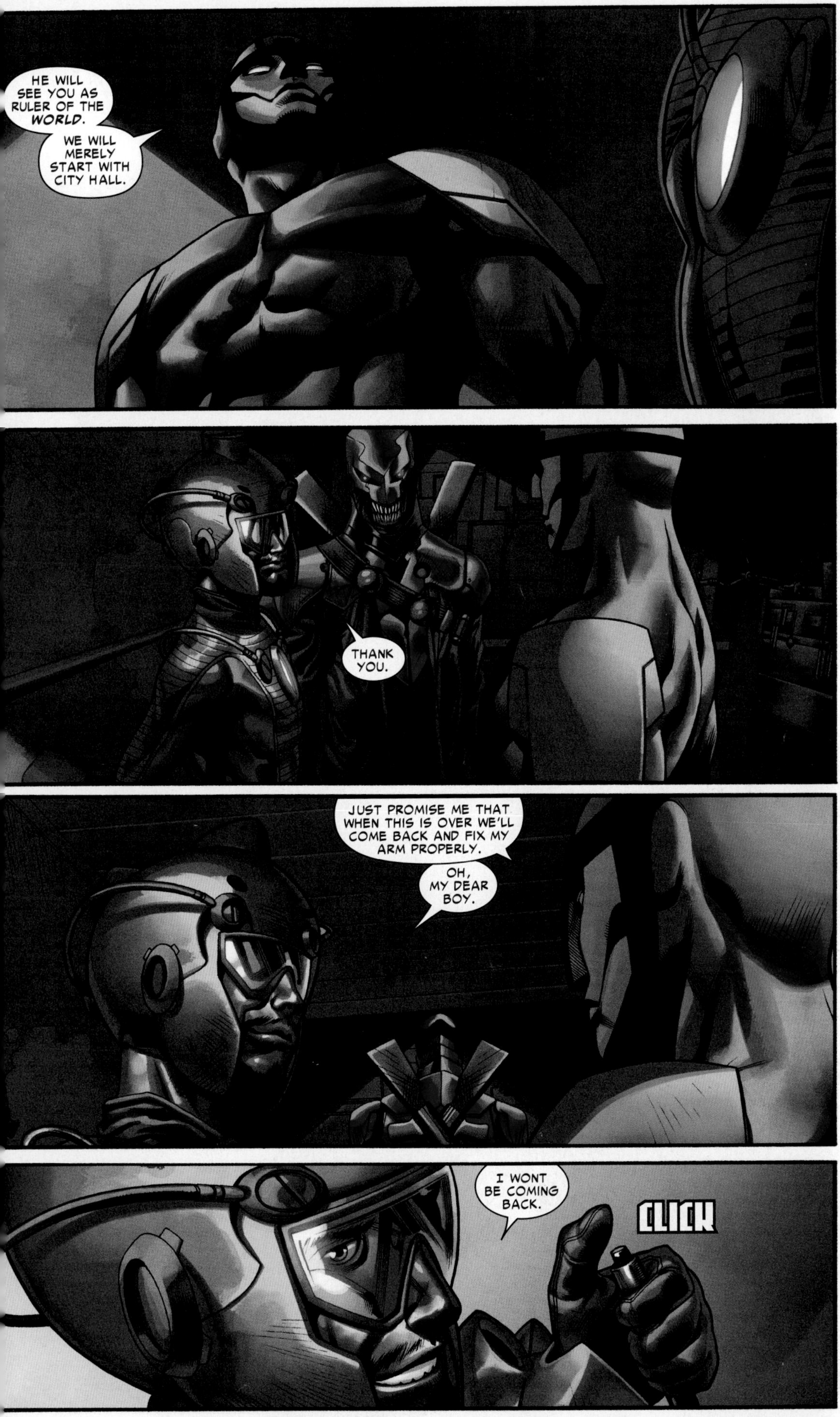
HE WILL SEE YOU AS RULER OF THE WORLD.
WE WILL MERELY START WITH CITY HALL.
THANK YOU.
JUST PROMISE ME THAT WHEN THIS IS OVER WE'LL COME BACK AND FIX MY ARM PROPERLY.
OH, MY DEAR BOY.
I WONT BE COMING BACK.
CLICK

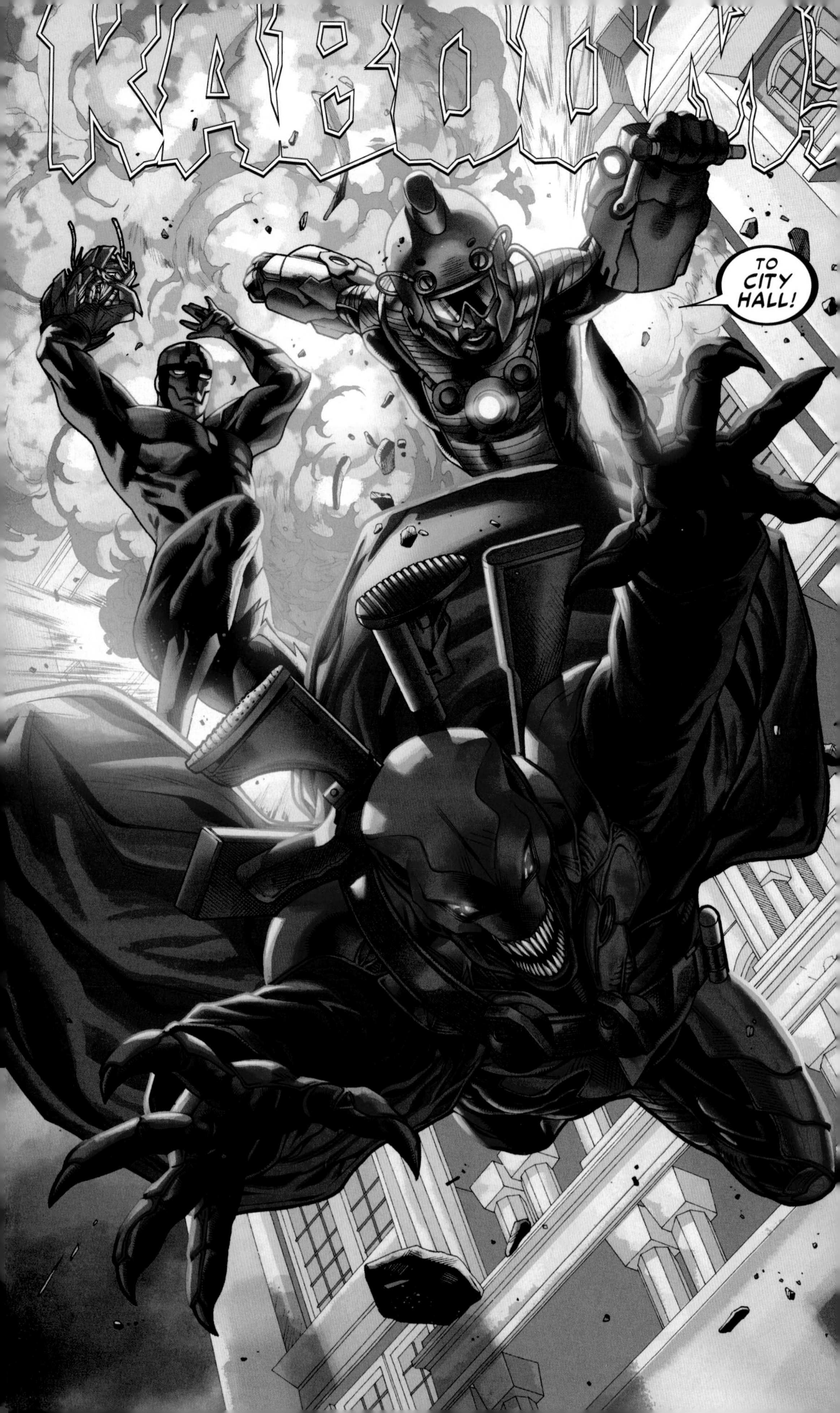
TO CITY HALL!

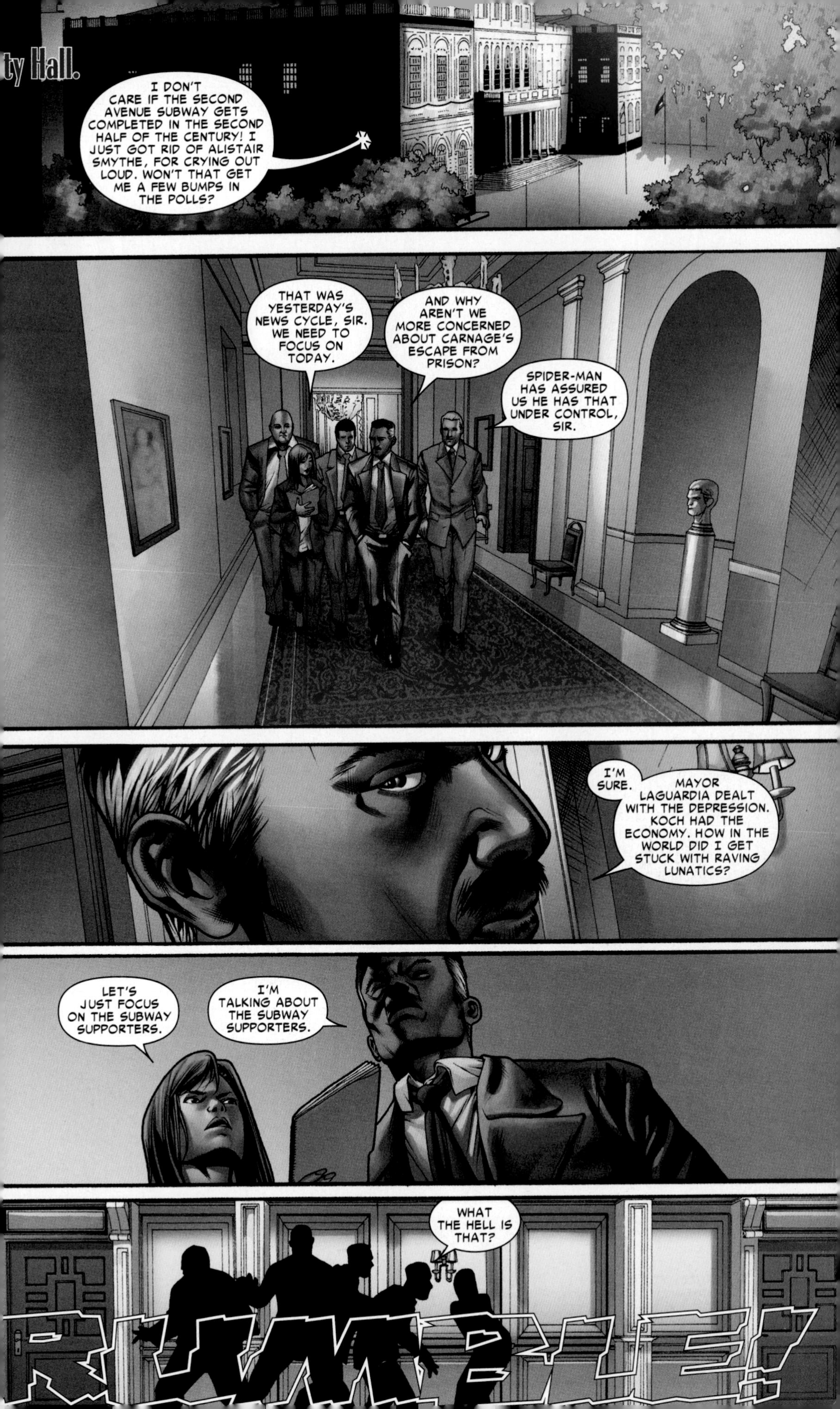

ty Hall.
I DON'T CARE IF THE SECOND AVENUE SUBWAY GETS COMPLETED IN THE SECOND HALF OF THE CENTURY! I JUST GOT RID OF ALISTAIR SMYTHE, FOR CRYING OUT LOUD. WON'T THAT GET ME A FEW BUMPS IN THE POLLS?
THAT WAS YESTERDAY'S NEWS CYCLE, SIR. WE NEED TO FOCUS ON TODAY.
AND WHY AREN'T WE MORE CONCERNED ABOUT CARNAGE'S ESCAPE FROM PRISON?
SPIDER-MAN HAS ASSURED US HE HAS THAT UNDER CONTROL, SIR.
I'M SURE.
MAYOR LAGUARDIA DEALT WITH THE DEPRESSION. KOCH HAD THE ECONOMY. HOW IN THE WORLD DID I GET STUCK WITH RAVING LUNATICS?
LET'S JUST FOCUS ON THE SUBWAY SUPPORTERS.
I'M TALKING ABOUT THE SUBWAY SUPPORTERS.
WHAT THE HELL IS THAT?

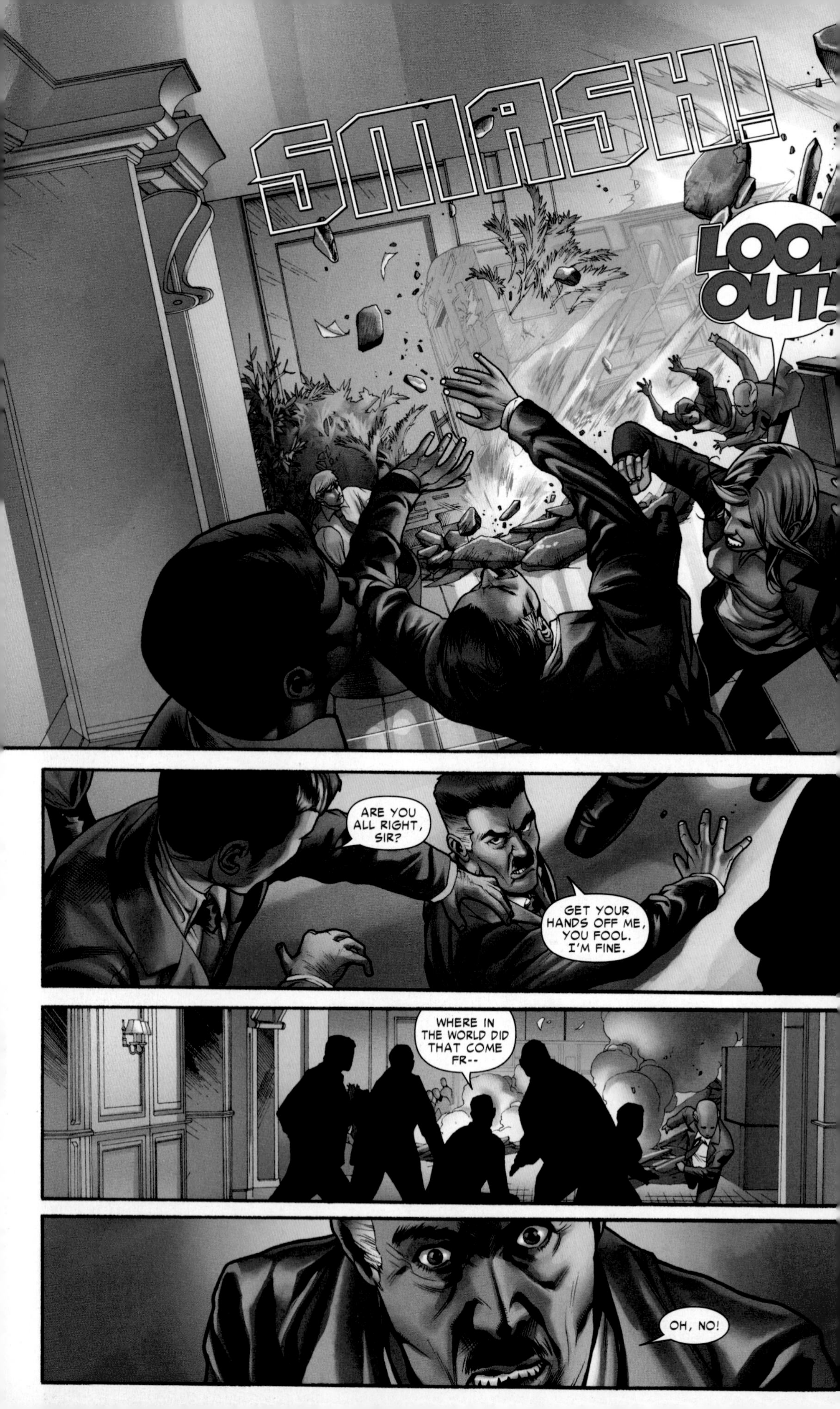
SMASH!
LOOK OUT!
ARE YOU ALL RIGHT, SIR?
GET YOUR HANDS OFF ME, YOU FOOL. I'M FINE.
WHERE IN THE WORLD DID THAT COME FR--
OH, NO!

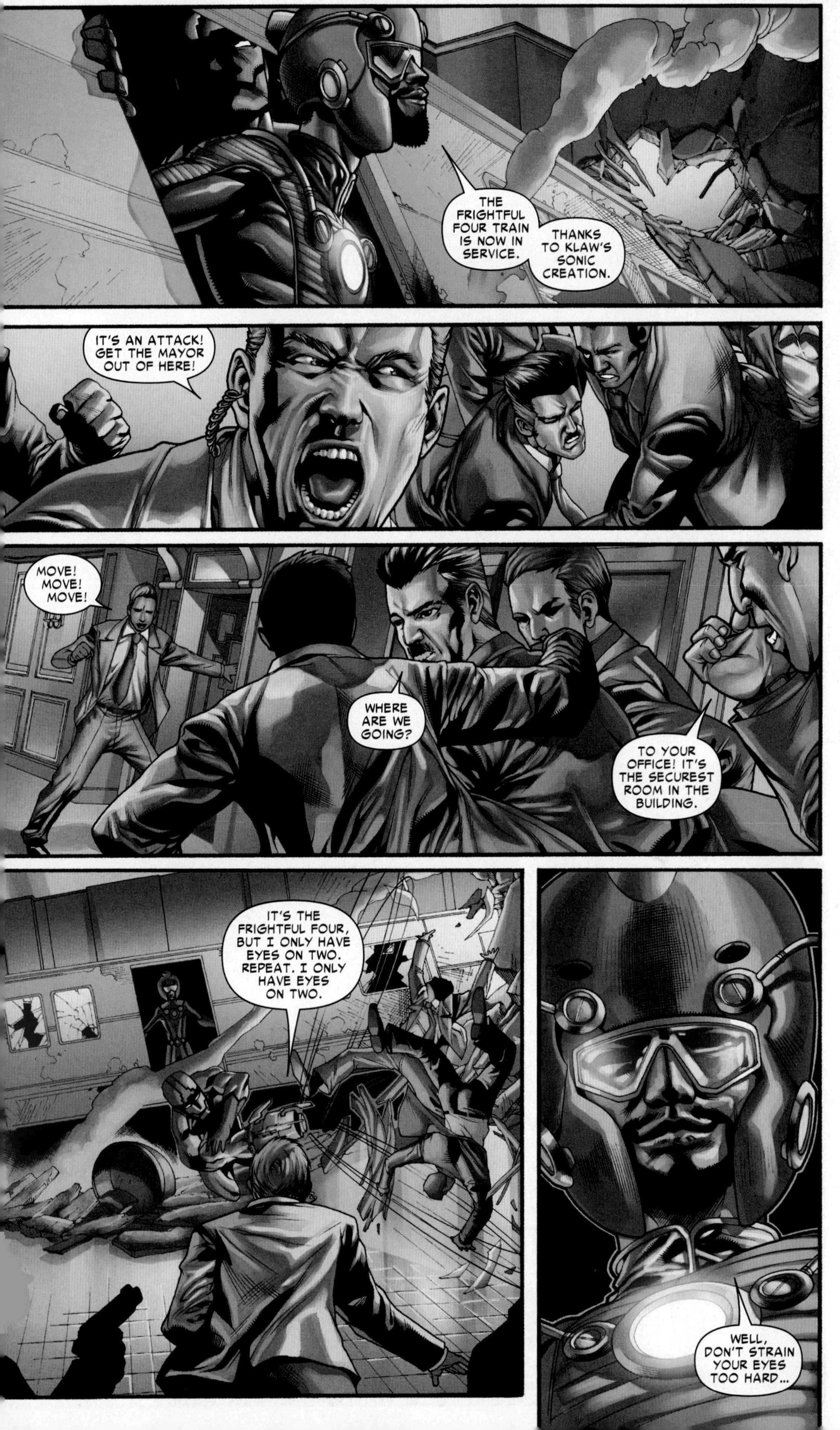
THE FRIGHTFUL FOUR TRAIN IS NOW IN SERVICE.
THANKS TO KLAW'S SONIC CREATION.
IT'S AN ATTACK! GET THE MAYOR OUT OF HERE!
MOVE! MOVE! MOVE!
WHERE ARE WE GOING?
TO YOUR OFFICE! IT'S THE SECUREST ROOM IN THE BUILDING.
IT'S THE FRIGHTFUL FOUR, BUT I ONLY HAVE EYES ON TWO. REPEAT. I ONLY HAVE EYES ON TWO.
WELL, DON'T STRAIN YOUR EYES TOO HARD...

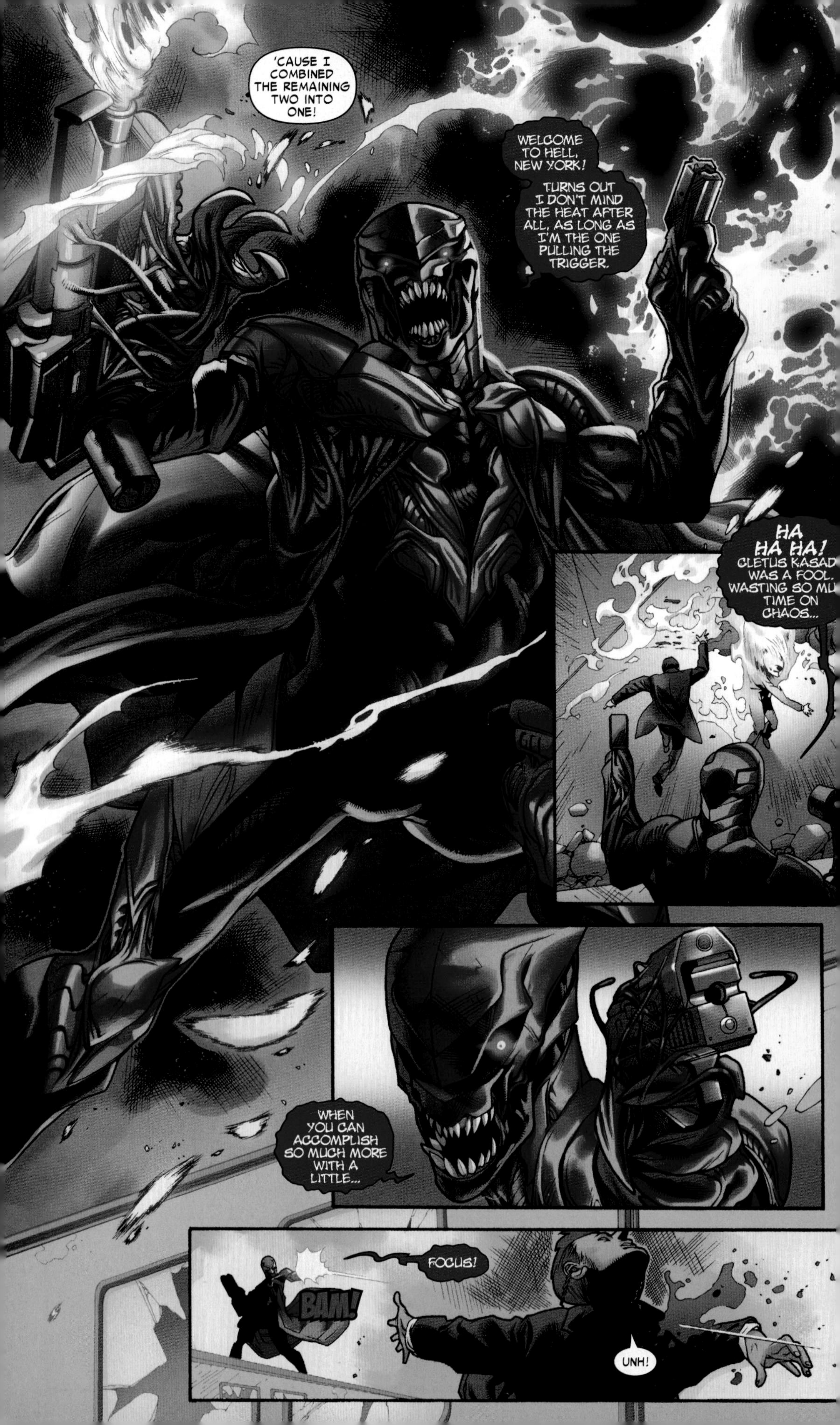
'CAUSE I COMBINED THE REMAINING TWO INTO ONE!
WELCOME TO HELL, NEW YORK!
TURNS OUT I DON'T MIND THE HEAT AFTER ALL, AS LONG AS I'M THE ONE PULLING THE TRIGGER.
HA HA HA! CLETUS KASAD WAS A FOOL, WASTING SO MU TIME ON CHAOS...
WHEN YOU CAN ACCOMPLISH SO MUCH MORE WITH A LITTLE...
BAM!
FOCUS!
UNH!

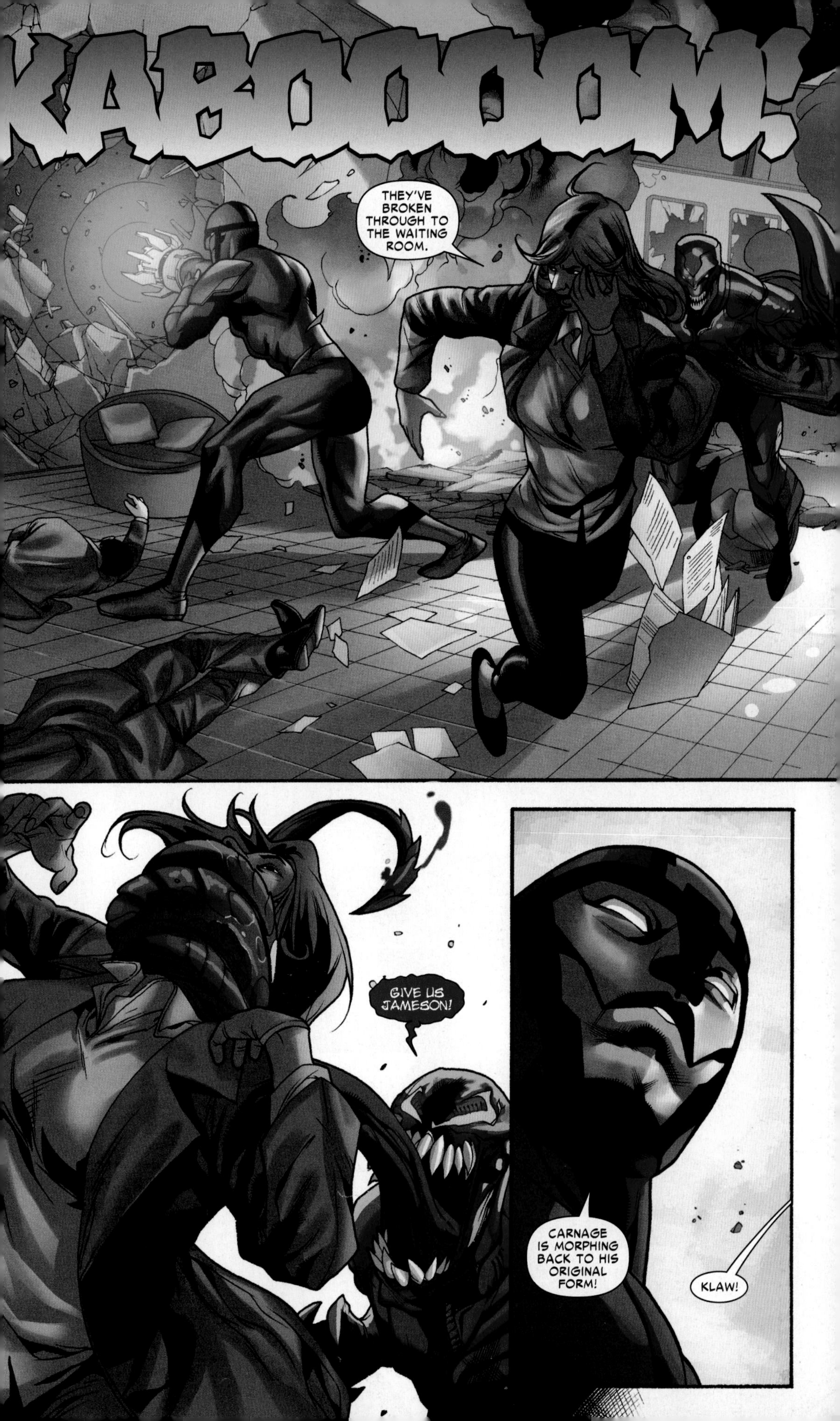
KABOOOOM!
THEY'VE BROKEN THROUGH TO THE WAITING ROOM.
GIVE US JAMESON!
CARNAGE IS MORPHING BACK TO HIS ORIGINAL FORM!
KLAW!

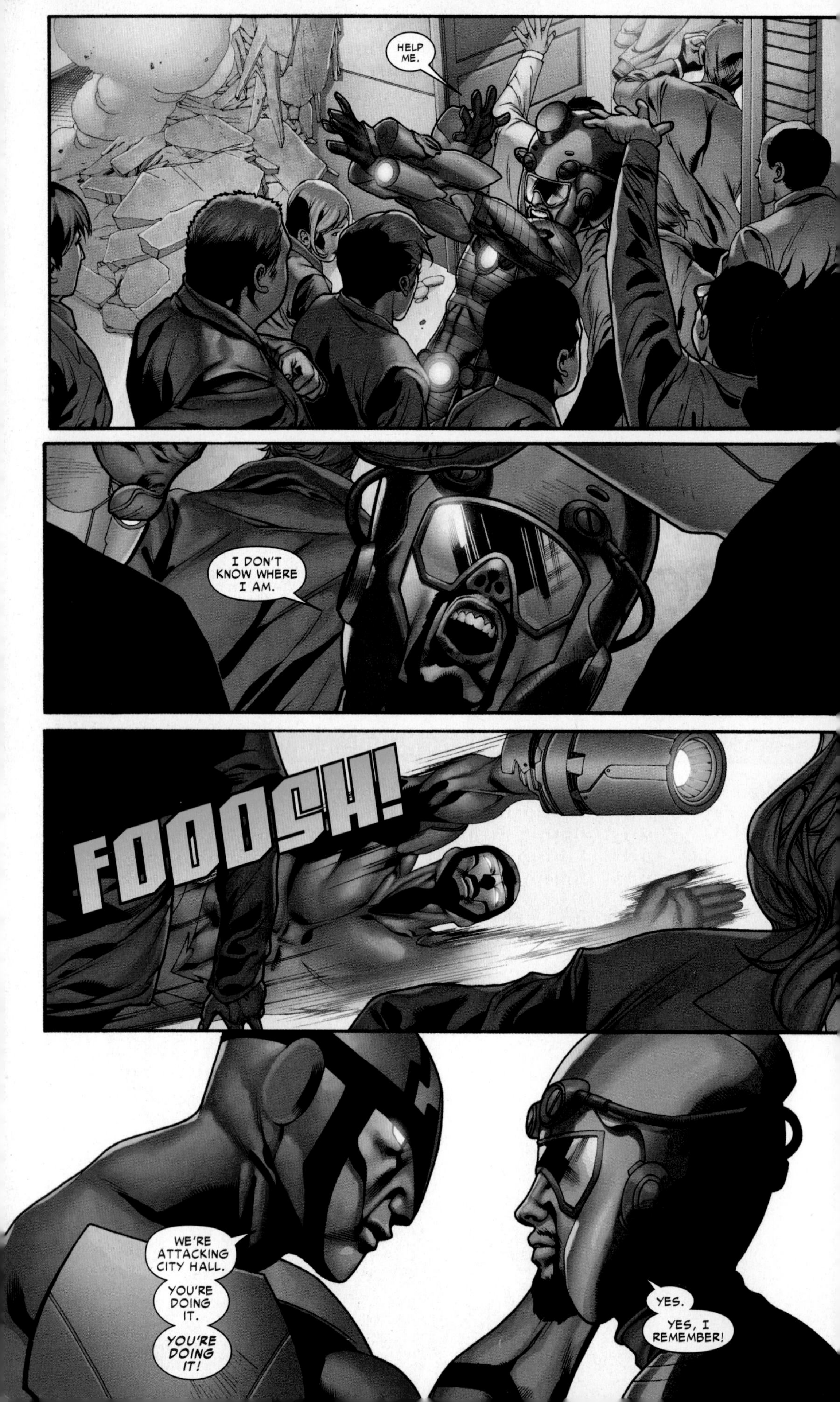
HELP ME.
I DON'T KNOW WHERE I AM.
FOOOSH!
WE'RE ATTACKING CITY HALL.
YOU'RE DOING IT.
YOU'RE DOING IT!
YES.
YES, I REMEMBER!

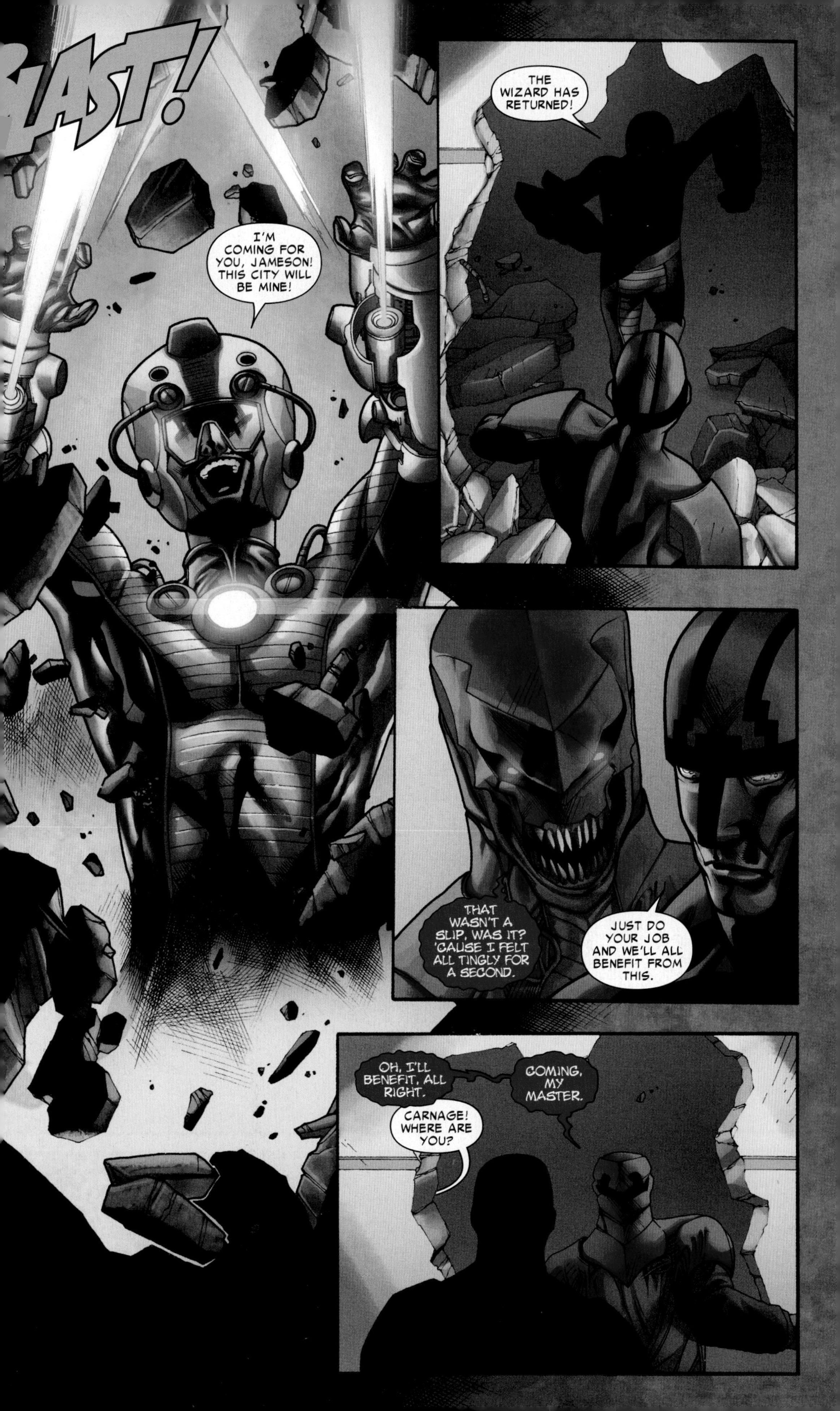
BLAST!
I'M COMING FOR YOU, JAMESON! THIS CITY WILL BE MINE!
THE WIZARD HAS RETURNED!
THAT WASN'T A SLIP, WAS IT? 'CAUSE I FELT ALL TINGLY FOR A SECOND.
JUST DO YOUR JOB AND WE'LL ALL BENEFIT FROM THIS.
OH, I'LL BENEFIT, ALL RIGHT.
COMING, MY MASTER.
CARNAGE! WHERE ARE YOU?

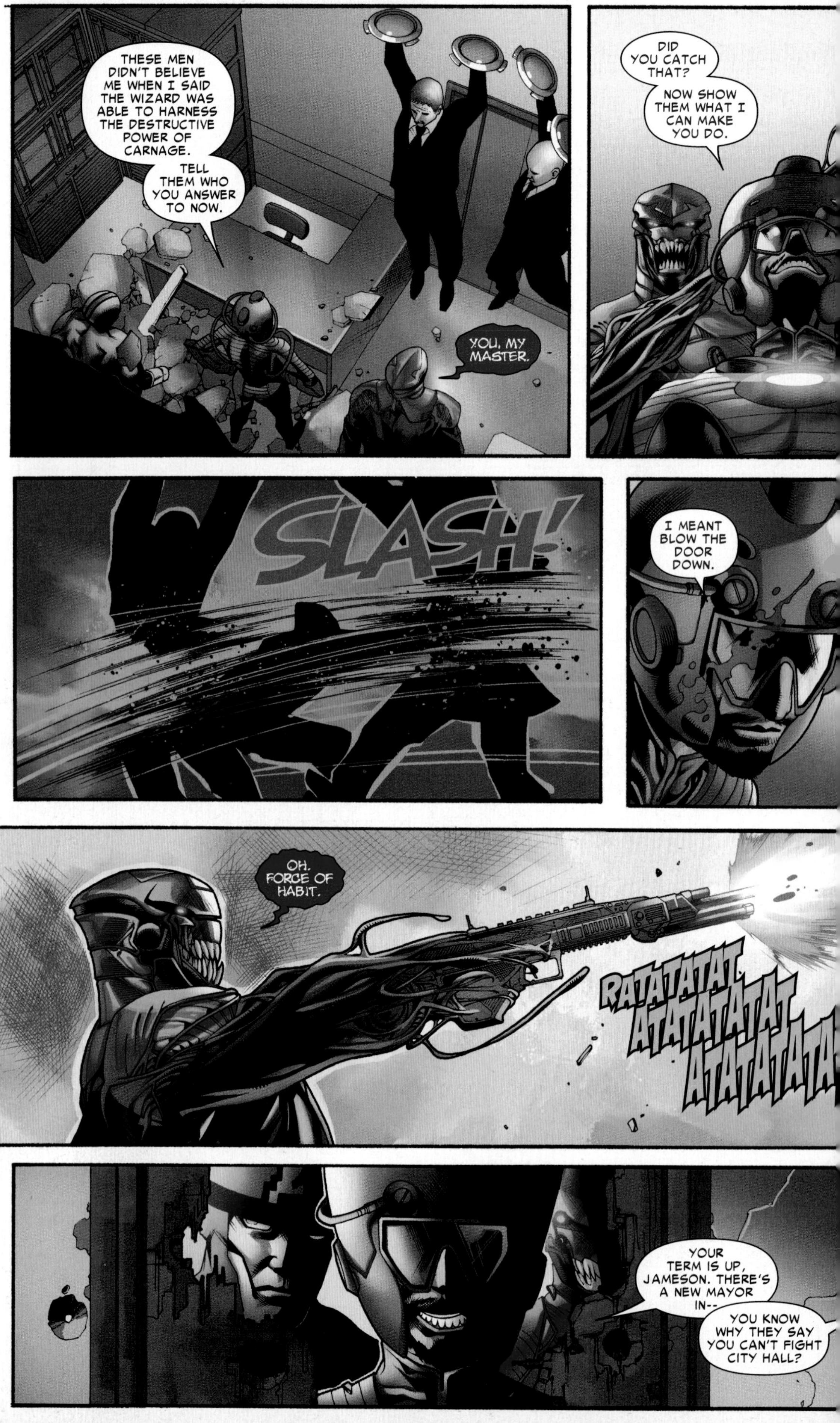
THESE MEN DIDN'T BELIEVE ME WHEN I SAID THE WIZARD WAS ABLE TO HARNESS THE DESTRUCTIVE POWER OF CARNAGE.
TELL THEM WHO YOU ANSWER TO NOW.
YOU, MY MASTER.
DID YOU CATCH THAT?
NOW SHOW THEM WHAT I CAN MAKE YOU DO.
SLASH!
I MEANT BLOW THE DOOR DOWN.
OH. FORCE OF HABIT.
RATATATAT ATATATATAT ATATATATA
YOUR TERM IS UP, JAMESON. THERE'S A NEW MAYOR IN--
YOU KNOW WHY THEY SAY YOU CAN'T FIGHT CITY HALL?

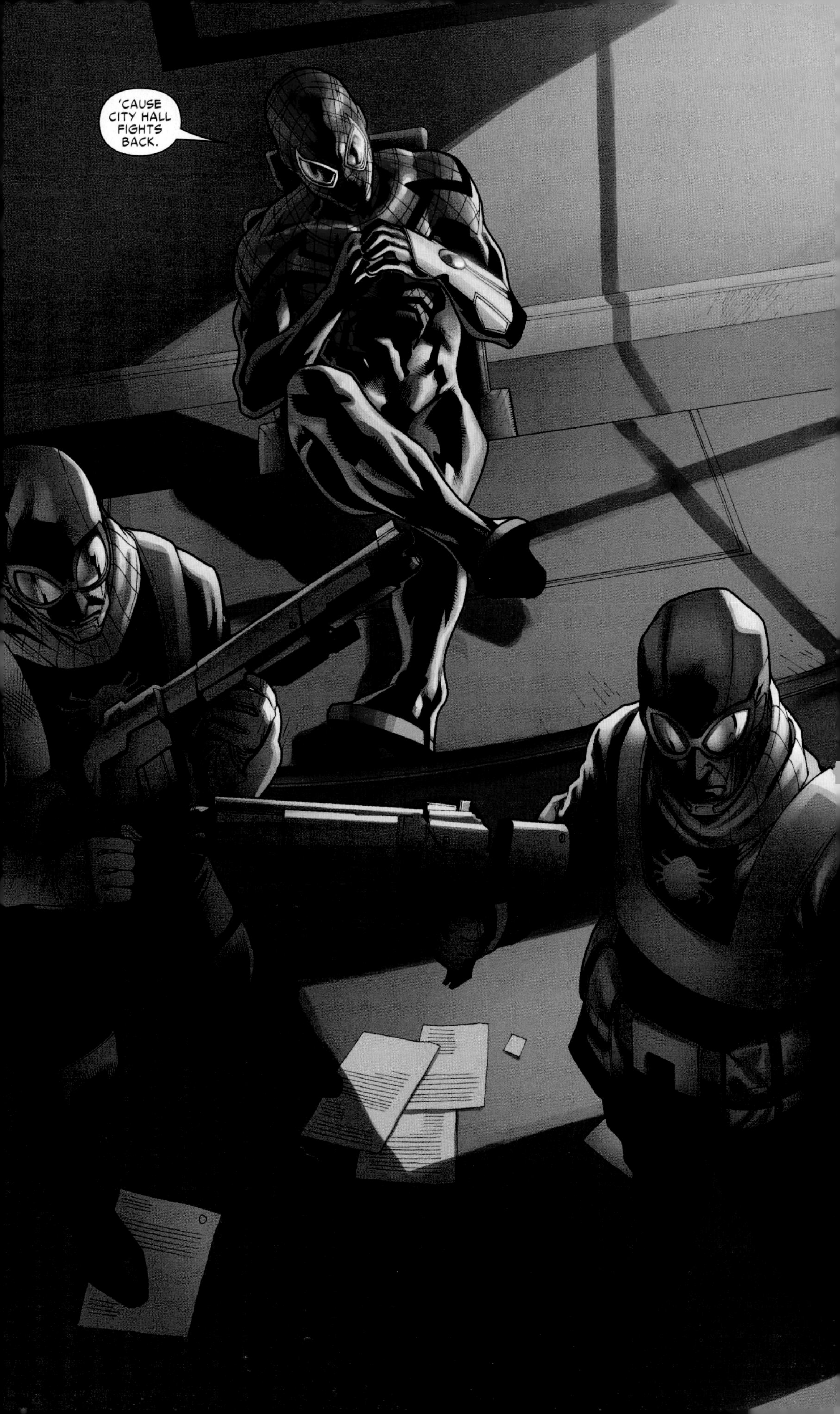
'CAUSE CITY HALL FIGHTS BACK.

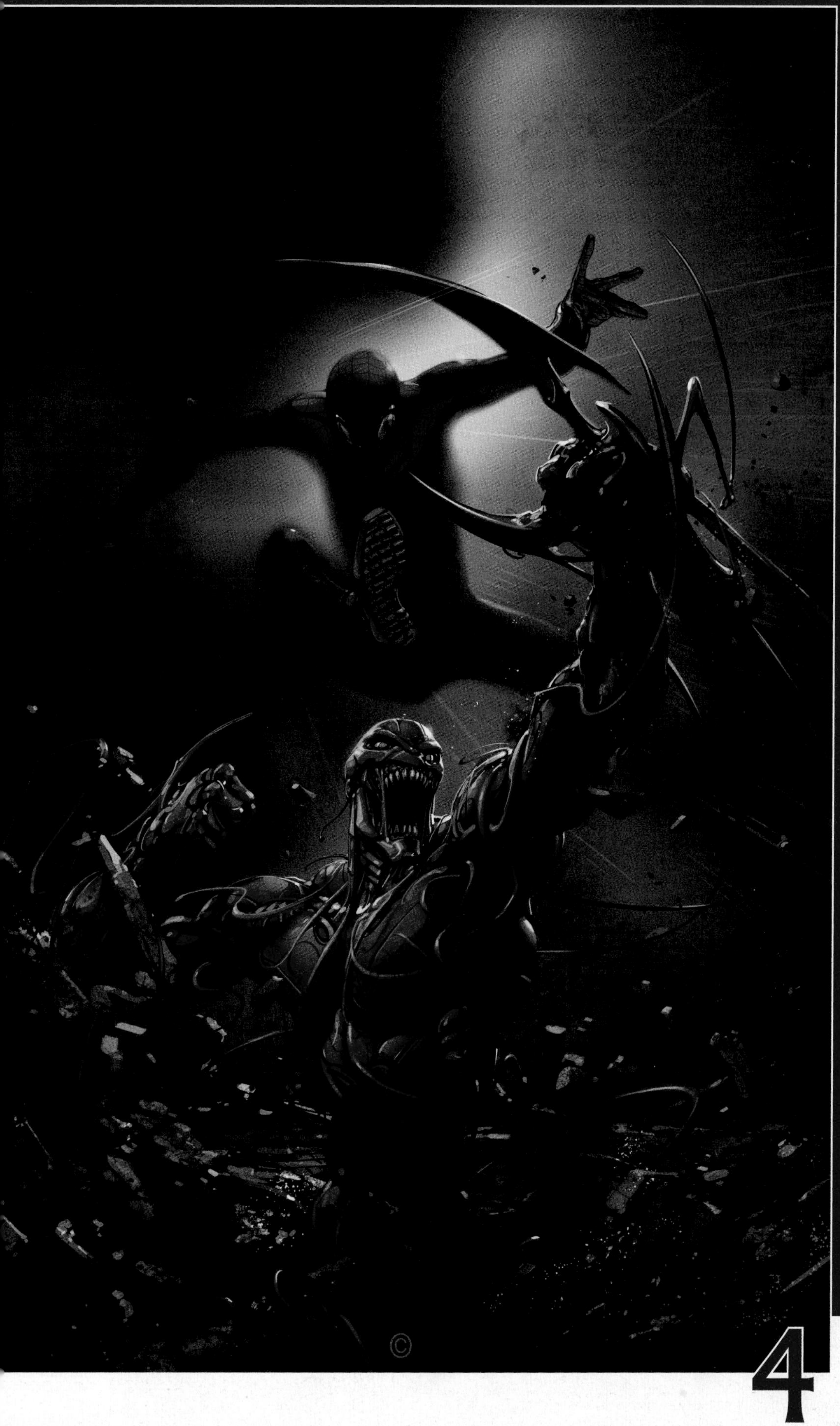

4

IT'S NO SURPRISE TO SAY I'M ALMOST ALWAYS THE SMARTEST PERSON IN THE ROOM.

I DO NOT **NEED** TO BE PROTECTED! I AM THE MAYOR! I HELPED YOU BRING DOWN THE **SPIDER-SLAYER**, FOR GOD'S SAKE!

YOU ARE A LIABILITY, JAME AND YOU'LL W IN THE SECUR BUNKER AS I H DICTATED.

SCRATCH THE "ALMOST." I'M **ALWAYS** THE SMARTEST PERSON IN THE ROOM.

TO THE POINT WHERE SURPRISES ARE ACTUALLY A RARE OCCURRENCE FOR ME.

WHEN, AS THE GREAT OTTO OCTAVIUS, I BEAT THE TRILLION-TO-ONE ODDS OF SUCCESSFULLY TRANSFERRING MY MIND WITH THAT OF THE ORIGINAL, OR SHOULD I SAY INFERIOR SPIDER-MAN, I WAS NOT SURPRISED.

IN A MATTER OF SECONDS, THE WIZARD AND HIS CRONIES WILL BE COMING THROUGH THAT DOOR.

HE IS A FEEBLE OLD MAN WHO HAS HOURS IF NOT MINUTES LEFT BEFORE HIS BRAIN SUCCUMBS TO DEMENTIA.

WHEN I HEARD THAT ANOTHER AGING VILLAIN WITH ONLY DAYS TO LIVE WAS ATTEMPTING TO SECURE A LEGACY OF HIS OWN, I WAS ALSO NOT SURPRISED.

WITH HIM WILL BE CLETUS KASADY, A SERIAL KILLER WHOM YOU'LL BE HAPPY TO HEAR, DESPITE BEING ATTACHED TO THE SAVAGE CARNAGE SYMBIOTE, HAS ALSO BEEN LOBOTOMIZED.

YOU ARE EQUIPPED WITH ALL THE NECESSARY ITEMS TO TAKE THEM, AND THEIR ASSOCIATE KLAW, DOWN.

I HAVE ESTIMATED THIS SHOULD TAKE SEVEN MINUTES.

SO WHEN TH BUMBLING EG MANIACS MAKE THE WAY TO HALL LOOKIN THEY DO NC

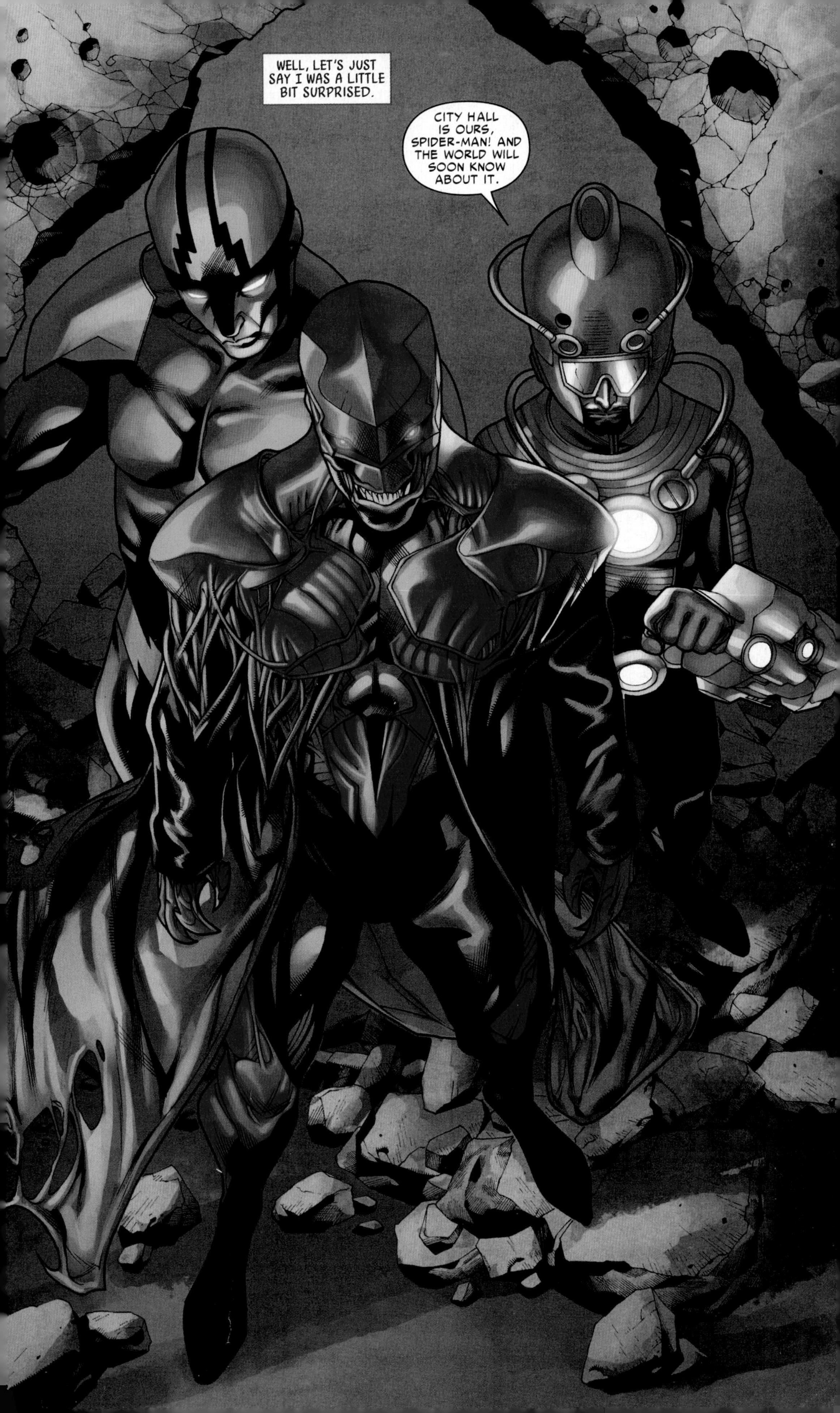
WELL, LET'S JUST SAY I WAS A LITTLE BIT SURPRISED.
CITY HALL IS OURS, SPIDER-MAN! AND THE WORLD WILL SOON KNOW ABOUT IT.

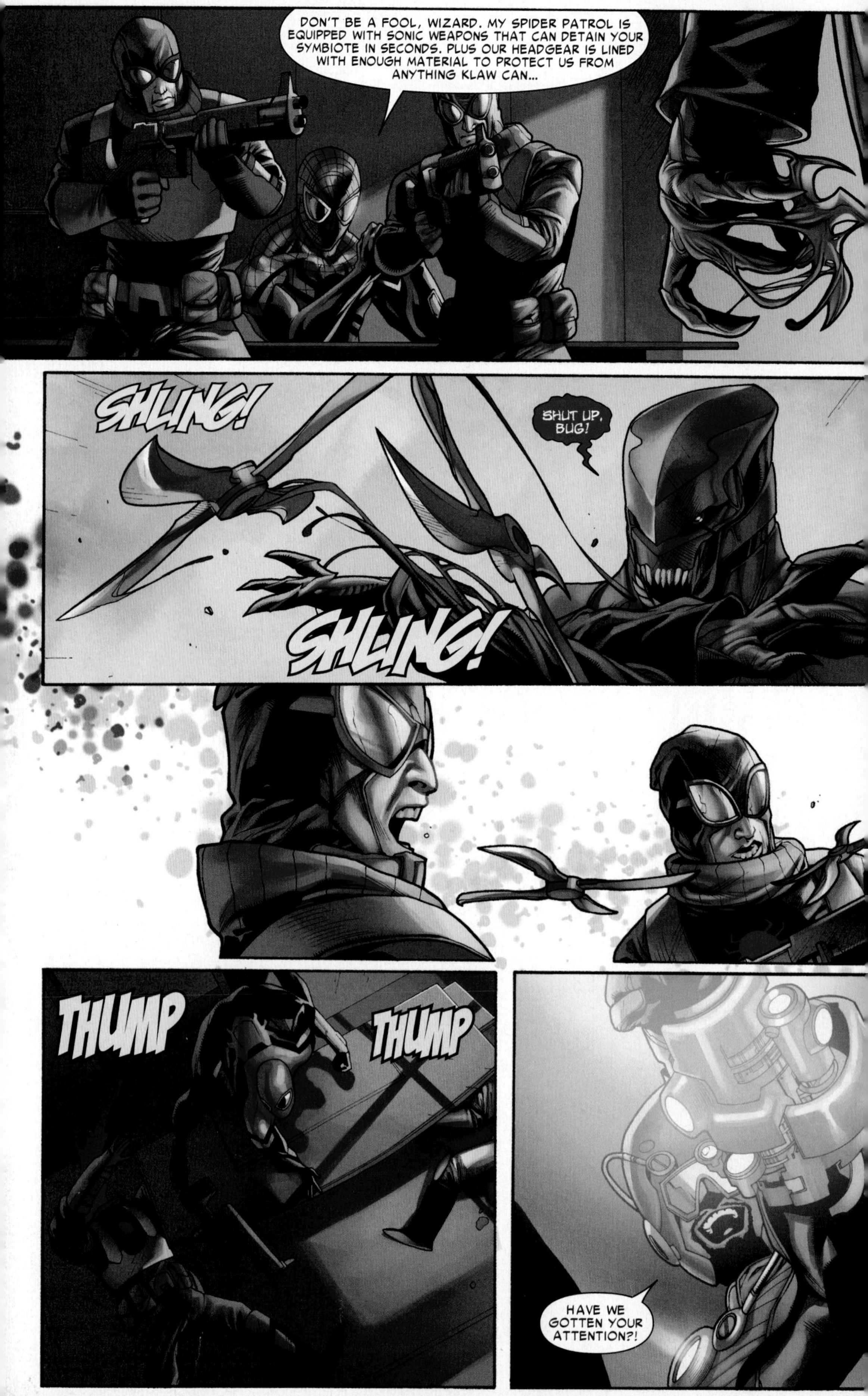
DON'T BE A FOOL, WIZARD. MY SPIDER PATROL IS EQUIPPED WITH SONIC WEAPONS THAT CAN DETAIN YOUR SYMBIOTE IN SECONDS. PLUS OUR HEADGEAR IS LINED WITH ENOUGH MATERIAL TO PROTECT US FROM ANYTHING KLAW CAN...
SHLING!
SHUT UP, BUG!
SHLING!
THUMP
THUMP
HAVE WE GOTTEN YOUR ATTENTION?!

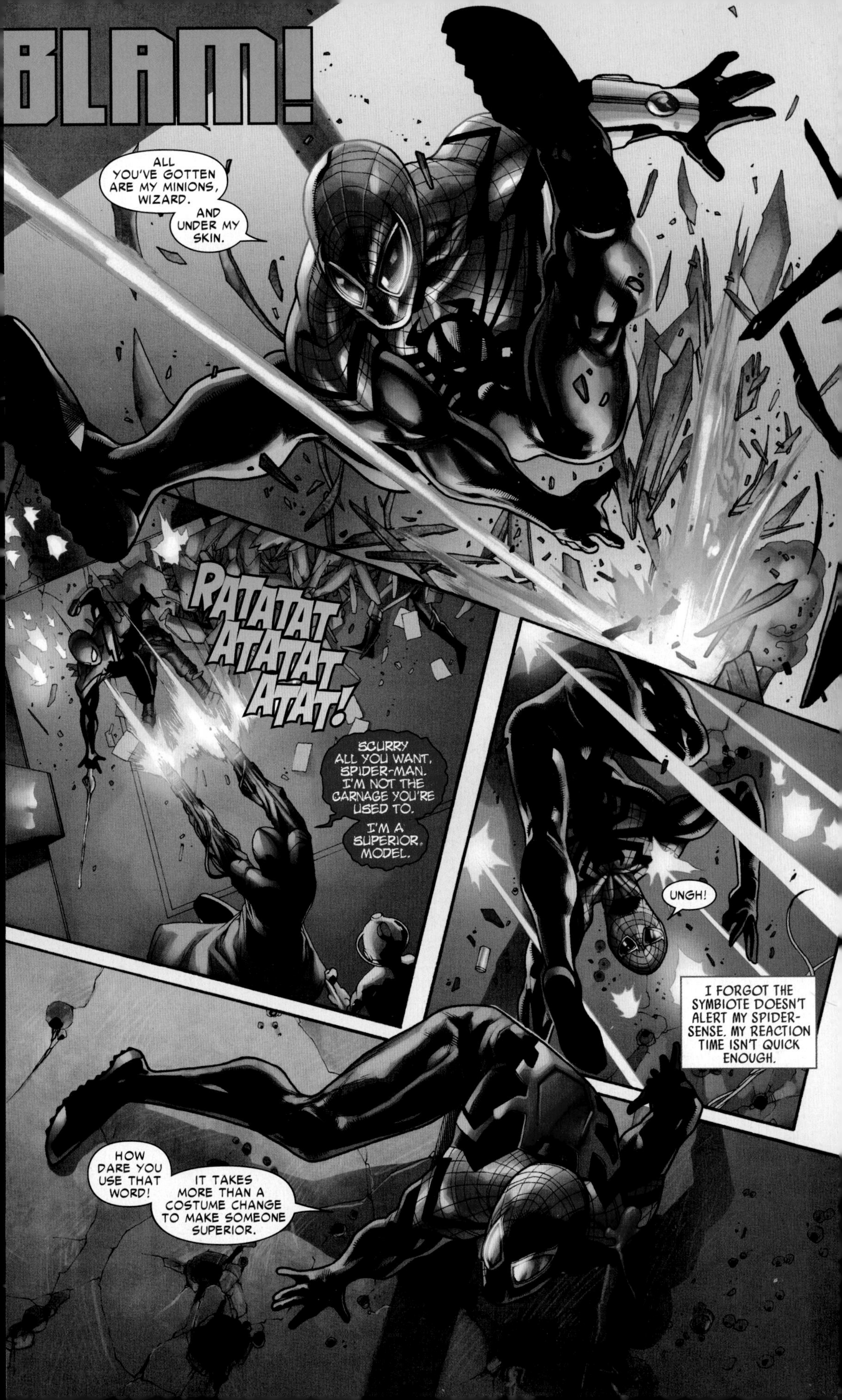
BLAM!
ALL YOU'VE GOTTEN ARE MY MINIONS, WIZARD.
AND UNDER MY SKIN.
RATATAT ATATAT ATAT!
SCURRY ALL YOU WANT, SPIDER-MAN. I'M NOT THE CARNAGE YOU'RE USED TO.
I'M A SUPERIOR MODEL.
UNGH!
I FORGOT THE SYMBIOTE DOESN'T ALERT MY SPIDER-SENSE. MY REACTION TIME ISN'T QUICK ENOUGH.
HOW DARE YOU USE THAT WORD!
IT TAKES MORE THAN A COSTUME CHANGE TO MAKE SOMEONE SUPERIOR.

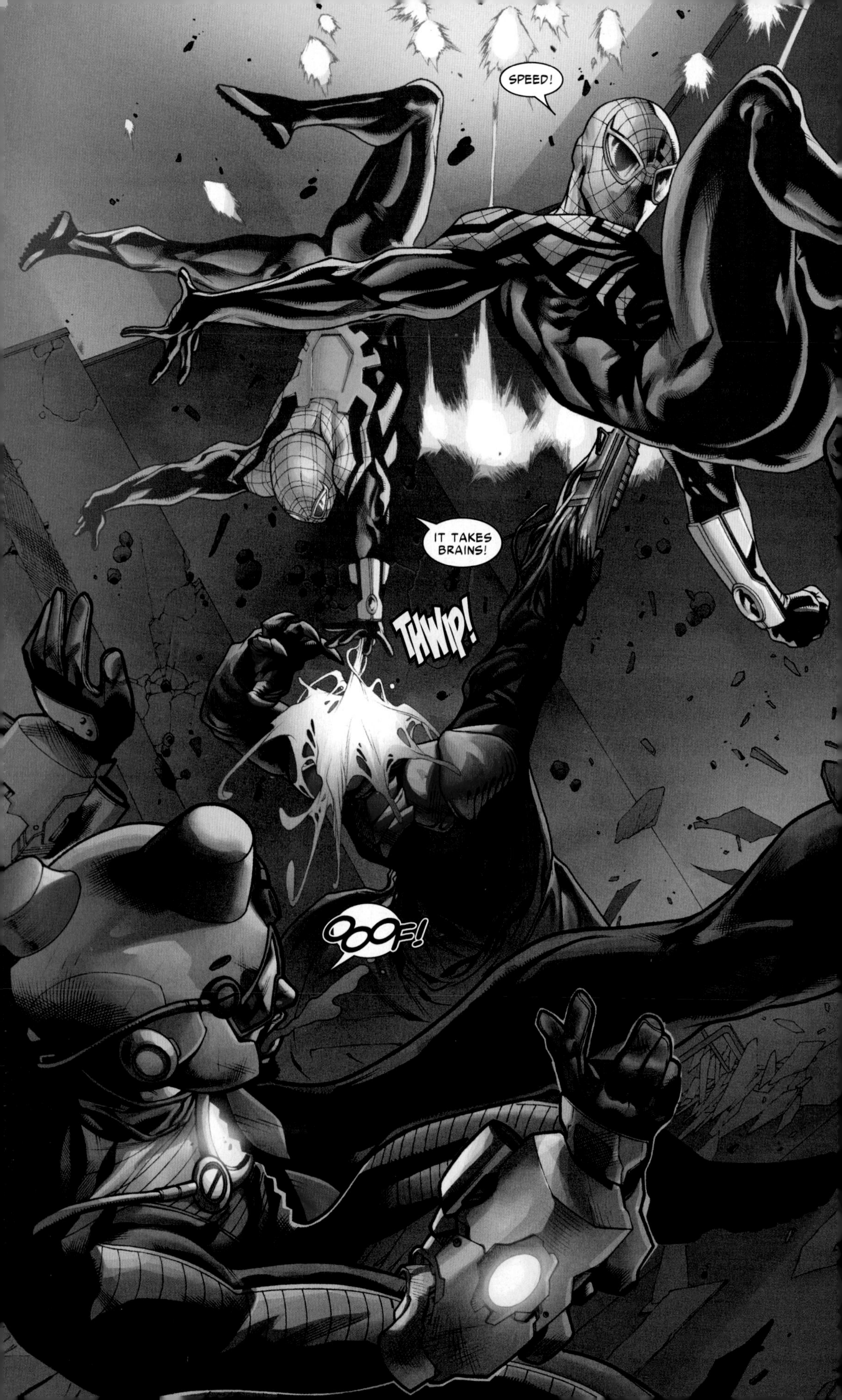
SPEED!
IT TAKES BRAINS!
THWIP!
OOOF!

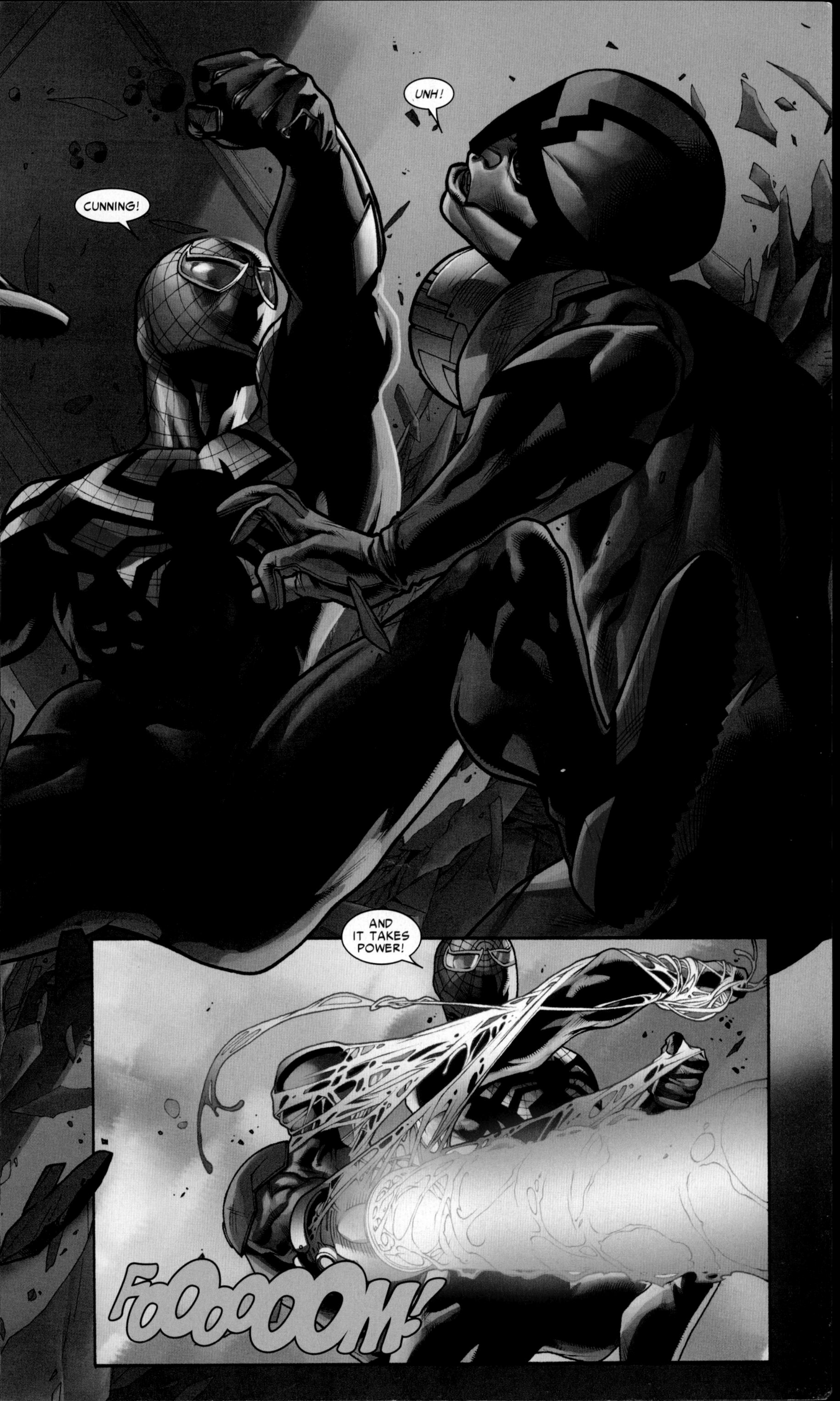
UNH!
CUNNING!
AND IT TAKES POWER!
FOOOOOOM!

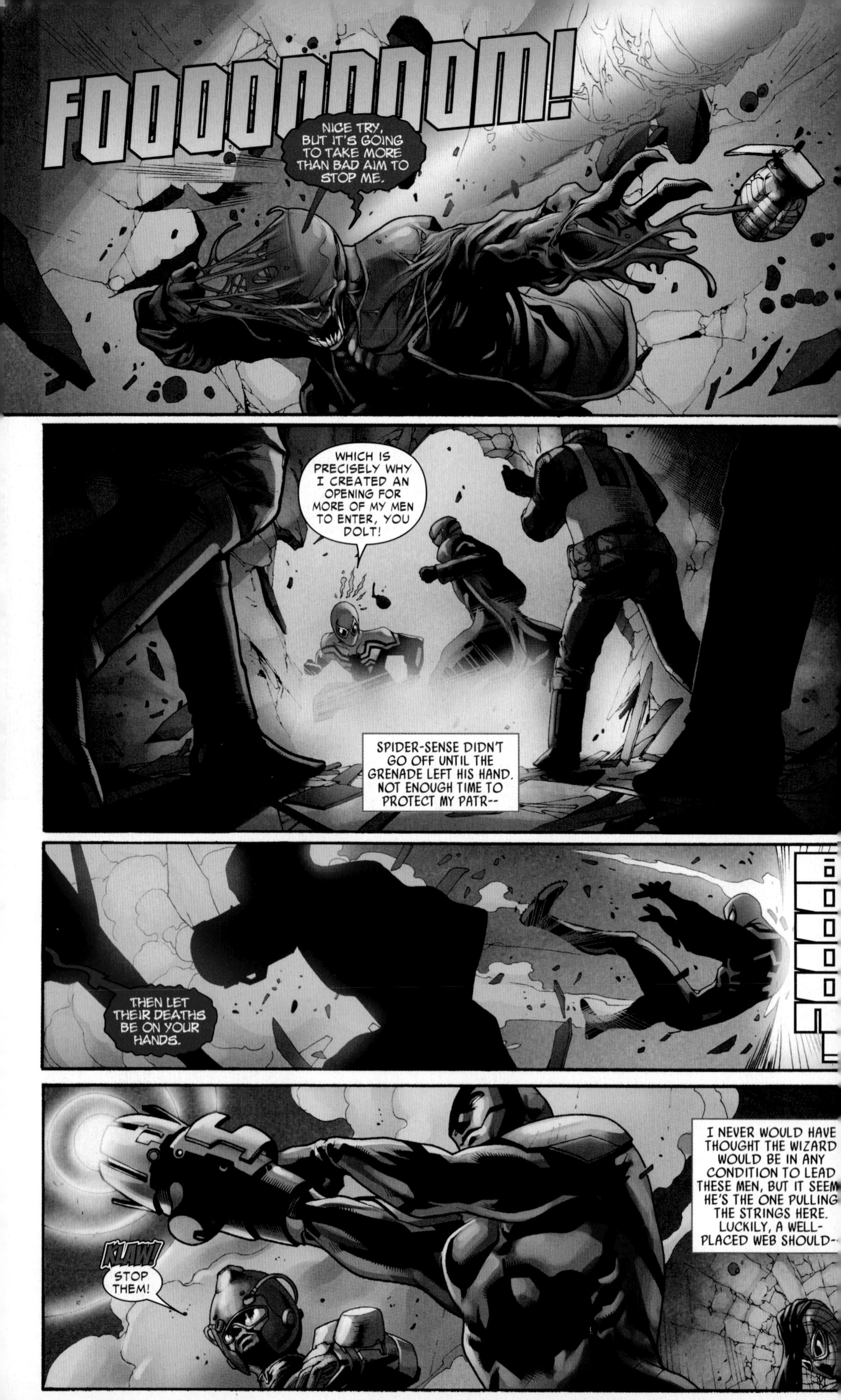
FOOOOMMMOM!
NICE TRY, BUT IT'S GOING TO TAKE MORE THAN BAD AIM TO STOP ME.
WHICH IS PRECISELY WHY I CREATED AN OPENING FOR MORE OF MY MEN TO ENTER, YOU DOLT!
SPIDER-SENSE DIDN'T GO OFF UNTIL THE GRENADE LEFT HIS HAND. NOT ENOUGH TIME TO PROTECT MY PATR--
THEN LET THEIR DEATHS BE ON YOUR HANDS.
I NEVER WOULD HAVE THOUGHT THE WIZARD WOULD BE IN ANY CONDITION TO LEAD THESE MEN, BUT IT SEEM HE'S THE ONE PULLING THE STRINGS HERE. LUCKILY, A WELL-PLACED WEB SHOULD--
KLAW! STOP THEM!

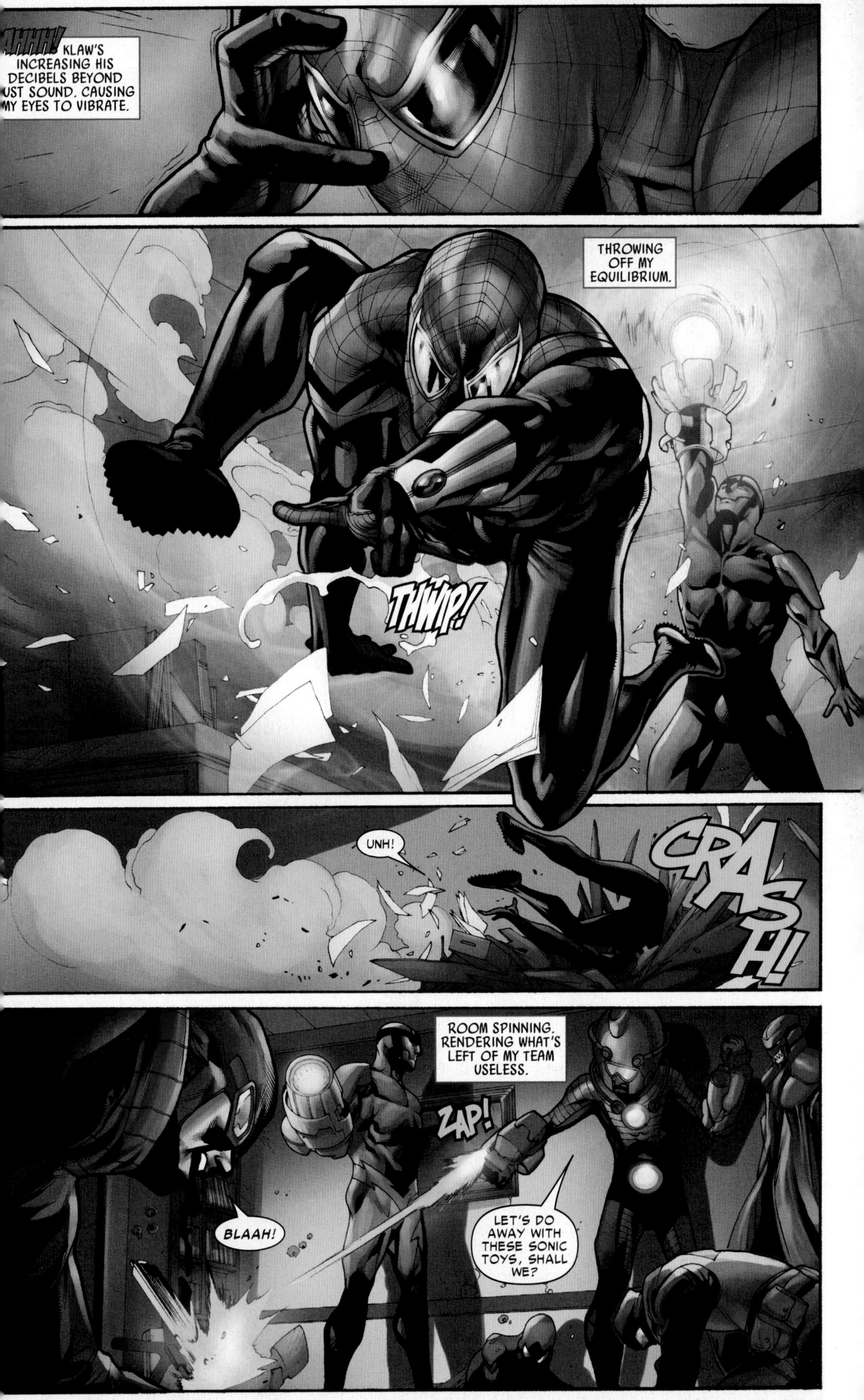
AHHH!
KLAW'S INCREASING HIS DECIBELS BEYOND JUST SOUND. CAUSING MY EYES TO VIBRATE.
THROWING OFF MY EQUILIBRIUM.
THWIP!
UNH!
CRASH!
ROOM SPINNING. RENDERING WHAT'S LEFT OF MY TEAM USELESS.
ZAP!
BLAAH!
LET'S DO AWAY WITH THESE SONIC TOYS, SHALL WE?

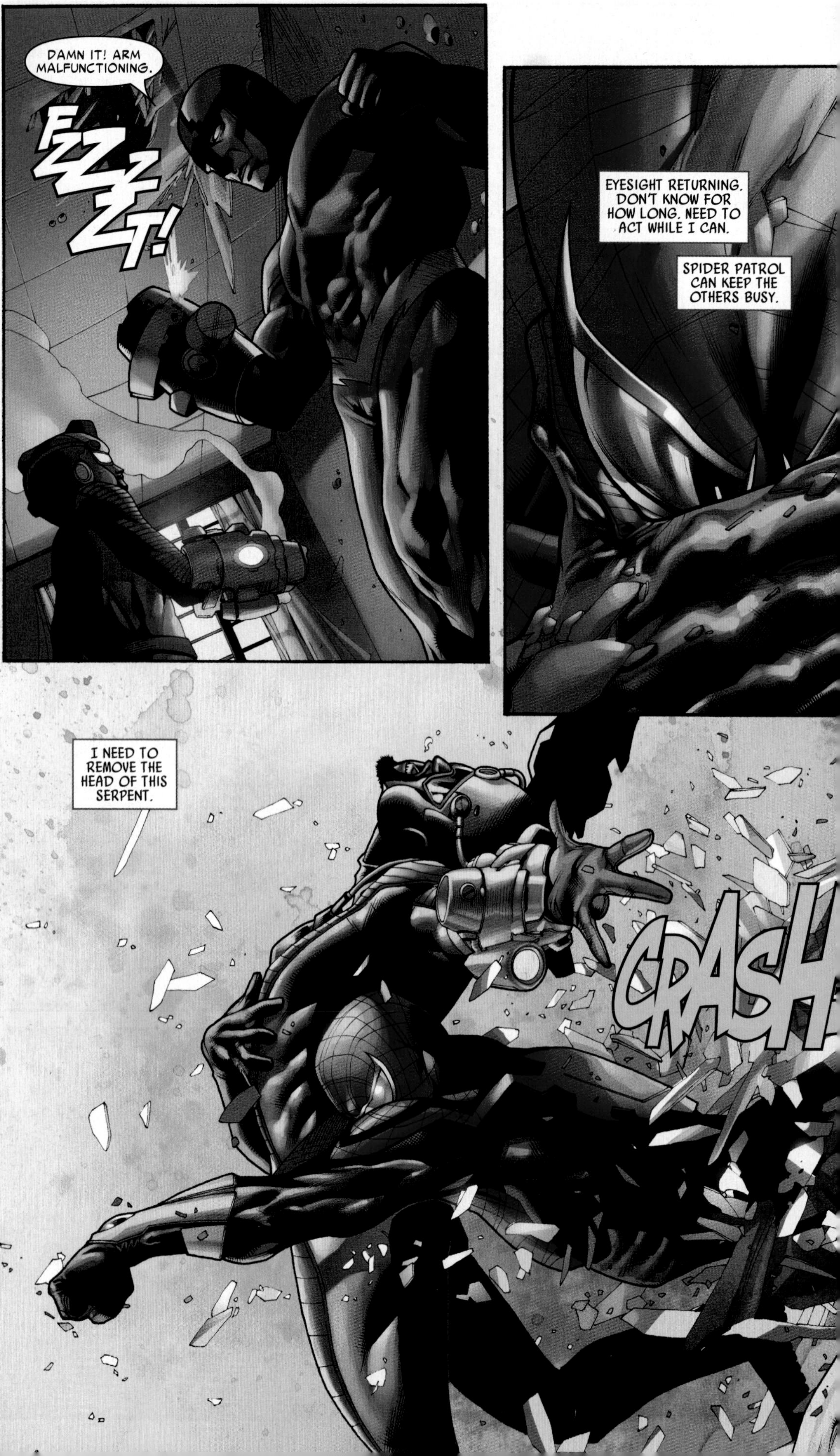
DAMN IT! ARM MALFUNCTIONING.
FZZZZT!
EYESIGHT RETURNING. DON'T KNOW FOR HOW LONG. NEED TO ACT WHILE I CAN.
SPIDER PATROL CAN KEEP THE OTHERS BUSY.
I NEED TO REMOVE THE HEAD OF THIS SERPENT.
CRASH

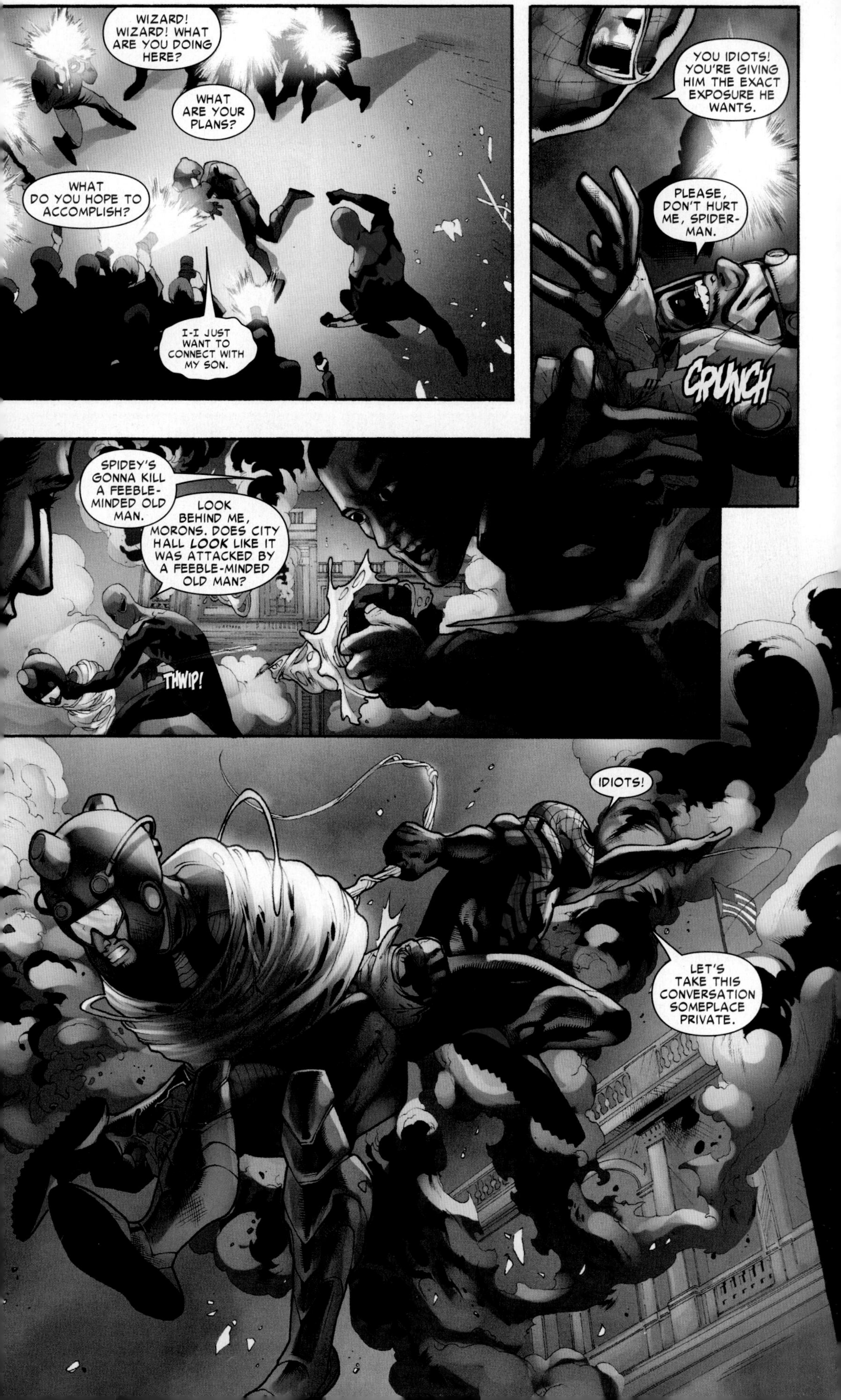
WIZARD! WIZARD! WHAT ARE YOU DOING HERE?
WHAT ARE YOUR PLANS?
WHAT DO YOU HOPE TO ACCOMPLISH?
I-I JUST WANT TO CONNECT WITH MY SON.
YOU IDIOTS! YOU'RE GIVING HIM THE EXACT EXPOSURE HE WANTS.
PLEASE, DON'T HURT ME, SPIDER-MAN.
CRUNCH
SPIDEY'S GONNA KILL A FEEBLE-MINDED OLD MAN.
LOOK BEHIND ME, MORONS. DOES CITY HALL LOOK LIKE IT WAS ATTACKED BY A FEEBLE-MINDED OLD MAN?
THWIP!
IDIOTS!
LET'S TAKE THIS CONVERSATION SOMEPLACE PRIVATE.

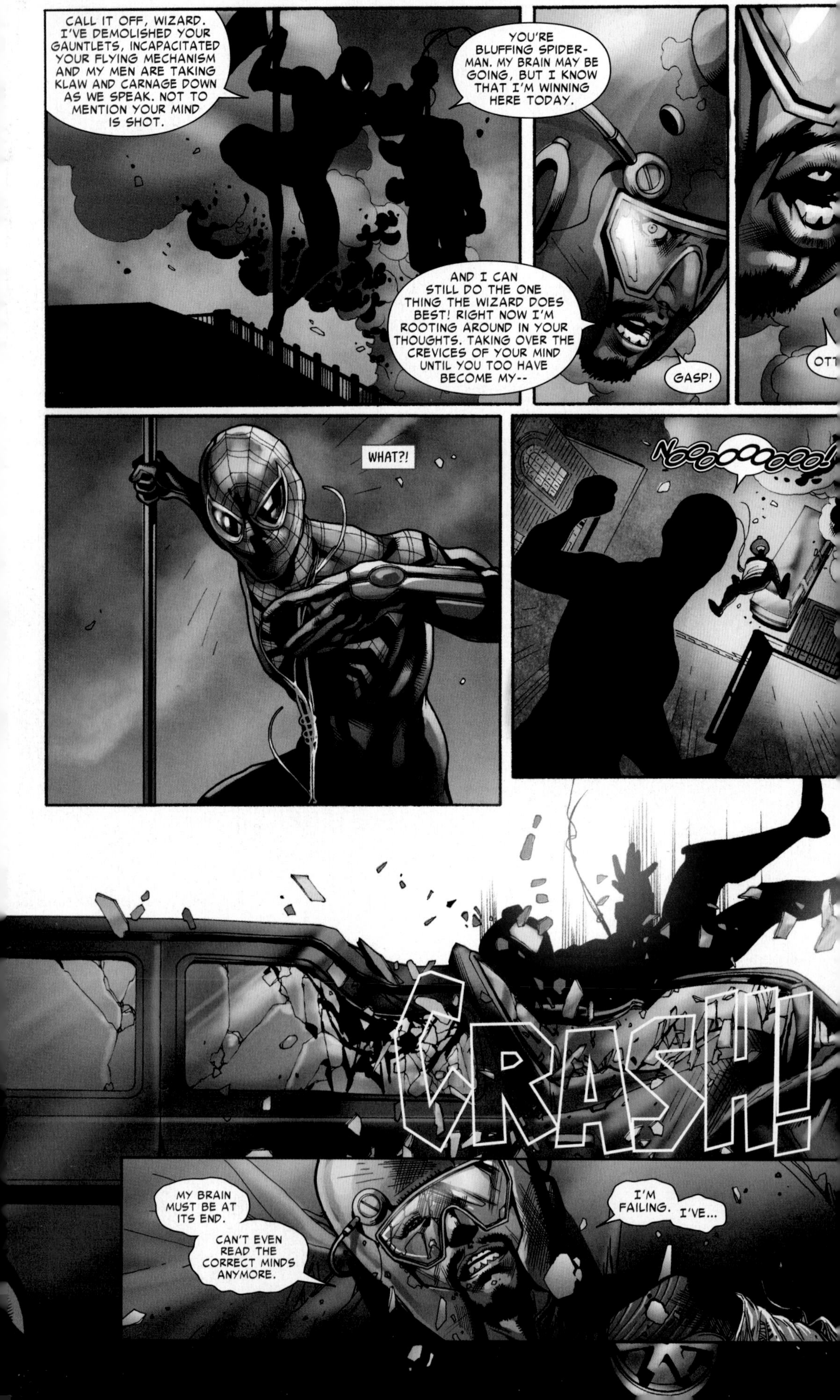
CALL IT OFF, WIZARD. I'VE DEMOLISHED YOUR GAUNTLETS, INCAPACITATED YOUR FLYING MECHANISM AND MY MEN ARE TAKING KLAW AND CARNAGE DOWN AS WE SPEAK. NOT TO MENTION YOUR MIND IS SHOT.
YOU'RE BLUFFING SPIDER-MAN. MY BRAIN MAY BE GOING, BUT I KNOW THAT I'M WINNING HERE TODAY.
AND I CAN STILL DO THE ONE THING THE WIZARD DOES BEST! RIGHT NOW I'M ROOTING AROUND IN YOUR THOUGHTS. TAKING OVER THE CREVICES OF YOUR MIND UNTIL YOU TOO HAVE BECOME MY--
GASP!
WHAT?!
NOOOOOOOOO!
CRASH!
MY BRAIN MUST BE AT ITS END.
CAN'T EVEN READ THE CORRECT MINDS ANYMORE.
I'M FAILING.
I'VE...

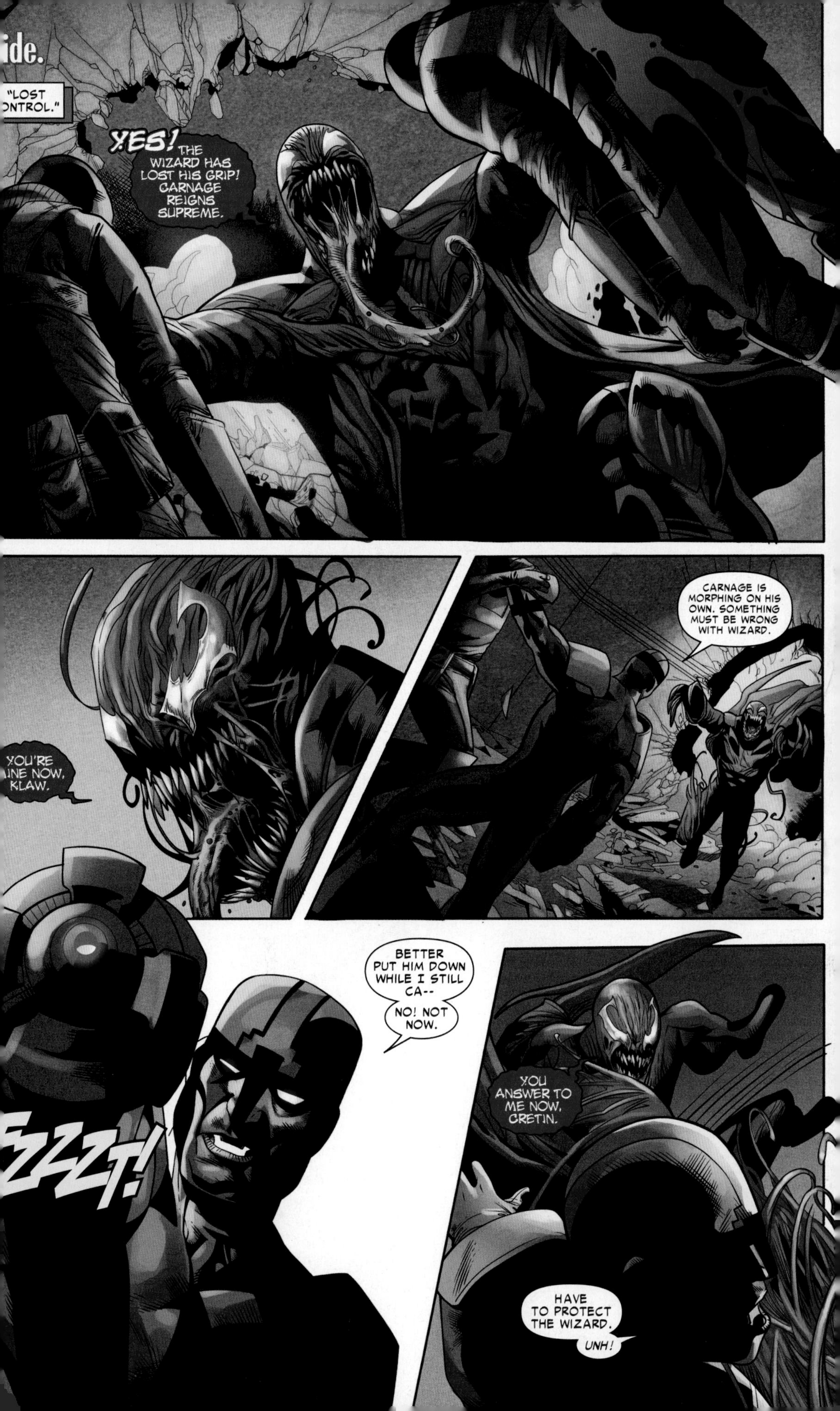

ide.
"LOST
ONTROL."
YES! THE WIZARD HAS LOST HIS GRIP! CARNAGE REIGNS SUPREME.
YOU'RE INE NOW, KLAW.
CARNAGE IS MORPHING ON HIS OWN. SOMETHING MUST BE WRONG WITH WIZARD.
BETTER PUT HIM DOWN WHILE I STILL CA--
NO! NOT NOW.
ZZZT!
YOU ANSWER TO ME NOW, CRETIN.
HAVE TO PROTECT THE WIZARD.
UNH!

Outside.

DAMN IT, WHY DID I LET THAT HAPPEN?

I WAS THREATENED BY WHAT HE KNEW AND NOW I MAY HAVE LOST AN IMPORTANT ASSET BECAUSE OF IT.

WANTED TO SEE MY SON ONE MORE TIME.

WIZARD! LISTEN TO ME. YOU'RE NOT WRONG! IT IS ME...OTTO OCTAVIUS!

GET CARNAGE TO STAND DOWN AND I'LL LET YOU SEE YOUR SON.

ARE-- ARE YOU HELPING ME?

THE THING TO SA YES. THAT I WAS C IN YOUR SHOES DYING MAN DESPE FOR ONE LAST CH AT A LEGACY.

BUT THE TRUTH LYING. I'M JUST YOU TO WIN A COST. MAKING PROMISES BEC KNOW YOU'LL DEAD SOO

I SMELL FEAR, SPIDER-MAN.

AHHHHHHH!

KEEP FORGETTING THE SYMBIOTE DOESN'T SET OFF MY SPIDER-SENSE.

SPIDER PATROL, SOUTH LAWN.

DON'T EXPECT A RESPONSE, SPIDER-MAN.

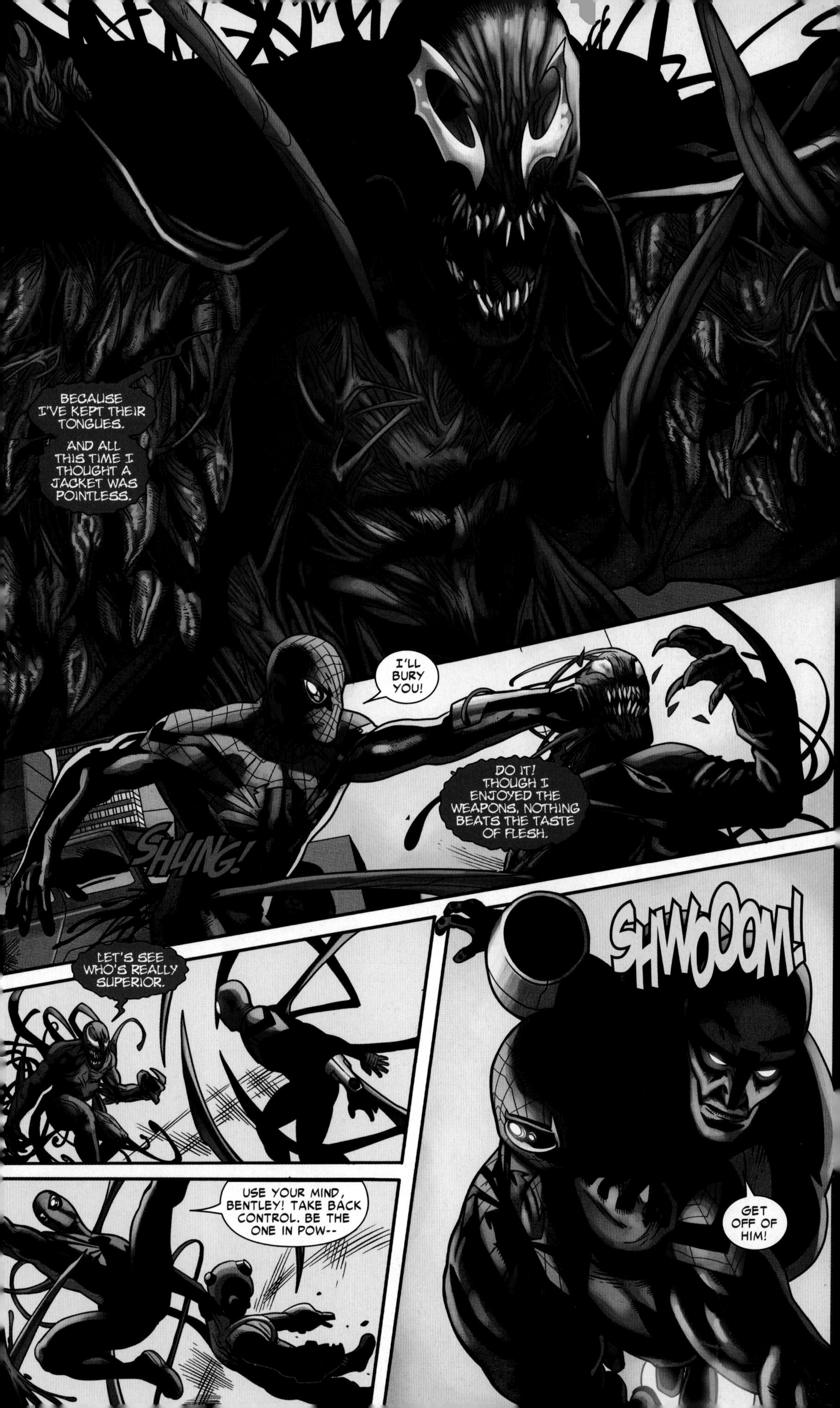
BECAUSE I'VE KEPT THEIR TONGUES.
AND ALL THIS TIME I THOUGHT A JACKET WAS POINTLESS.
I'LL BURY YOU!
DO IT! THOUGH I ENJOYED THE WEAPONS, NOTHING BEATS THE TASTE OF FLESH.
SHUNG!
SHWOOOM!
LET'S SEE WHO'S REALLY SUPERIOR.
USE YOUR MIND, BENTLEY! TAKE BACK CONTROL. BE THE ONE IN POW--
GET OFF OF HIM!

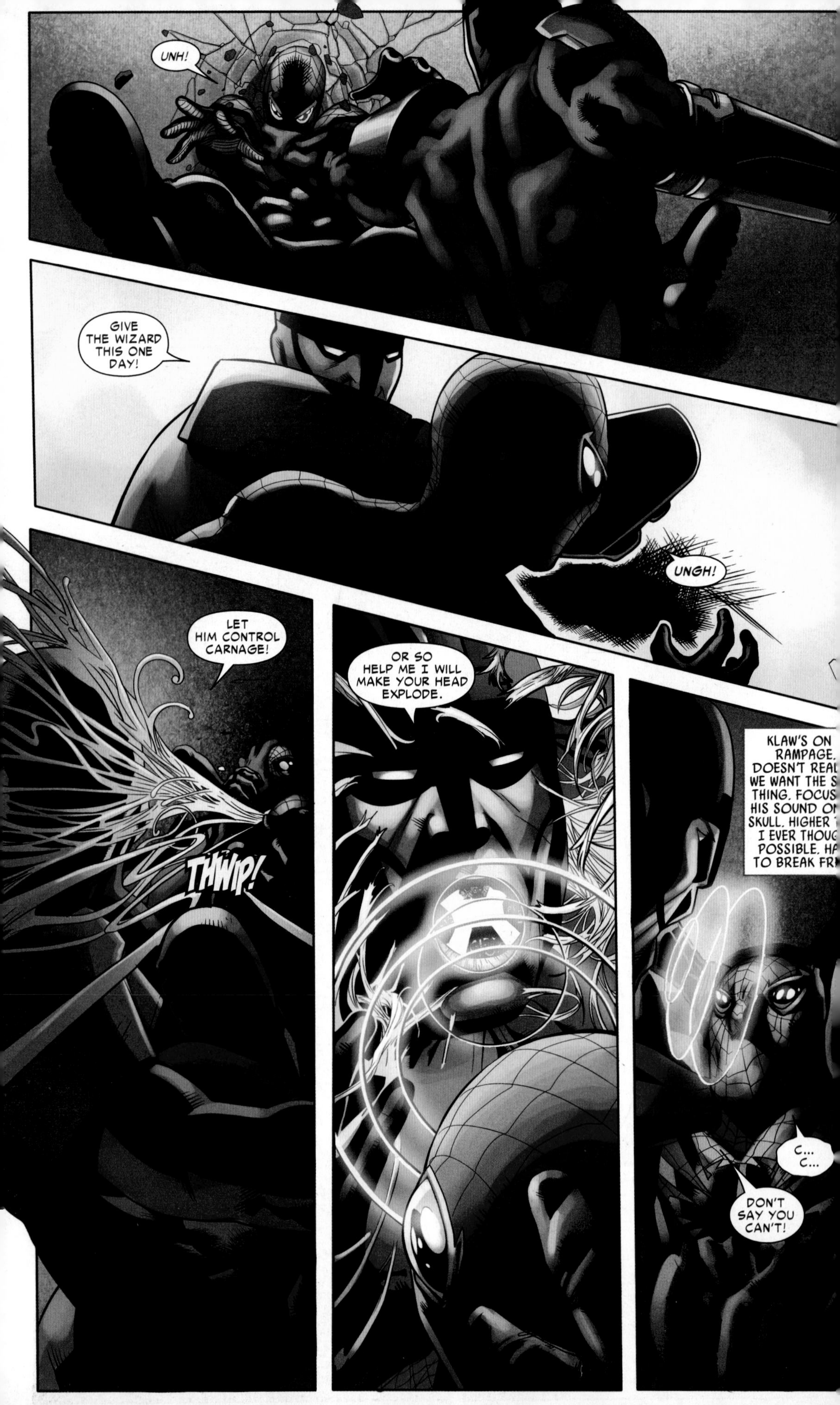
UNH!
GIVE THE WIZARD THIS ONE DAY!
UNGH!
LET HIM CONTROL CARNAGE!
THWIP!
OR SO HELP ME I WILL MAKE YOUR HEAD EXPLODE.
KLAW'S ON RAMPAGE. DOESN'T REAL WE WANT THE S THING. FOCUS HIS SOUND ON SKULL. HIGHER I EVER THOUG POSSIBLE. HA TO BREAK FR
C... C...
DON'T SAY YOU CAN'T!

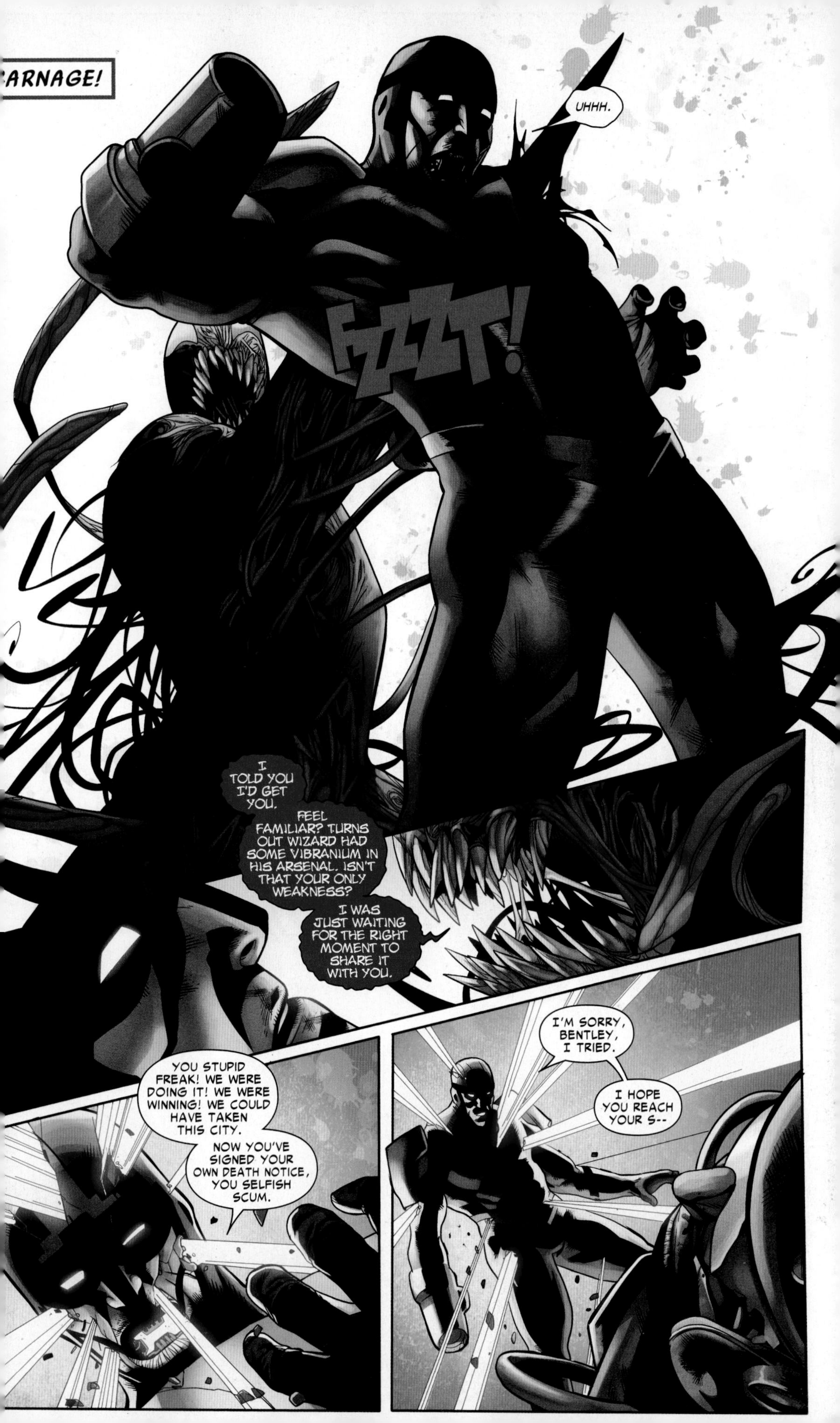
CARNAGE!
UHHH.
FZZZT!
I TOLD YOU I'D GET YOU.
FEEL FAMILIAR? TURNS OUT WIZARD HAD SOME VIBRANIUM IN HIS ARSENAL. ISN'T THAT YOUR ONLY WEAKNESS?
I WAS JUST WAITING FOR THE RIGHT MOMENT TO SHARE IT WITH YOU.
YOU STUPID FREAK! WE WERE DOING IT! WE WERE WINNING! WE COULD HAVE TAKEN THIS CITY.
NOW YOU'VE SIGNED YOUR OWN DEATH NOTICE, YOU SELFISH SCUM.
I'M SORRY, BENTLEY, I TRIED.
I HOPE YOU REACH YOUR S--

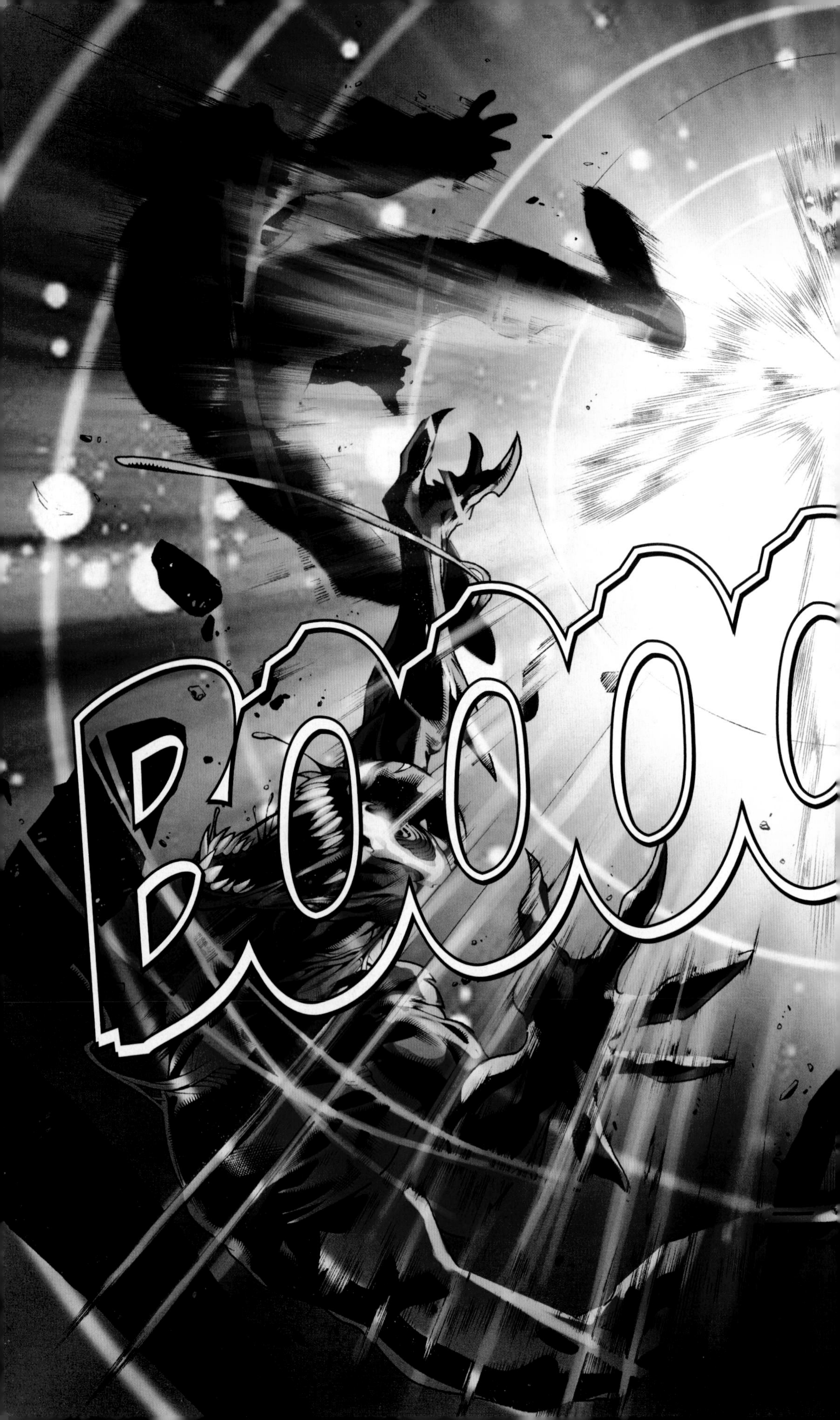
BOOOO

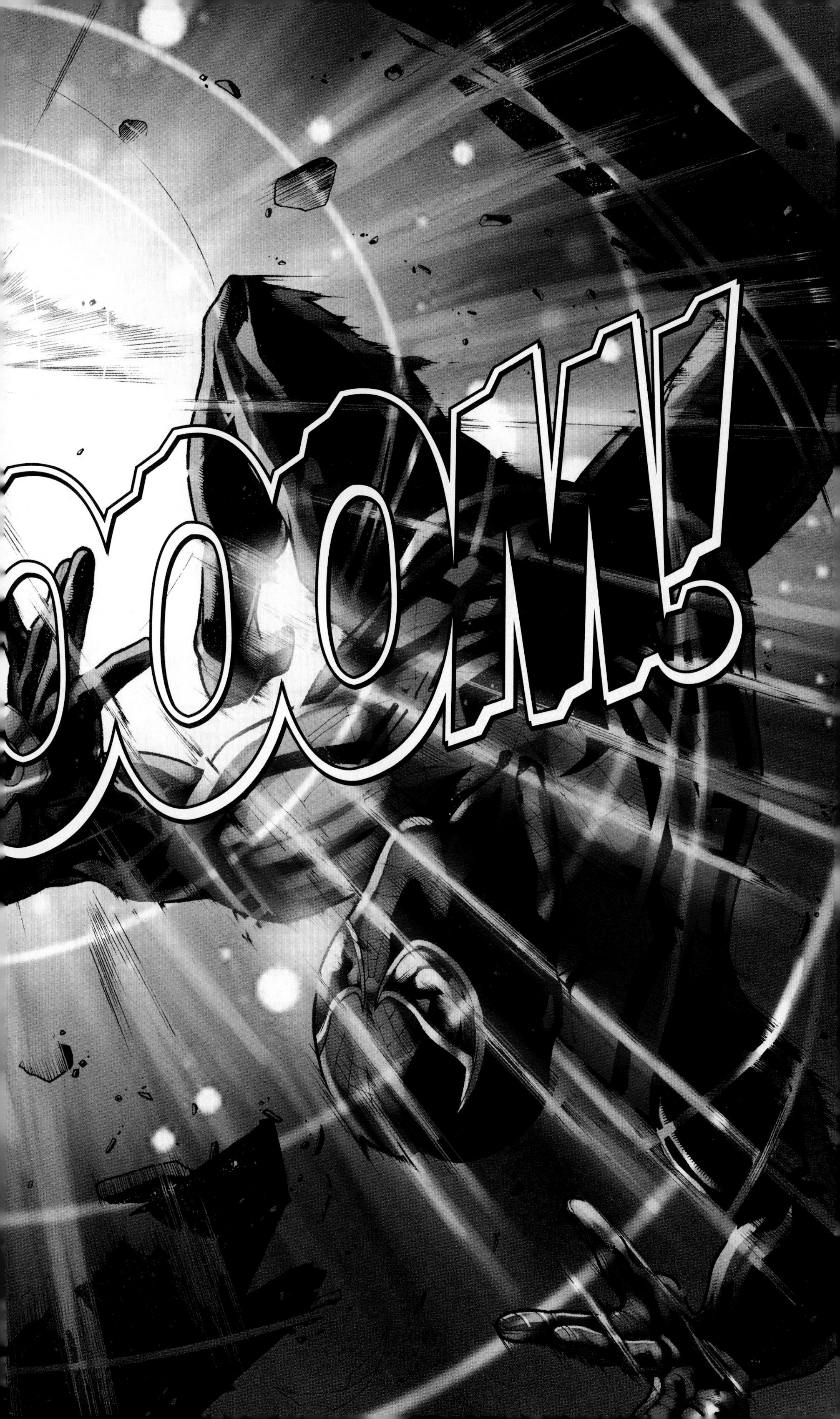
OOOM!

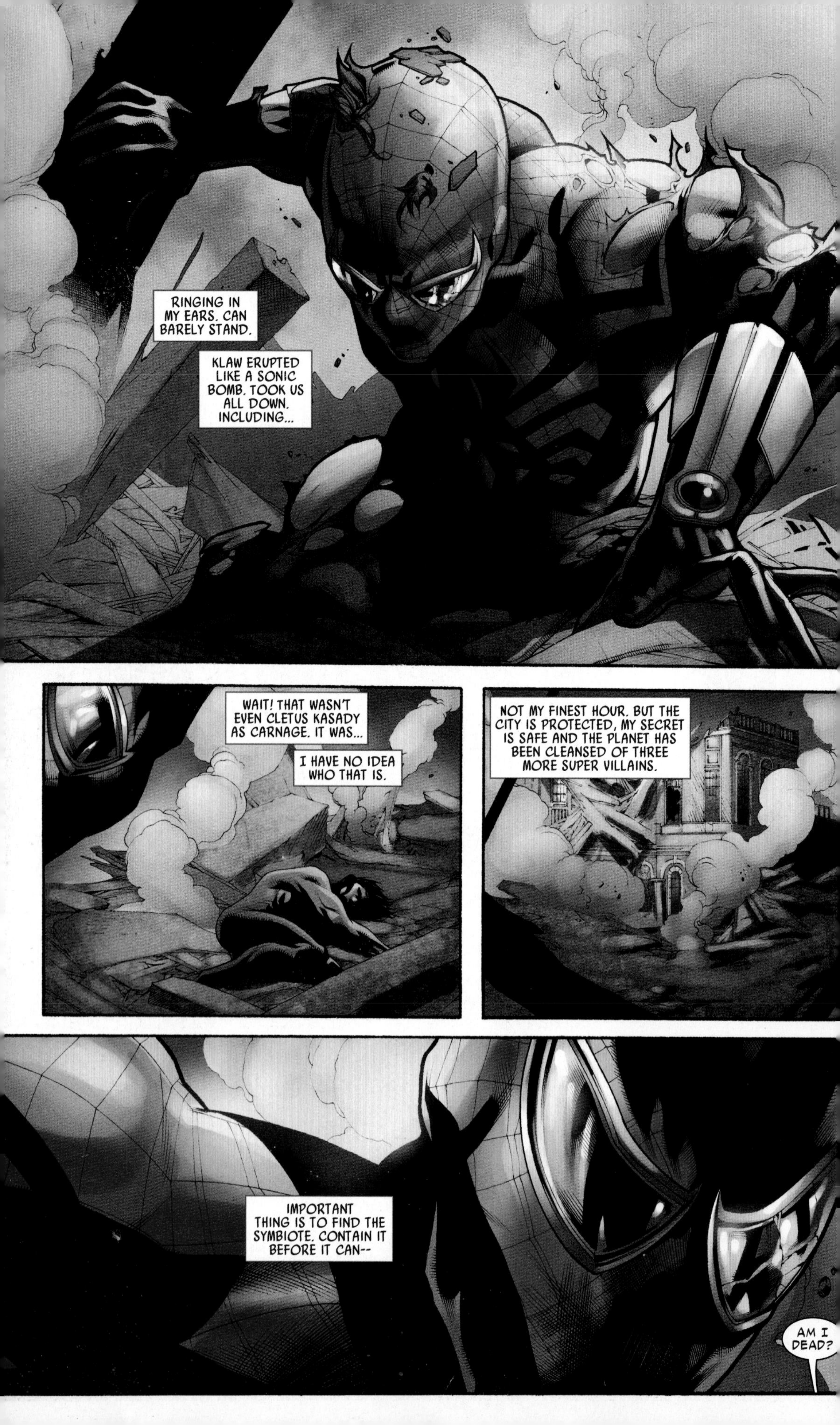
RINGING IN MY EARS. CAN BARELY STAND.
KLAW ERUPTED LIKE A SONIC BOMB. TOOK US ALL DOWN. INCLUDING...
WAIT! THAT WASN'T EVEN CLETUS KASADY AS CARNAGE. IT WAS...
I HAVE NO IDEA WHO THAT IS.
NOT MY FINEST HOUR. BUT THE CITY IS PROTECTED, MY SECRET IS SAFE AND THE PLANET HAS BEEN CLEANSED OF THREE MORE SUPER VILLAINS.
IMPORTANT THING IS TO FIND THE SYMBIOTE. CONTAIN IT BEFORE IT CAN--
AM I DEAD?

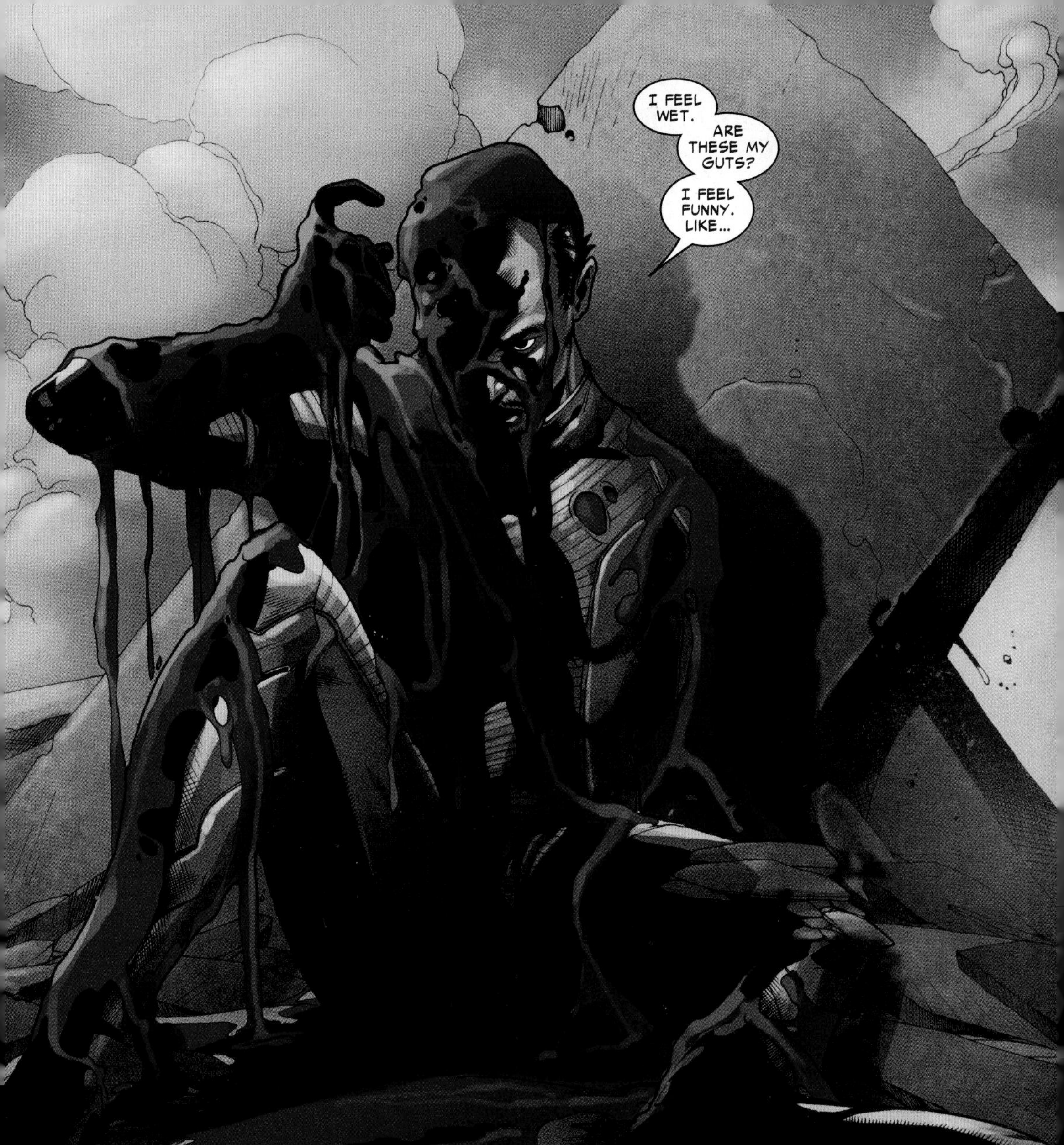
I FEEL WET.
ARE THESE MY GUTS?
I FEEL FUNNY. LIKE...

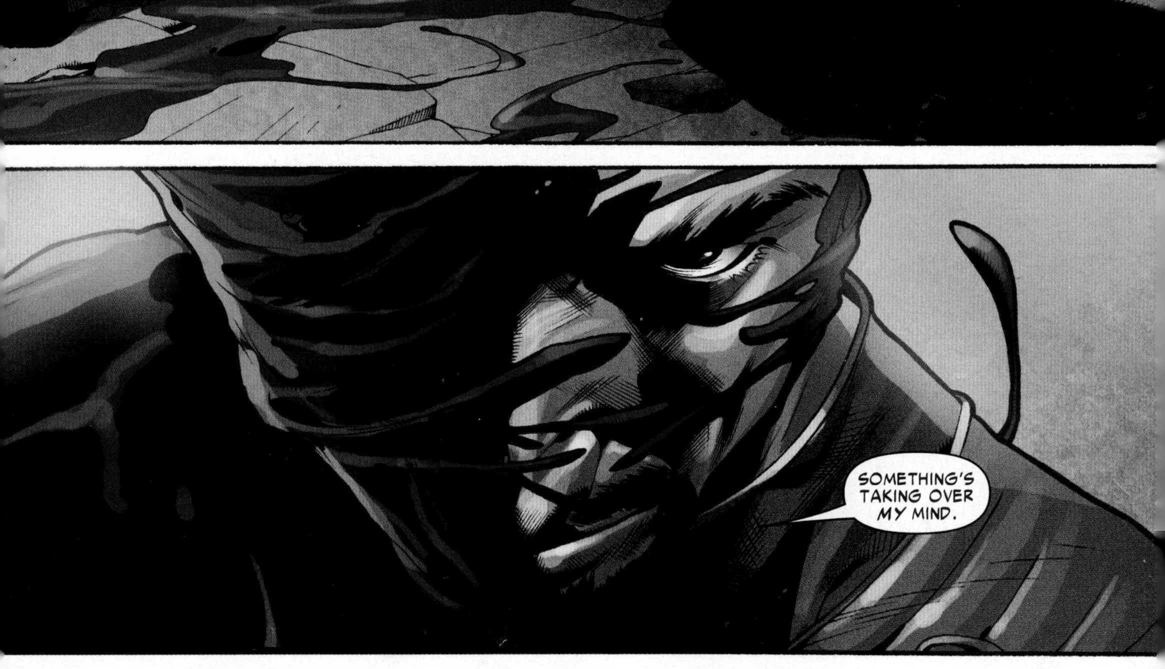
SOMETHING'S TAKING OVER MY MIND.

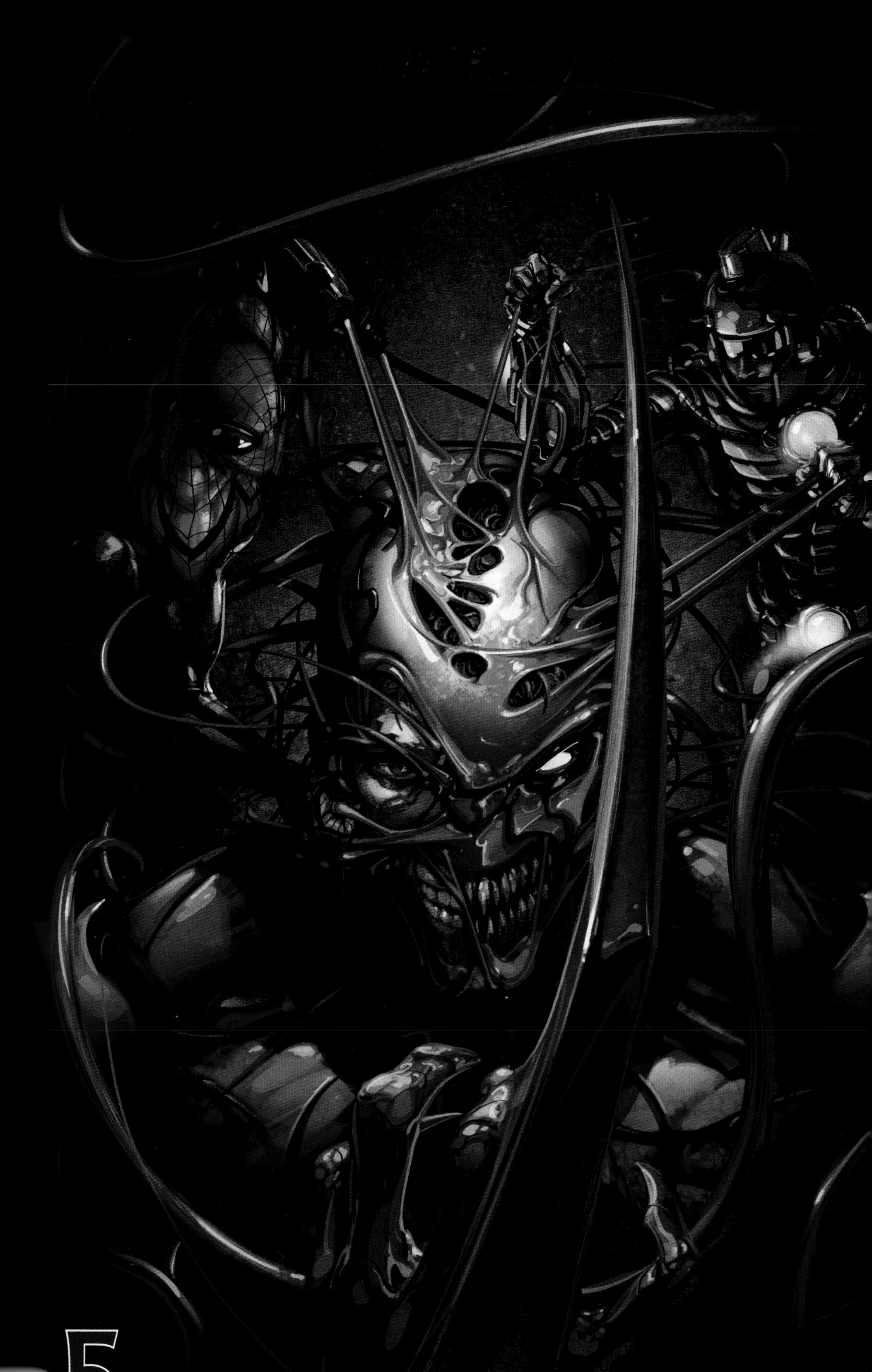

5

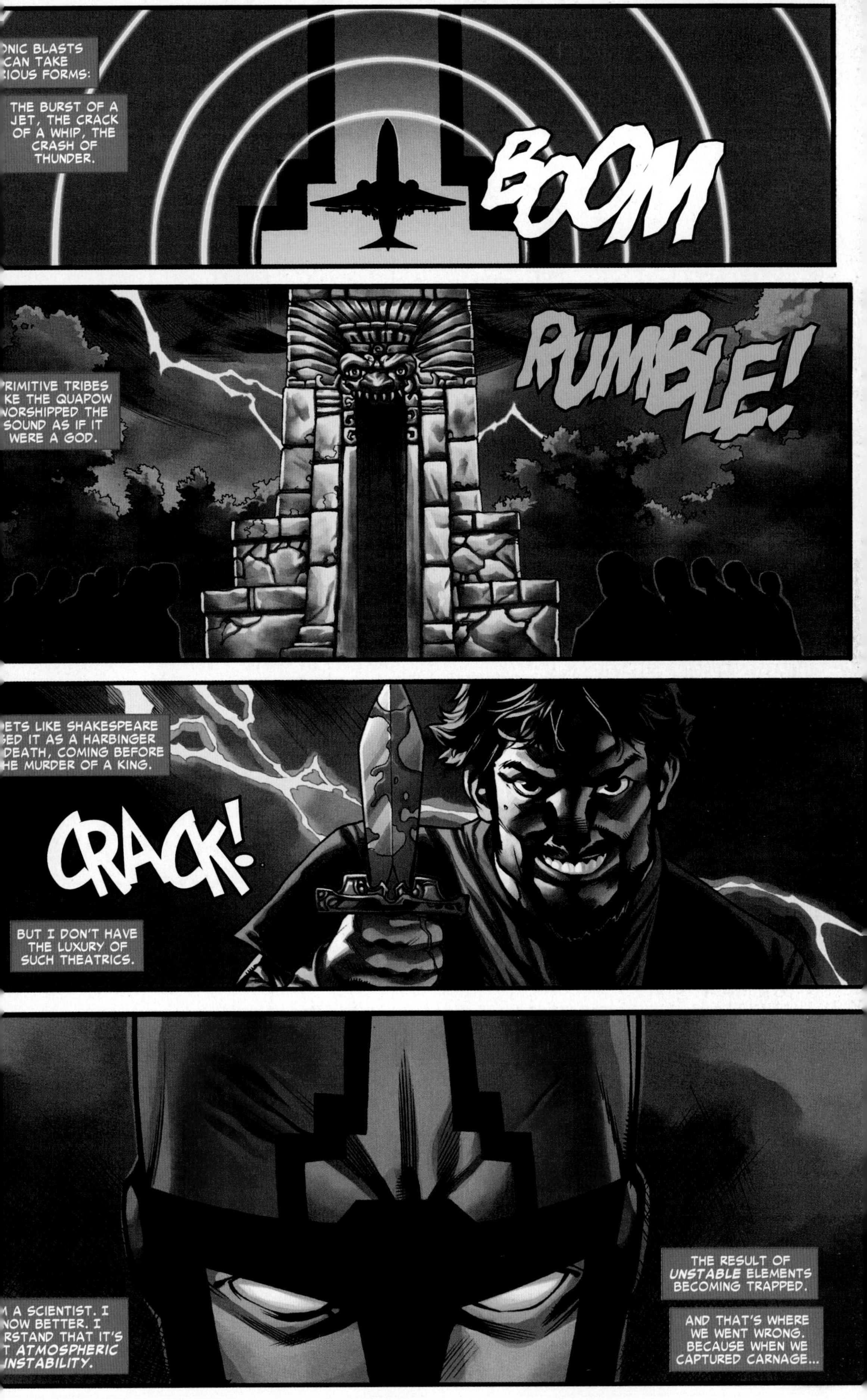
ONIC BLASTS CAN TAKE RIOUS FORMS:
THE BURST OF A JET, THE CRACK OF A WHIP, THE CRASH OF THUNDER.
BOOM
RUMBLE!
RIMITIVE TRIBES KE THE QUAPOW WORSHIPPED THE SOUND AS IF IT WERE A GOD.
ETS LIKE SHAKESPEARE SED IT AS A HARBINGER DEATH, COMING BEFORE HE MURDER OF A KING.
CRACK!
BUT I DON'T HAVE THE LUXURY OF SUCH THEATRICS.
M A SCIENTIST. I NOW BETTER. I RSTAND THAT IT'S T *ATMOSPHERIC INSTABILITY*.
THE RESULT OF *UNSTABLE* ELEMENTS BECOMING TRAPPED.
AND THAT'S WHERE WE WENT WRONG. BECAUSE WHEN WE CAPTURED CARNAGE...

...WE FORGOT *HE* WAS AN UNSTABLE ELEMENT.

UHH!

AND THAT'S THE THING ABOUT ELEMENTS. NO MATTER WHAT FORM THEY TAKE.

THE RESULTS ARE ALWAYS THE SAME.

BOOOOOOOOOM

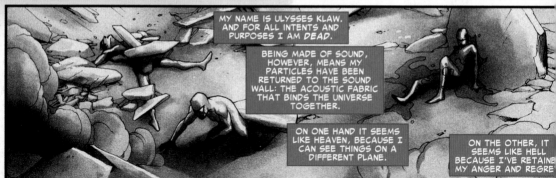

MY NAME IS ULYSSES KLAW. AND FOR ALL INTENTS AND PURPOSES I AM *DEAD*.

BEING MADE OF SOUND, HOWEVER, MEANS MY PARTICLES HAVE BEEN RETURNED TO THE SOUND WALL: THE ACOUSTIC FABRIC THAT BINDS THE UNIVERSE TOGETHER.

ON ONE HAND IT SEEMS LIKE HEAVEN, BECAUSE I CAN SEE THINGS ON A DIFFERENT PLANE.

ON THE OTHER, IT SEEMS LIKE HELL BECAUSE I'VE RETAINE MY ANGER AND REGRE

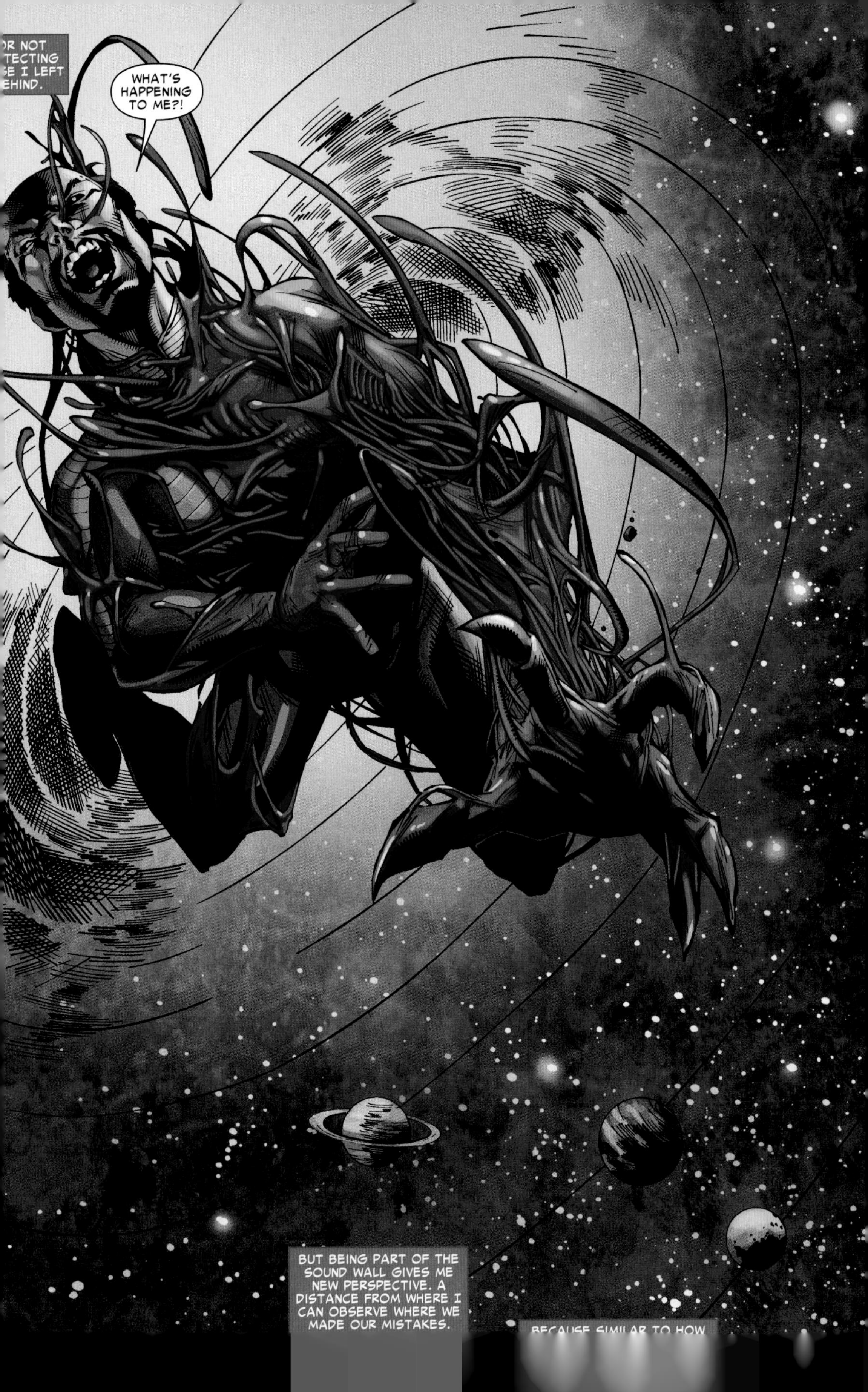

OR NOT
TECTING
SE I LEFT
EHIND.
WHAT'S HAPPENING TO ME?!
BUT BEING PART OF THE SOUND WALL GIVES ME NEW PERSPECTIVE. A DISTANCE FROM WHERE I CAN OBSERVE WHERE WE MADE OUR MISTAKES.
BECAUSE SIMILAR TO HOW

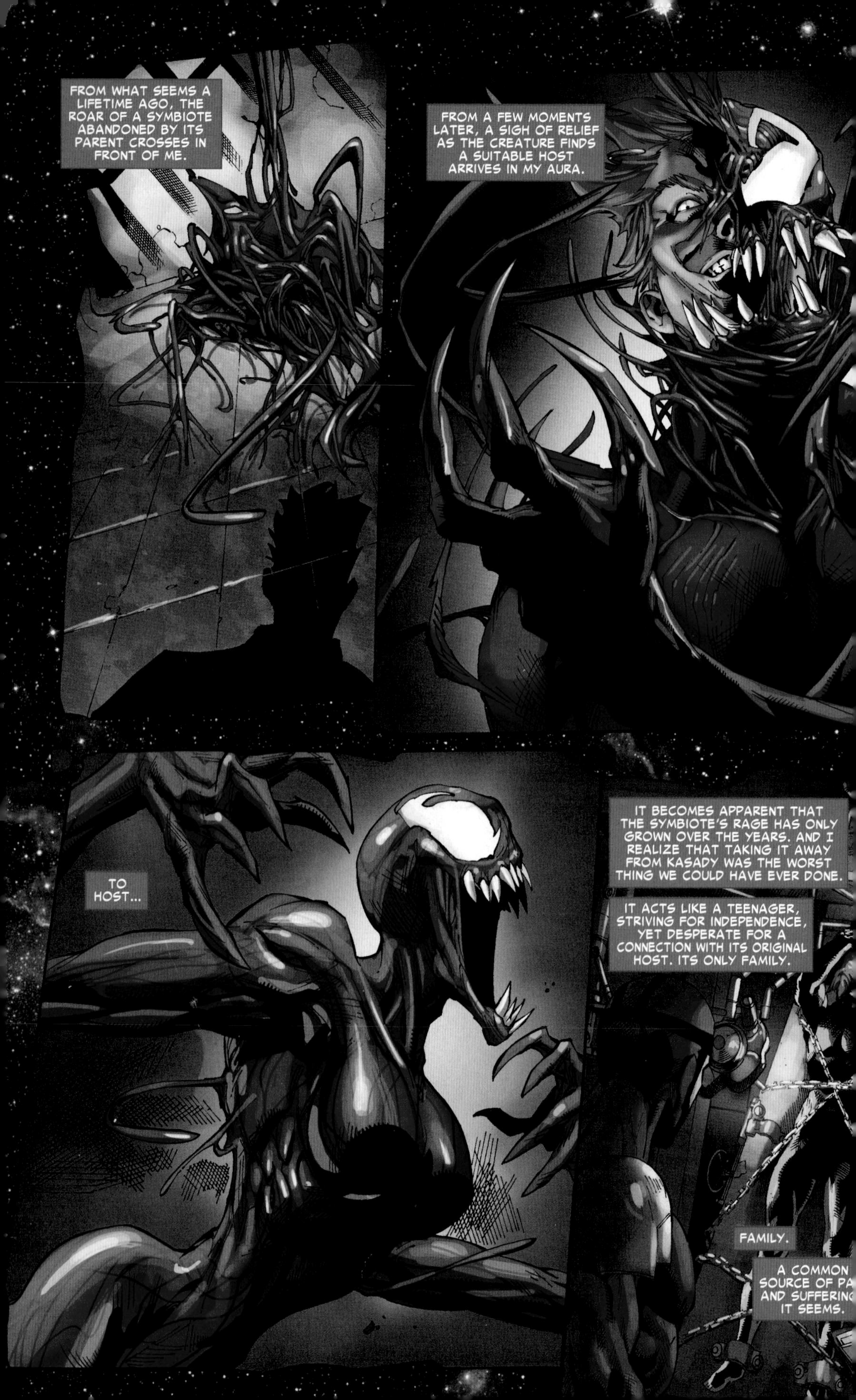
FROM WHAT SEEMS A LIFETIME AGO, THE ROAR OF A SYMBIOTE ABANDONED BY ITS PARENT CROSSES IN FRONT OF ME.
FROM A FEW MOMENTS LATER, A SIGH OF RELIEF AS THE CREATURE FINDS A SUITABLE HOST ARRIVES IN MY AURA.
TO HOST...
IT BECOMES APPARENT THAT THE SYMBIOTE'S RAGE HAS ONLY GROWN OVER THE YEARS. AND I REALIZE THAT TAKING IT AWAY FROM KASADY WAS THE WORST THING WE COULD HAVE EVER DONE.
IT ACTS LIKE A TEENAGER, STRIVING FOR INDEPENDENCE, YET DESPERATE FOR A CONNECTION WITH ITS ORIGINAL HOST. ITS ONLY FAMILY.
FAMILY.
A COMMON SOURCE OF PA AND SUFFERIN IT SEEMS.

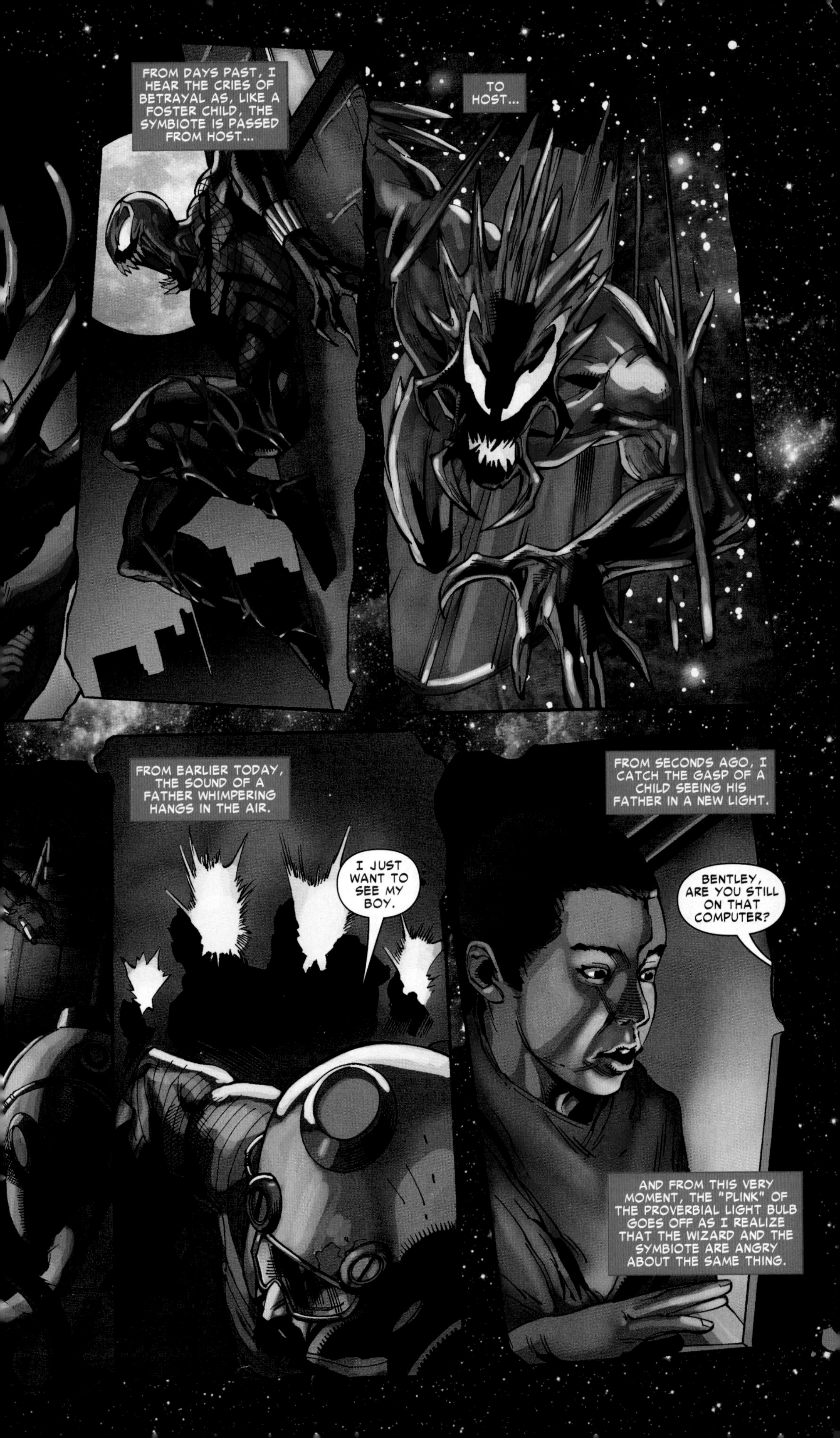
FROM DAYS PAST, I HEAR THE CRIES OF BETRAYAL AS, LIKE A FOSTER CHILD, THE SYMBIOTE IS PASSED FROM HOST...
TO HOST...
FROM EARLIER TODAY, THE SOUND OF A FATHER WHIMPERING HANGS IN THE AIR.
I JUST WANT TO SEE MY BOY.
FROM SECONDS AGO, I CATCH THE GASP OF A CHILD SEEING HIS FATHER IN A NEW LIGHT.
BENTLEY, ARE YOU STILL ON THAT COMPUTER?
AND FROM THIS VERY MOMENT, THE "PLINK" OF THE PROVERBIAL LIGHT BULB GOES OFF AS I REALIZE THAT THE WIZARD AND THE SYMBIOTE ARE ANGRY ABOUT THE SAME THING.

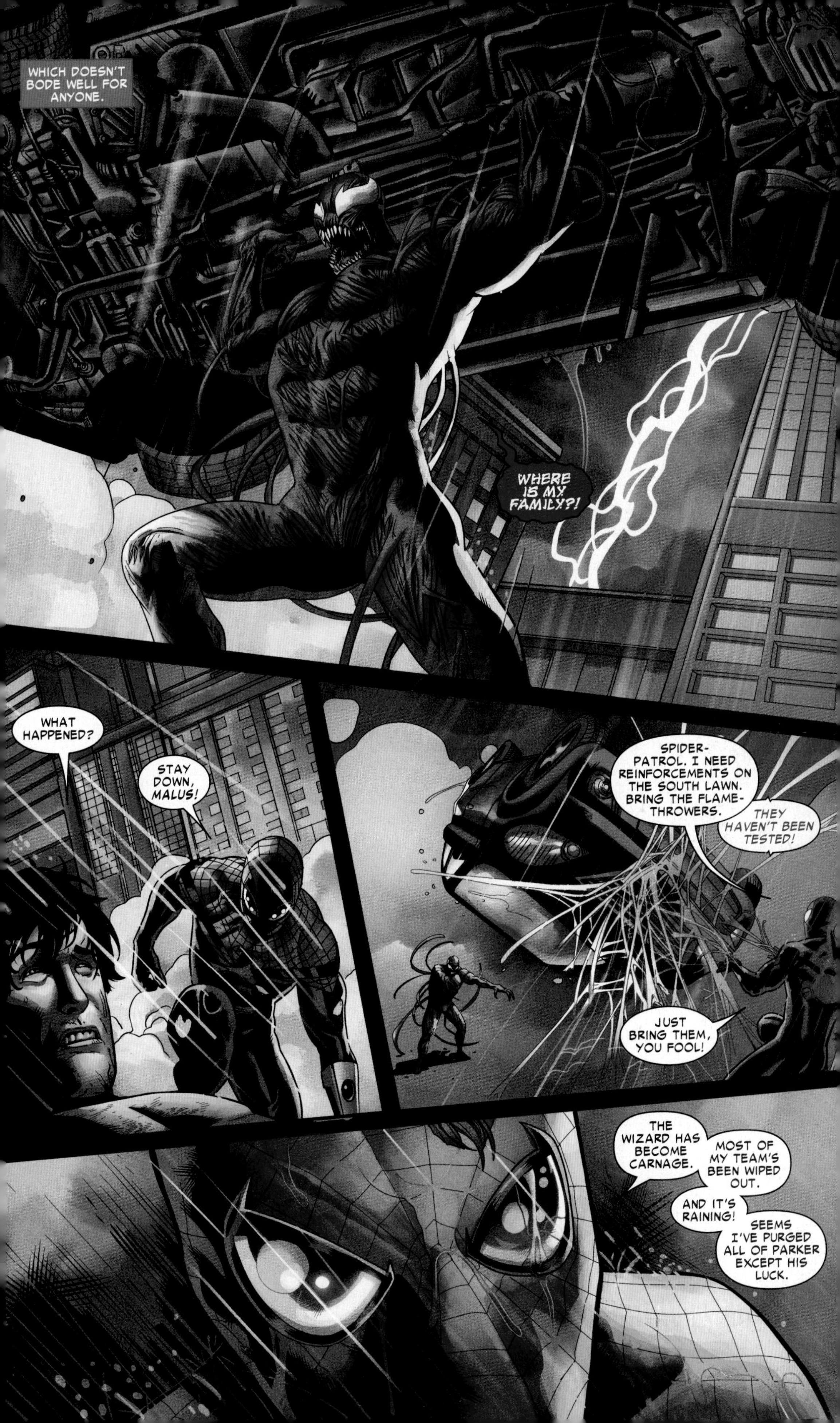

WHICH DOESN'T BODE WELL FOR ANYONE.
WHERE IS MY FAMILY?!
WHAT HAPPENED?
STAY DOWN, MALUS!
SPIDER-PATROL. I NEED REINFORCEMENTS ON THE SOUTH LAWN. BRING THE FLAME-THROWERS.
THEY HAVEN'T BEEN TESTED!
JUST BRING THEM, YOU FOOL!
THE WIZARD HAS BECOME CARNAGE.
MOST OF MY TEAM'S BEEN WIPED OUT.
AND IT'S RAINING!
SEEMS I'VE PURGED ALL OF PARKER EXCEPT HIS LUCK.

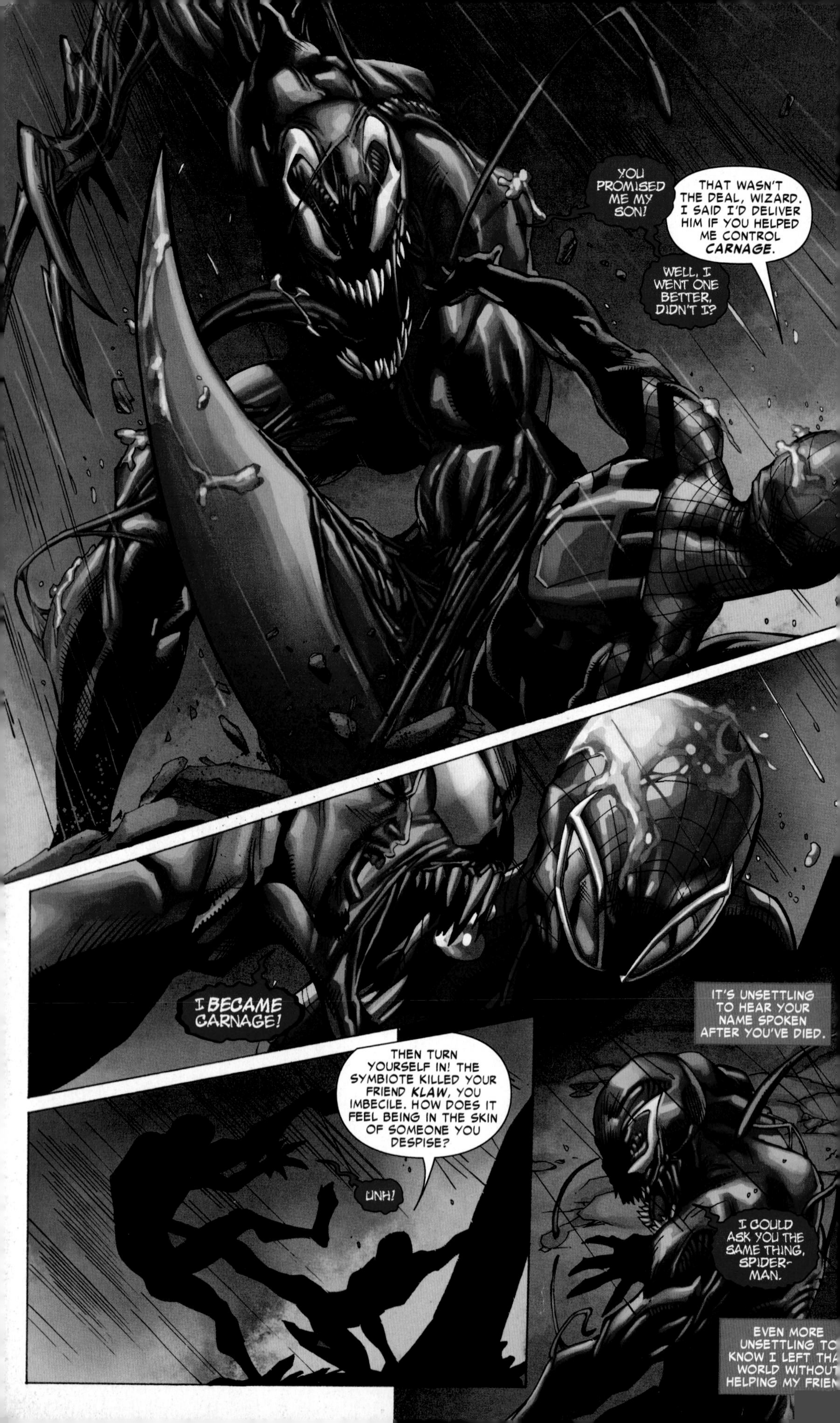
YOU PROMISED ME MY SON!
THAT WASN'T THE DEAL, WIZARD. I SAID I'D DELIVER HIM IF YOU HELPED ME CONTROL CARNAGE.
WELL, I WENT ONE BETTER, DIDN'T I?
I BECAME CARNAGE!
IT'S UNSETTLING TO HEAR YOUR NAME SPOKEN AFTER YOU'VE DIED.
THEN TURN YOURSELF IN! THE SYMBIOTE KILLED YOUR FRIEND KLAW, YOU IMBECILE. HOW DOES IT FEEL BEING IN THE SKIN OF SOMEONE YOU DESPISE?
UNH!
I COULD ASK YOU THE SAME THING, SPIDER-MAN.
EVEN MORE UNSETTLING TO KNOW I LEFT THA WORLD WITHOUT HELPING MY FRIEN

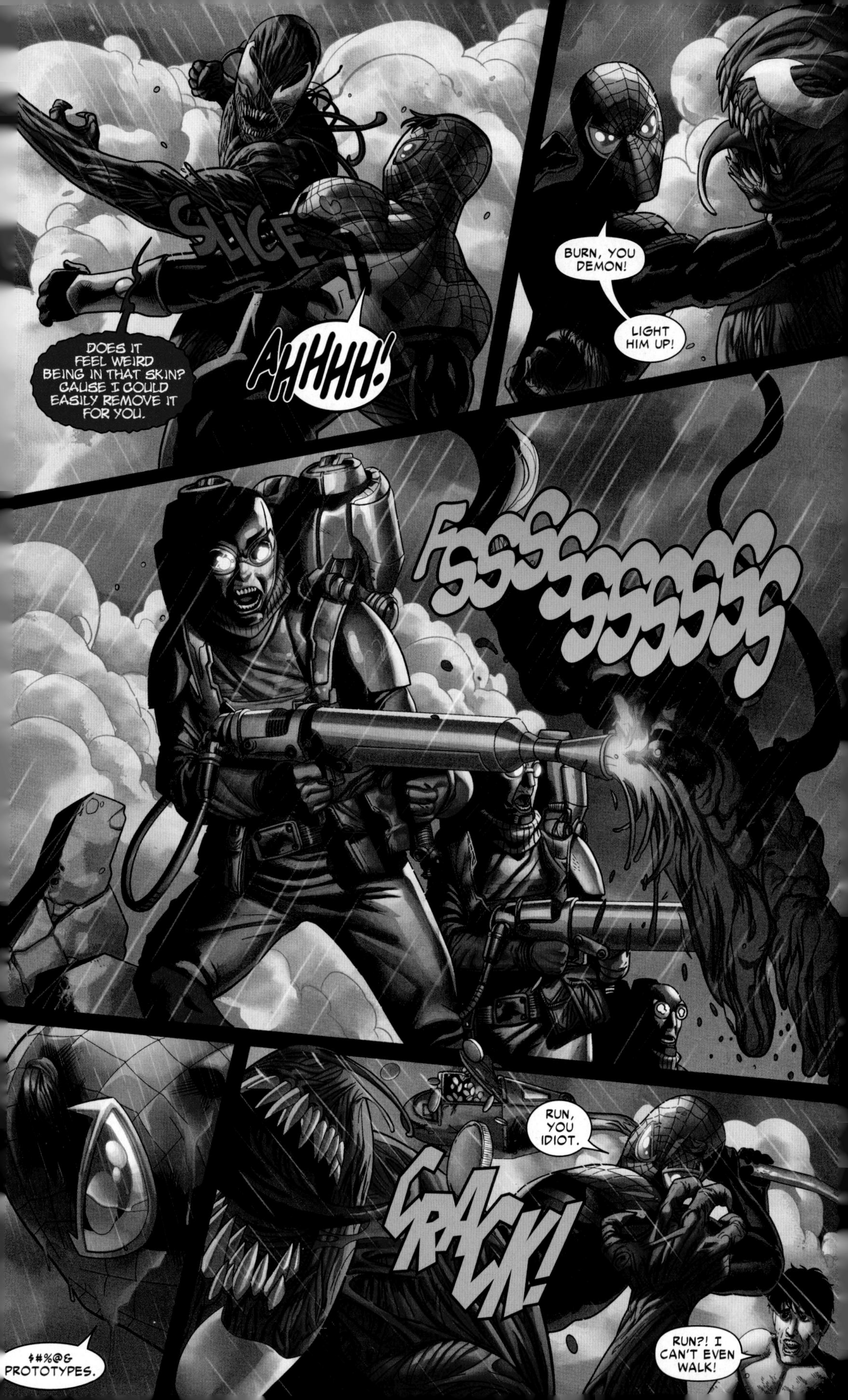
SLICE
AHHHH!
DOES IT FEEL WEIRD BEING IN THAT SKIN? CAUSE I COULD EASILY REMOVE IT FOR YOU.
BURN, YOU DEMON!
LIGHT HIM UP!
FSSSSSSSSSS
RUN, YOU IDIOT.
CRACK!
$#%@&
PROTOTYPES.
RUN?! I CAN'T EVEN WALK!

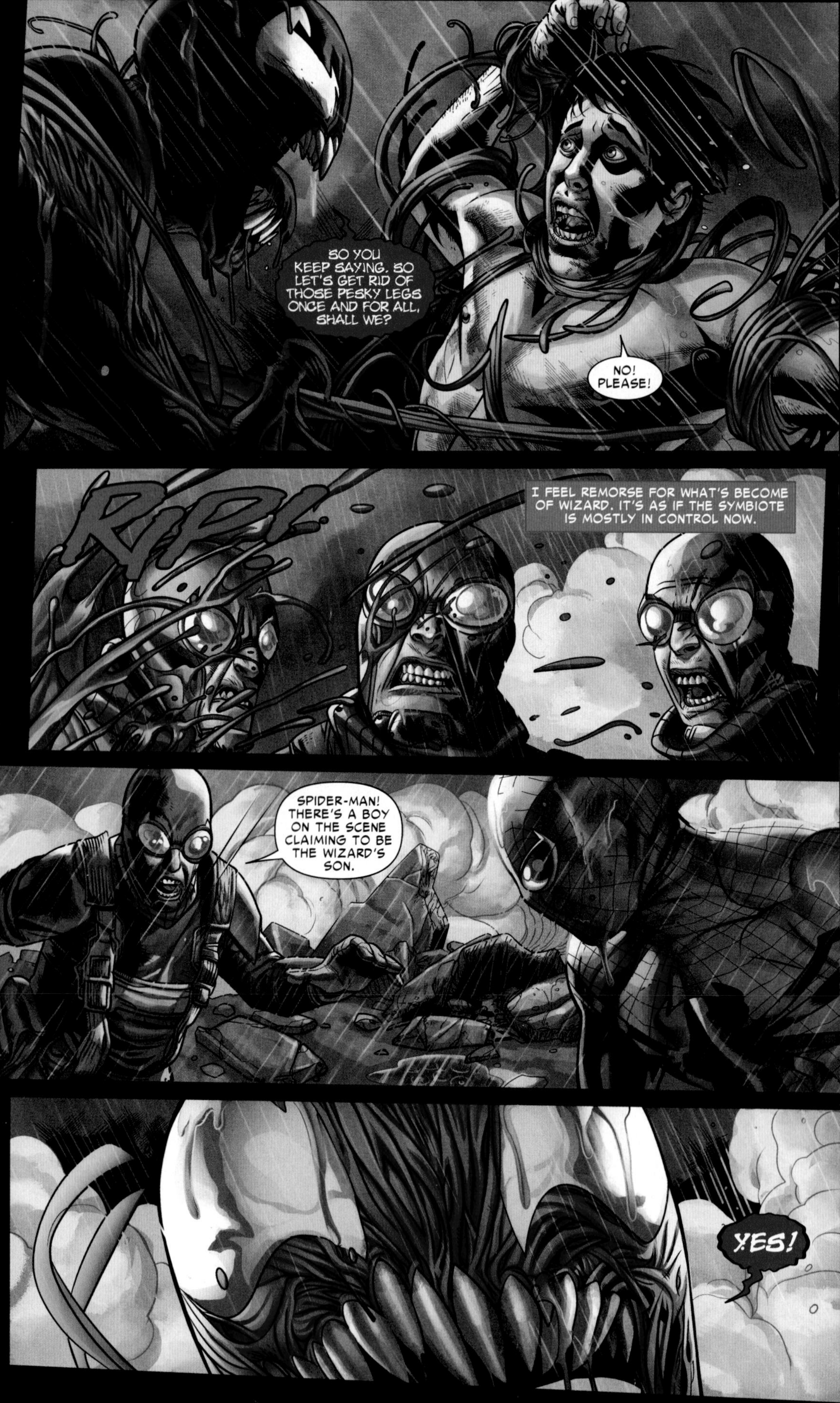
SO YOU KEEP SAYING. SO LET'S GET RID OF THOSE PESKY LEGS ONCE AND FOR ALL, SHALL WE?
NO! PLEASE!
RIP!
I FEEL REMORSE FOR WHAT'S BECOME OF WIZARD. IT'S AS IF THE SYMBIOTE IS MOSTLY IN CONTROL NOW.
SPIDER-MAN! THERE'S A BOY ON THE SCENE CLAIMING TO BE THE WIZARD'S SON.
YES!

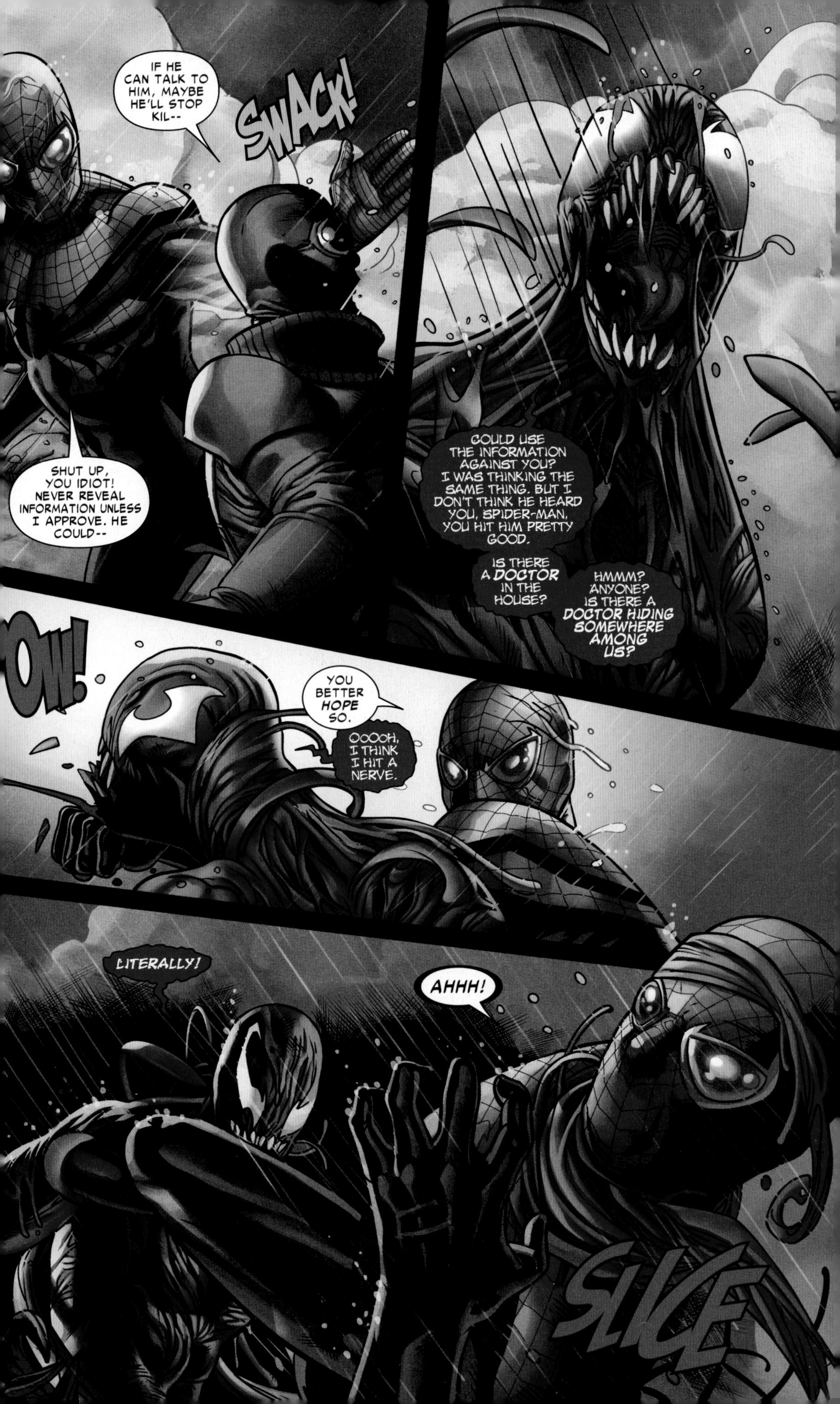
IF HE CAN TALK TO HIM, MAYBE HE'LL STOP KIL--
SWACK!
SHUT UP, YOU IDIOT! NEVER REVEAL INFORMATION UNLESS I APPROVE. HE COULD--
COULD USE THE INFORMATION AGAINST YOU? I WAS THINKING THE SAME THING. BUT I DON'T THINK HE HEARD YOU, SPIDER-MAN. YOU HIT HIM PRETTY GOOD.
IS THERE A DOCTOR IN THE HOUSE?
HMMM? ANYONE? IS THERE A DOCTOR HIDING SOMEWHERE AMONG US?
YOU BETTER HOPE SO.
OOOOH, I THINK I HIT A NERVE.
LITERALLY!
AHHH!
SLICE

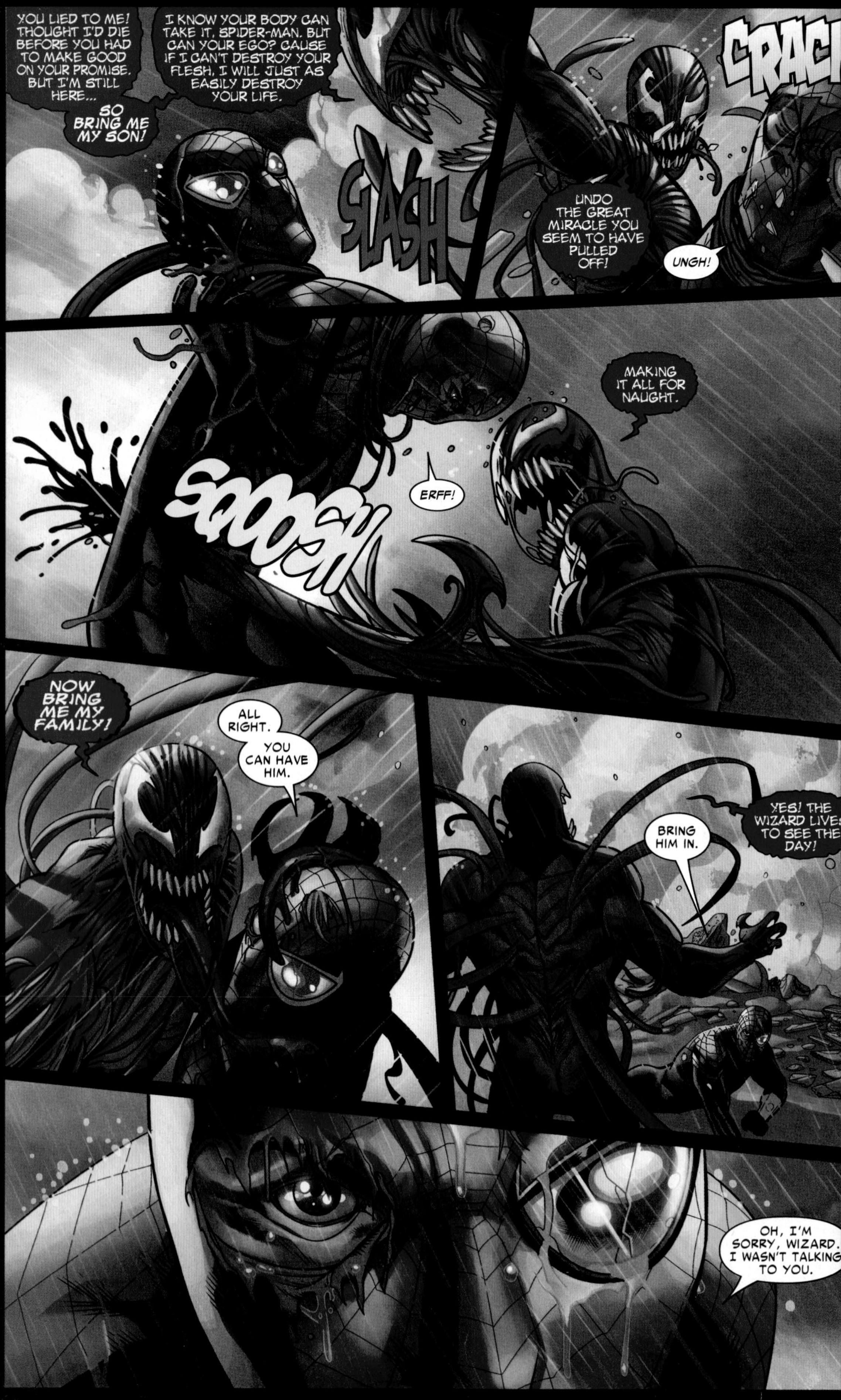

YOU LIED TO ME! THOUGHT I'D DIE BEFORE YOU HAD TO MAKE GOOD ON YOUR PROMISE. BUT I'M STILL HERE...
SO BRING ME MY SON!
I KNOW YOUR BODY CAN TAKE IT, SPIDER-MAN. BUT CAN YOUR EGO? CAUSE IF I CAN'T DESTROY YOUR FLESH, I WILL JUST AS EASILY DESTROY YOUR LIFE.
SLASH
CRAC
UNDO THE GREAT MIRACLE YOU SEEM TO HAVE PULLED OFF!
UNGH!
MAKING IT ALL FOR NAUGHT.
ERFF!
SQOOSH
NOW BRING ME MY FAMILY!
ALL RIGHT.
YOU CAN HAVE HIM.
BRING HIM IN.
YES! THE WIZARD LIVE TO SEE THE DAY!
OH, I'M SORRY, WIZARD. I WASN'T TALKING TO YOU.

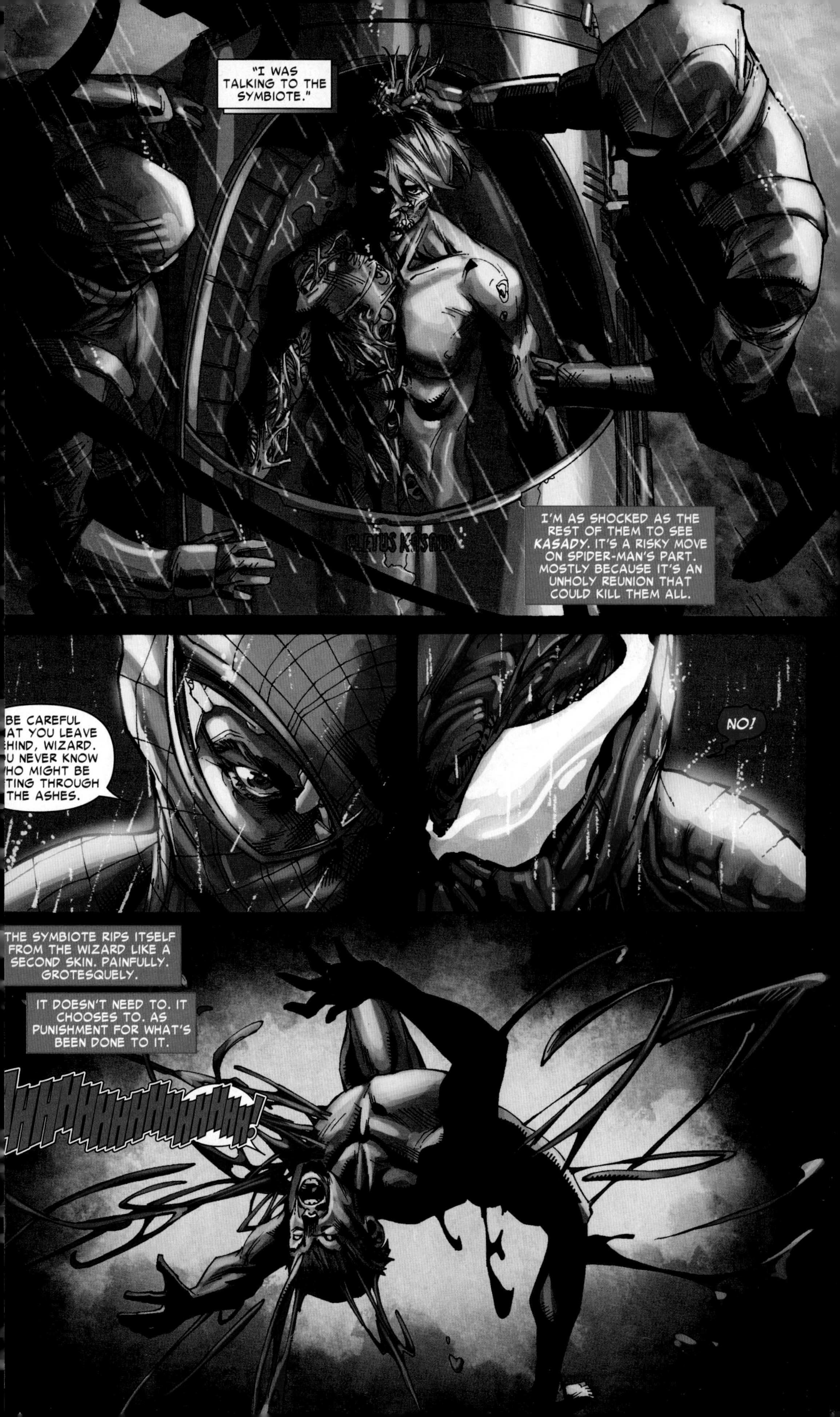
"I WAS TALKING TO THE SYMBIOTE."
I'M AS SHOCKED AS THE REST OF THEM TO SEE *KASADY*. IT'S A RISKY MOVE ON SPIDER-MAN'S PART. MOSTLY BECAUSE IT'S AN UNHOLY REUNION THAT COULD KILL THEM ALL.
BE CAREFUL AT YOU LEAVE HIND, WIZARD. U NEVER KNOW HO MIGHT BE TING THROUGH THE ASHES.
NO!
THE SYMBIOTE RIPS ITSELF FROM THE WIZARD LIKE A SECOND SKIN. PAINFULLY. GROTESQUELY.
IT DOESN'T NEED TO. IT CHOOSES TO. AS PUNISHMENT FOR WHAT'S BEEN DONE TO IT.

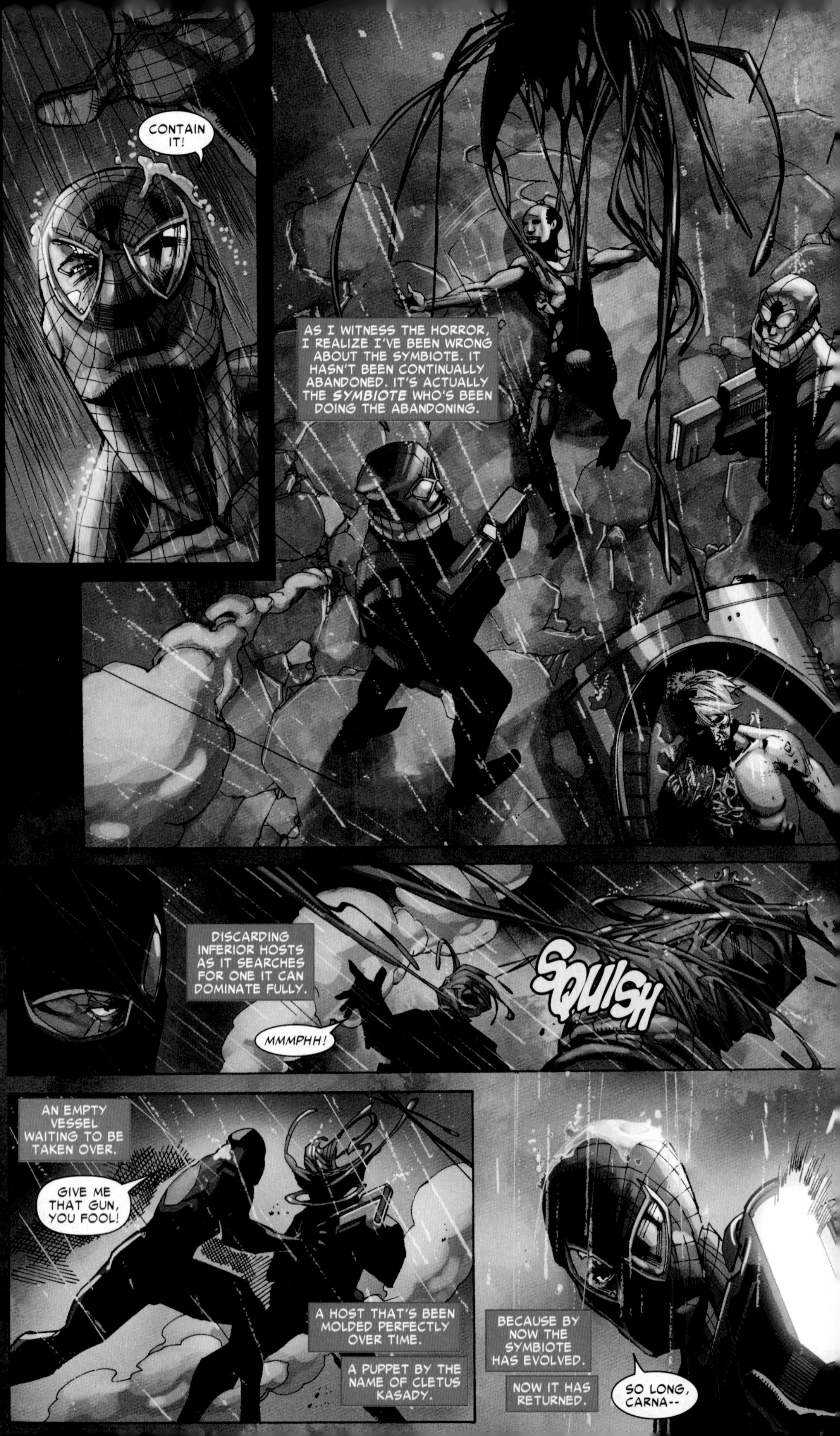
CONTAIN IT!
AS I WITNESS THE HORROR, I REALIZE I'VE BEEN WRONG ABOUT THE SYMBIOTE. IT HASN'T BEEN CONTINUALLY ABANDONED. IT'S ACTUALLY THE SYMBIOTE WHO'S BEEN DOING THE ABANDONING.
DISCARDING INFERIOR HOSTS AS IT SEARCHES FOR ONE IT CAN DOMINATE FULLY.
SQUISH
MMMPHH!
AN EMPTY VESSEL WAITING TO BE TAKEN OVER.
GIVE ME THAT GUN, YOU FOOL!
A HOST THAT'S BEEN MOLDED PERFECTLY OVER TIME.
A PUPPET BY THE NAME OF CLETUS KASADY.
BECAUSE BY NOW THE SYMBIOTE HAS EVOLVED.
NOW IT HAS RETURNED.
SO LONG, CARNA--

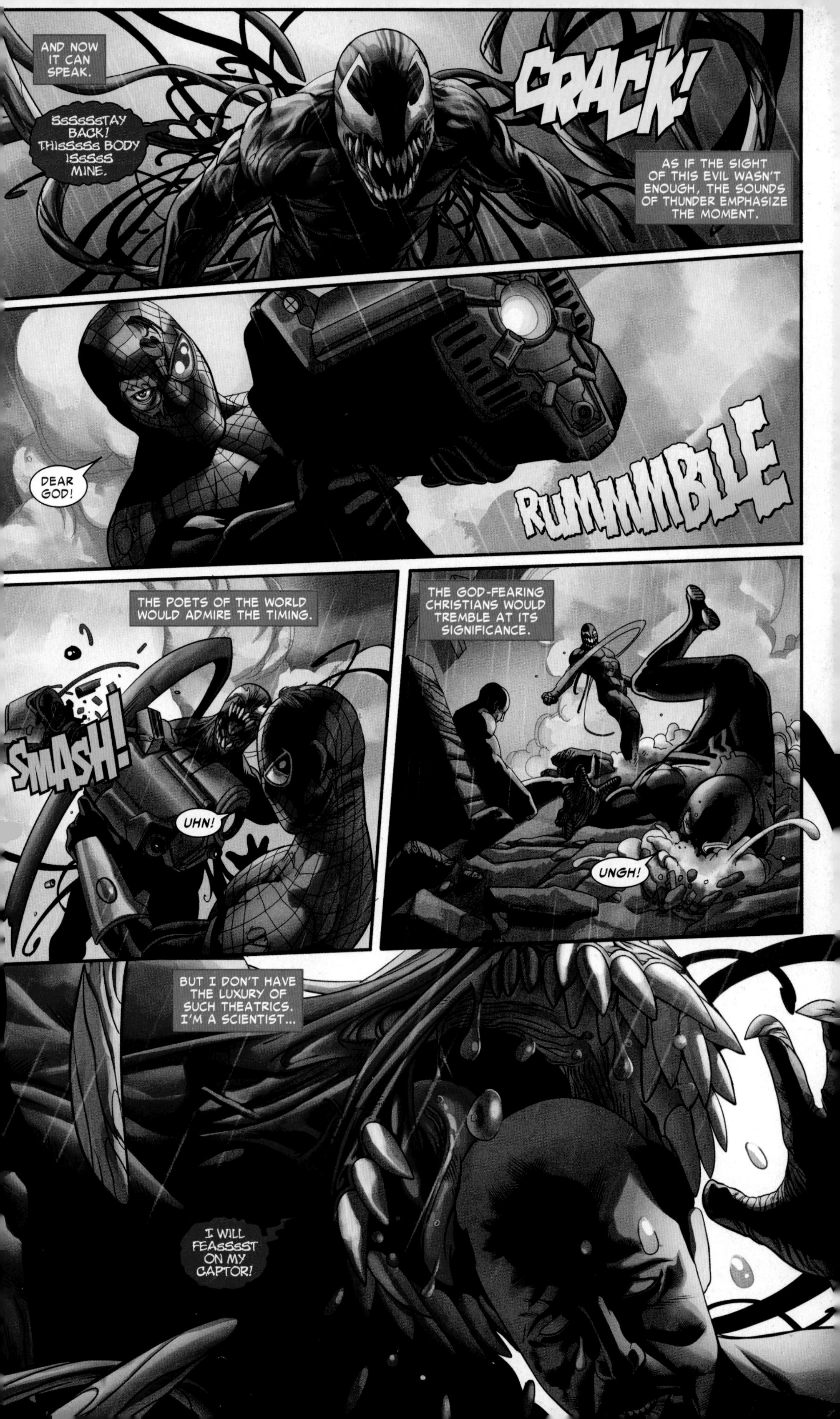
AND NOW IT CAN SPEAK.
SSSSSSTAY BACK! THISSSSS BODY ISSSSS MINE.
CRACK!
AS IF THE SIGHT OF THIS EVIL WASN'T ENOUGH, THE SOUNDS OF THUNDER EMPHASIZE THE MOMENT.
DEAR GOD!
RUMMMBLE
THE POETS OF THE WORLD WOULD ADMIRE THE TIMING.
SMASH!
UHN!
THE GOD-FEARING CHRISTIANS WOULD TREMBLE AT ITS SIGNIFICANCE.
UNGH!
BUT I DON'T HAVE THE LUXURY OF SUCH THEATRICS. I'M A SCIENTIST...
I WILL FEASSSST ON MY CAPTOR!

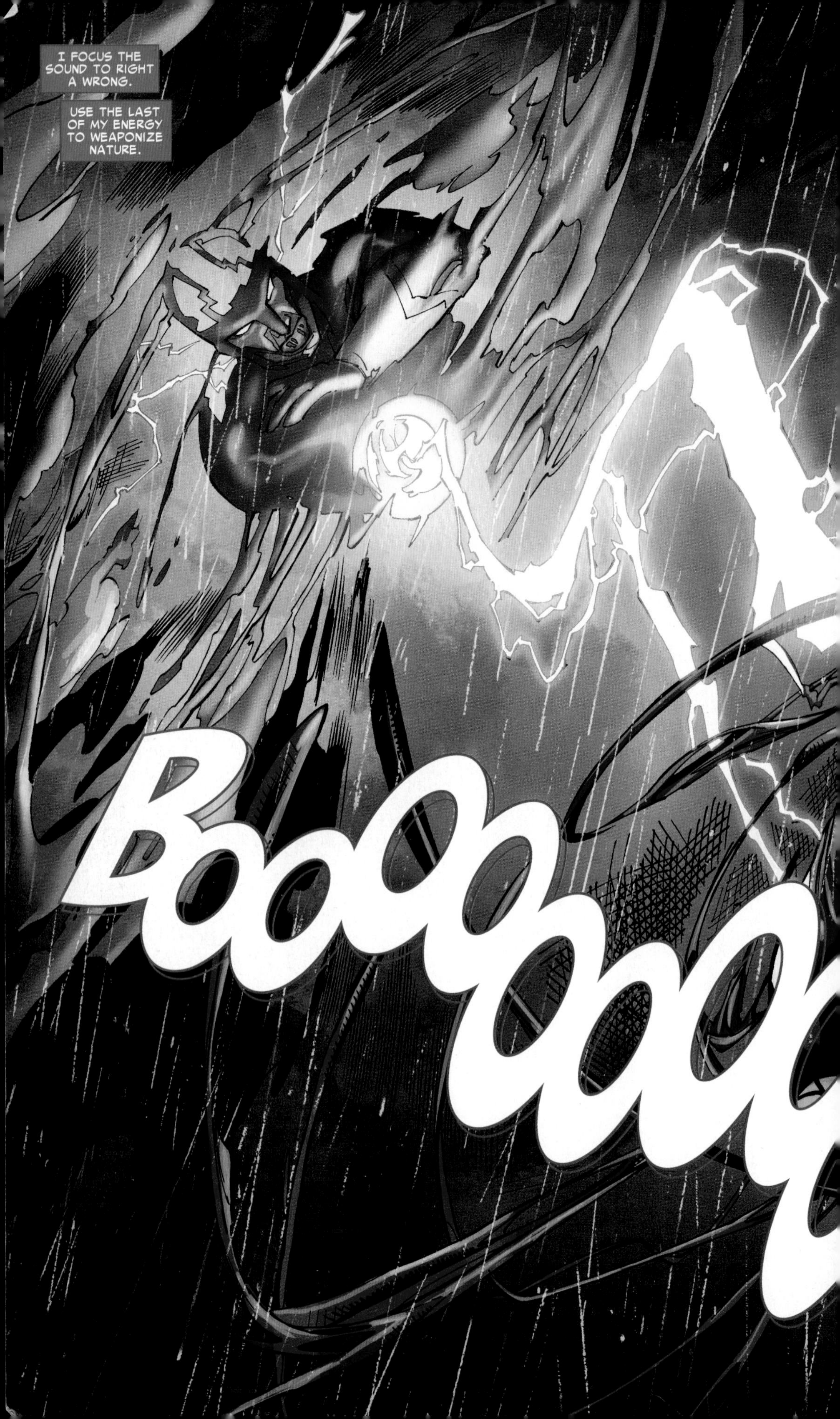
I FOCUS THE SOUND TO RIGHT A WRONG.
USE THE LAST OF MY ENERGY TO WEAPONIZE NATURE.
Booooooo

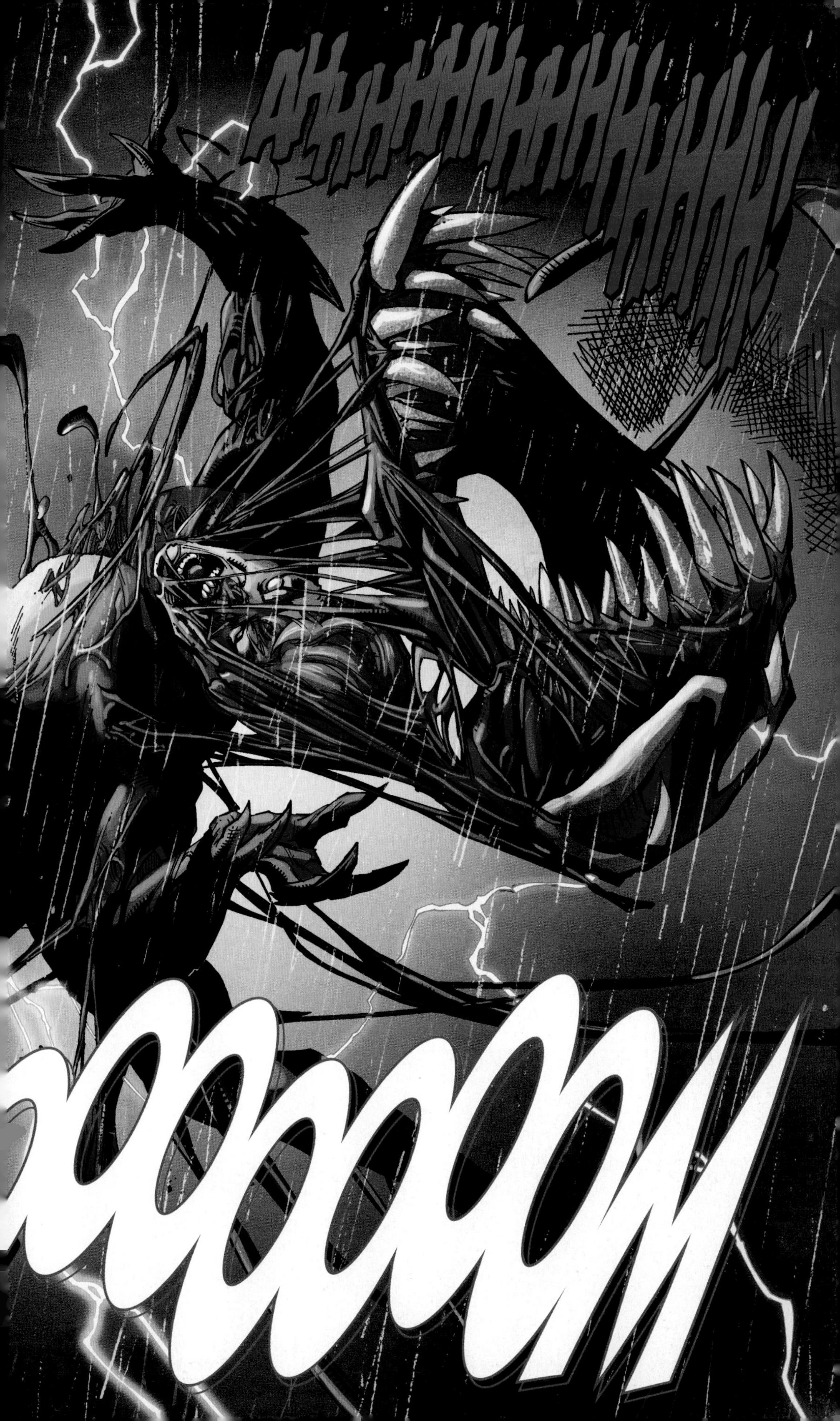
AHHHHHHHHHHHH!

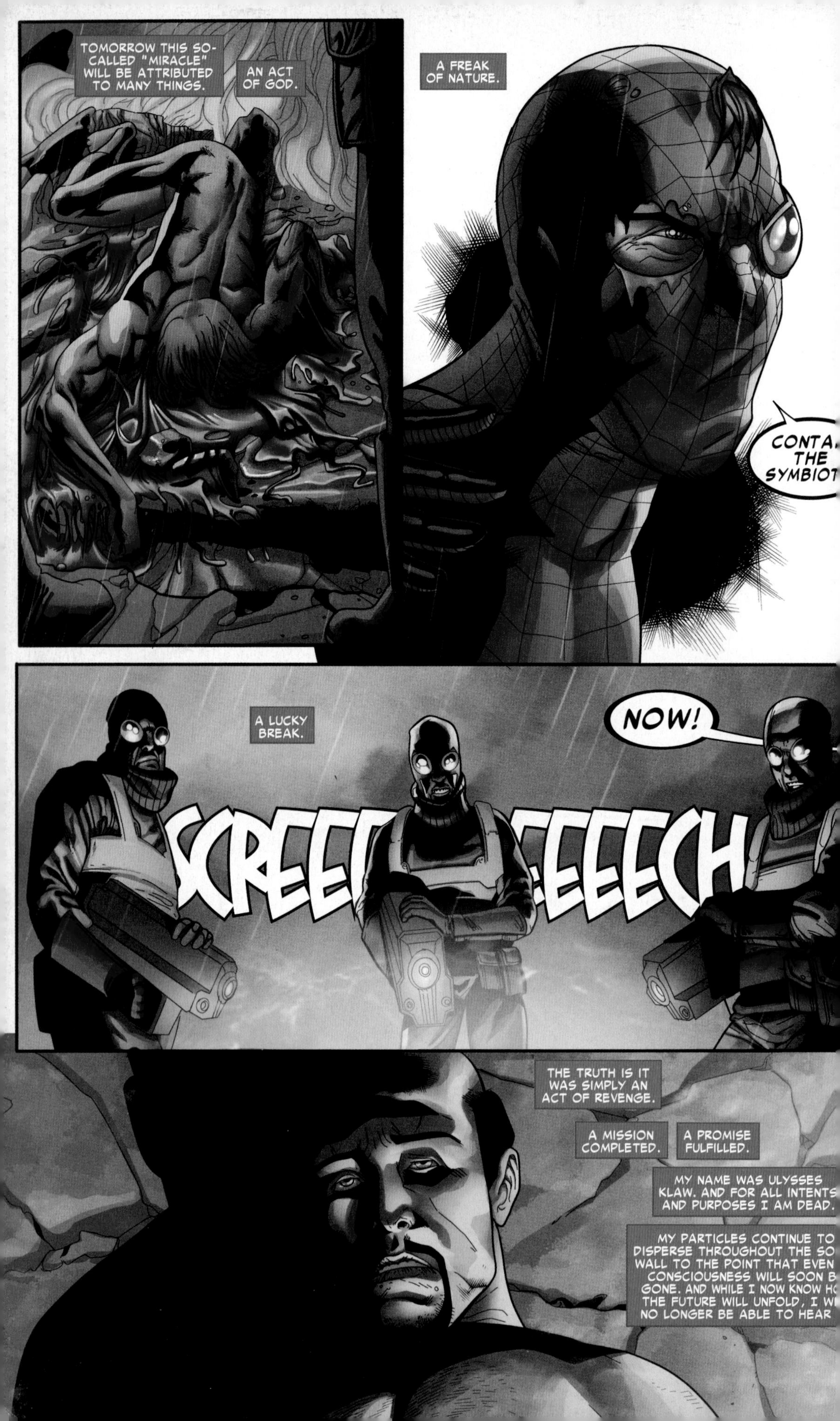
TOMORROW THIS SO-CALLED "MIRACLE" WILL BE ATTRIBUTED TO MANY THINGS.
AN ACT OF GOD.
A FREAK OF NATURE.
CONTA... THE SYMBIOT...
A LUCKY BREAK.
NOW!
SCREE...EEEECH
THE TRUTH IS IT WAS SIMPLY AN ACT OF REVENGE.
A MISSION COMPLETED.
A PROMISE FULFILLED.
MY NAME WAS ULYSSES KLAW. AND FOR ALL INTENTS AND PURPOSES I AM DEAD.
MY PARTICLES CONTINUE TO DISPERSE THROUGHOUT THE SO... WALL TO THE POINT THAT EVEN... CONSCIOUSNESS WILL SOON B... GONE. AND WHILE I NOW KNOW H... THE FUTURE WILL UNFOLD, I W... NO LONGER BE ABLE TO HEAR...

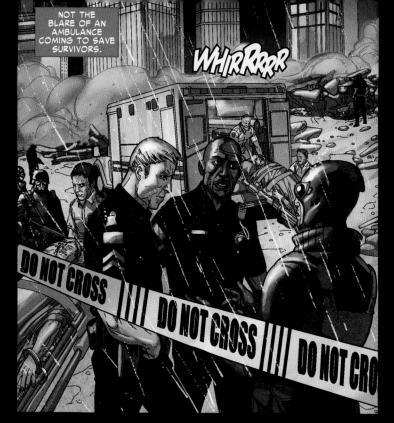

NOT THE BLARE OF AN AMBULANCE COMING TO SAVE SURVIVORS.

WHIRRRRR

DO NOT CROSS |||| DO NOT CROSS |||| DO NOT CRO

NOT THE CLANG OF ENTRAPMENT.

HISSSSSS

NOT THE WHISPER OF IMPENDING DOOM.

SO INSTEAD I FOCUS ON THE SOUND OF A WOMAN'S VOICE. A PASSAGE I OVERHEARD ONCE. A FAIRLY RANDOM THING, I ADMIT. BUT NO LESS RANDOM THAN LIFE, I SUPPOSE.

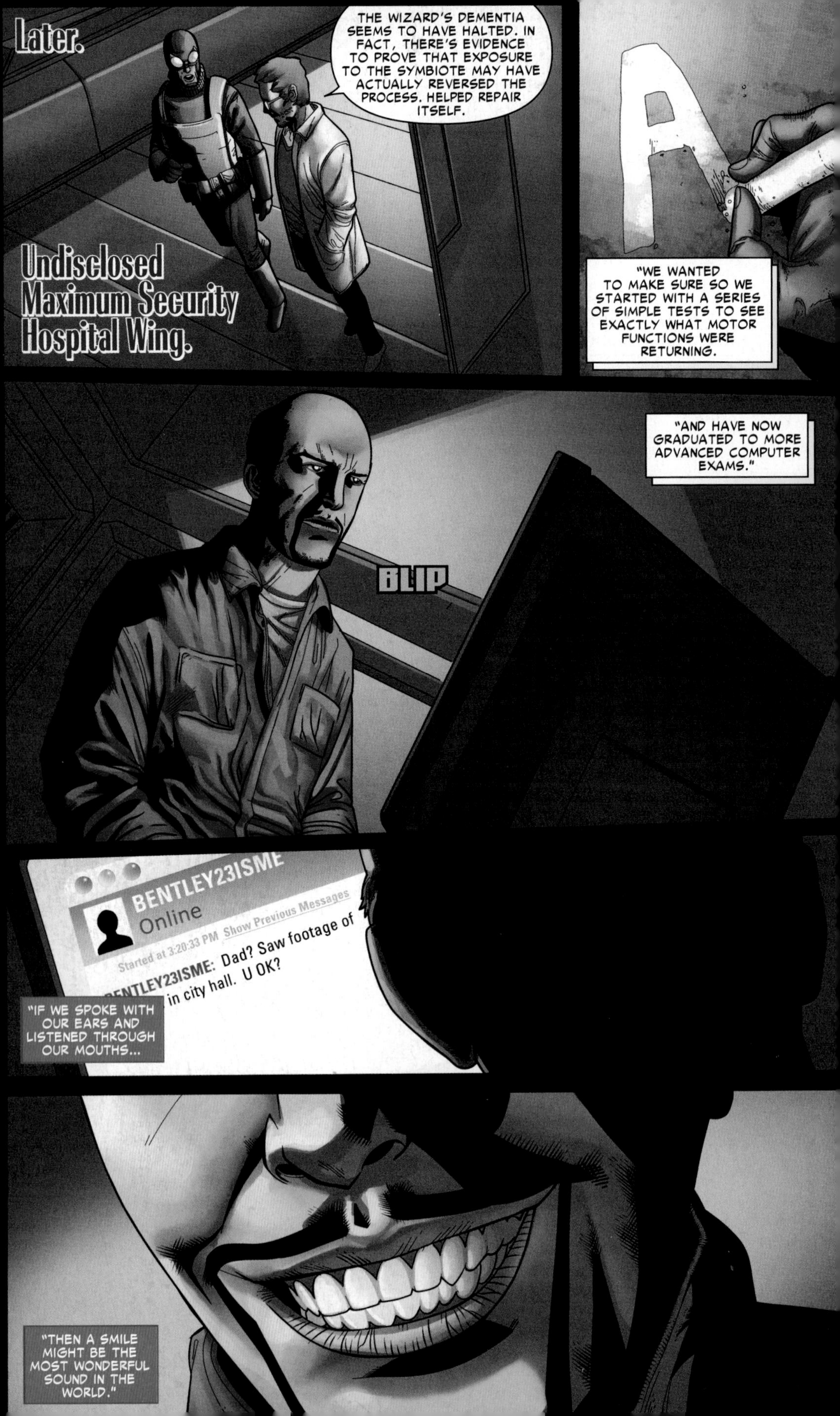
Later.
THE WIZARD'S DEMENTIA SEEMS TO HAVE HALTED. IN FACT, THERE'S EVIDENCE TO PROVE THAT EXPOSURE TO THE SYMBIOTE MAY HAVE ACTUALLY REVERSED THE PROCESS. HELPED REPAIR ITSELF.
Undisclosed Maximum Security Hospital Wing.
"WE WANTED TO MAKE SURE SO WE STARTED WITH A SERIES OF SIMPLE TESTS TO SEE EXACTLY WHAT MOTOR FUNCTIONS WERE RETURNING.
"AND HAVE NOW GRADUATED TO MORE ADVANCED COMPUTER EXAMS."
BLIP
BENTLEY23ISME
BENTLEY23ISME
Online
Show Previous Messages
Started at 3:20:33 PM
BENTLEY23ISME: Dad? Saw footage of ... in city hall. U OK?
"IF WE SPOKE WITH OUR EARS AND LISTENED THROUGH OUR MOUTHS...
"THEN A SMILE MIGHT BE THE MOST WONDERFUL SOUND IN THE WORLD."

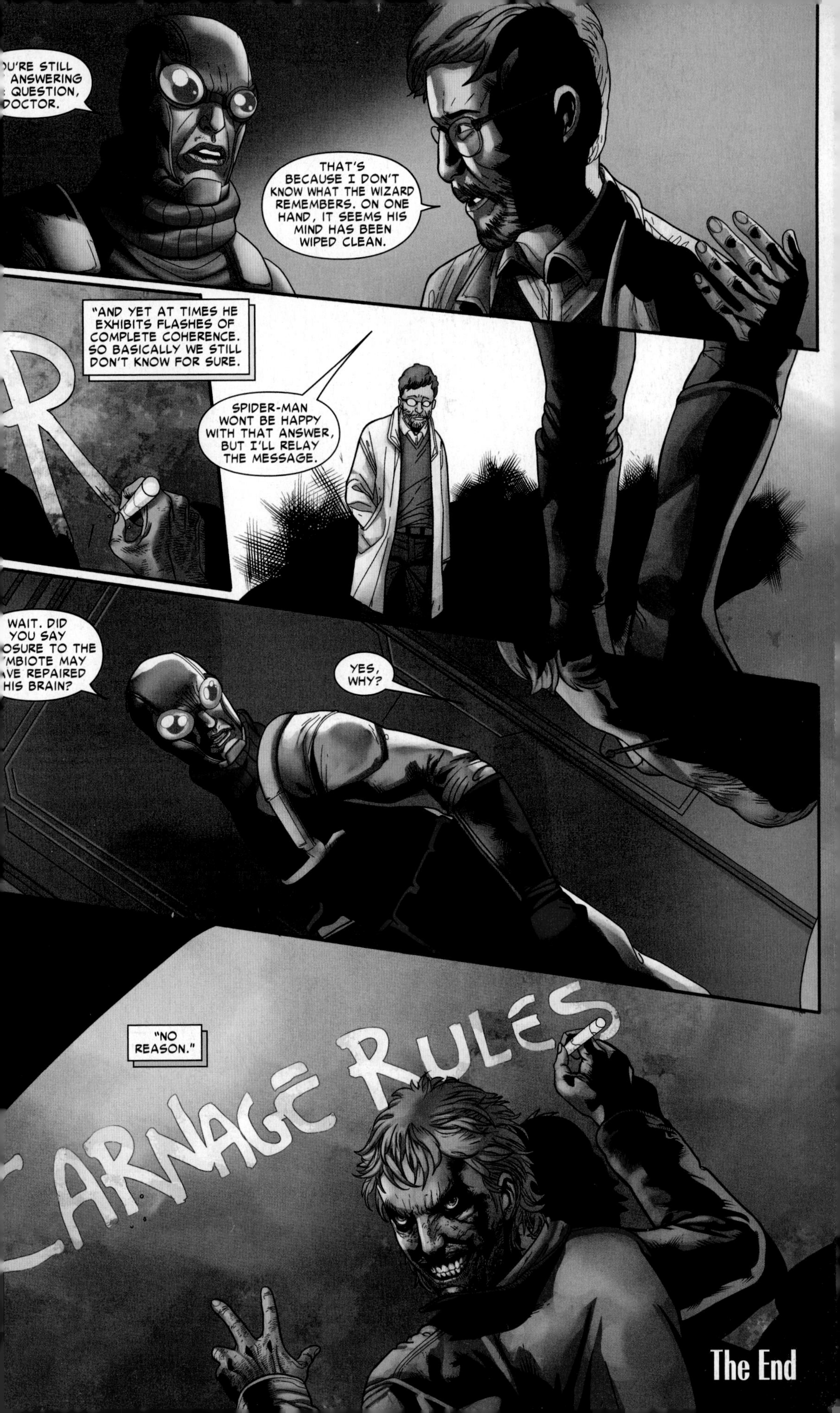

U'RE STILL ANSWERING QUESTION, DOCTOR.
THAT'S BECAUSE I DON'T KNOW WHAT THE WIZARD REMEMBERS. ON ONE HAND, IT SEEMS HIS MIND HAS BEEN WIPED CLEAN.
"AND YET AT TIMES HE EXHIBITS FLASHES OF COMPLETE COHERENCE. SO BASICALLY WE STILL DON'T KNOW FOR SURE.
SPIDER-MAN WONT BE HAPPY WITH THAT ANSWER, BUT I'LL RELAY THE MESSAGE.
WAIT. DID YOU SAY OSURE TO THE MBIOTE MAY VE REPAIRED HIS BRAIN?
YES, WHY?
"NO REASON."
CARNAGE RULES
The End

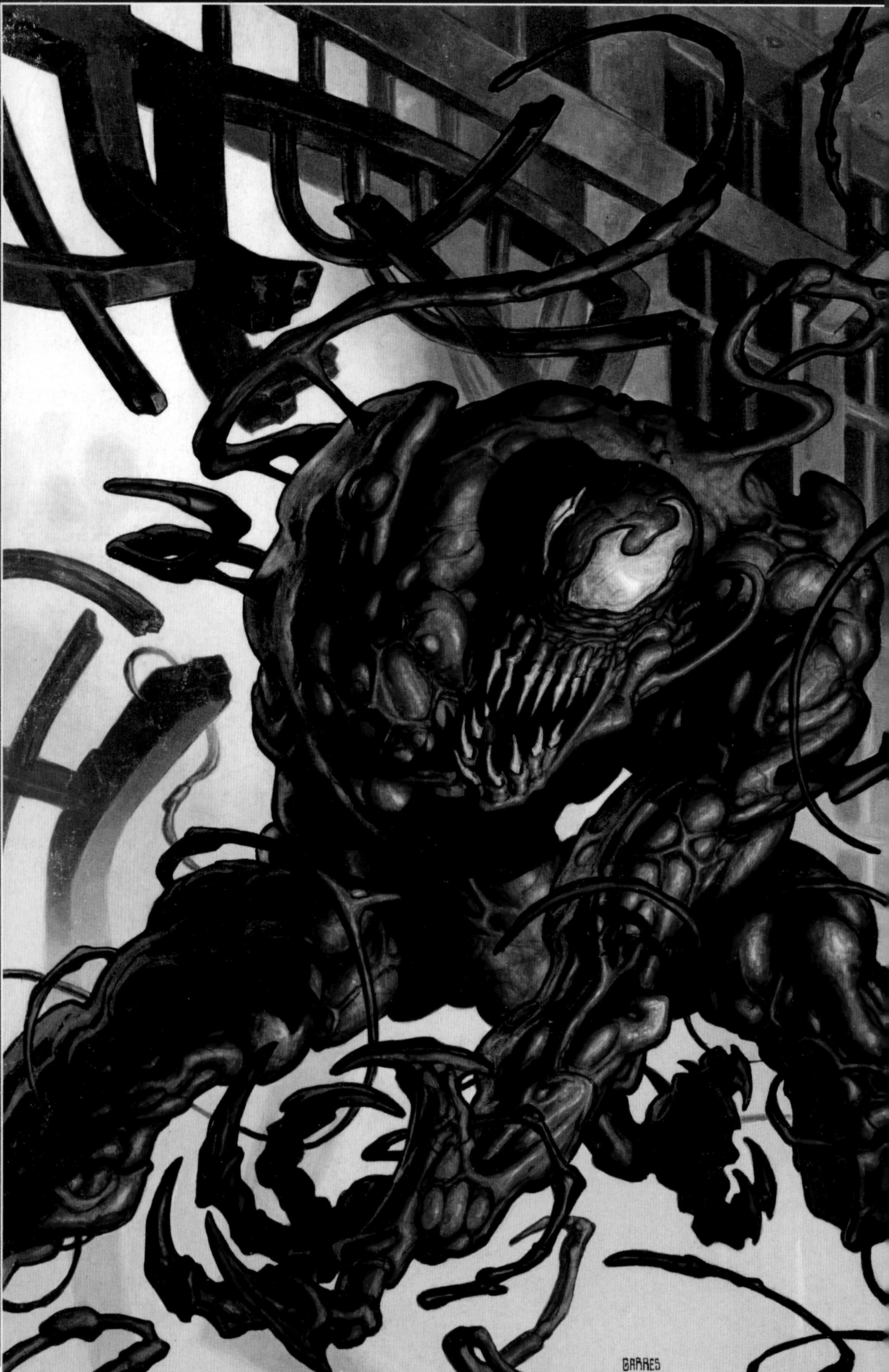
GARRES

#2 VARIANT BY RAFA GARRES